TEACHINGS OF PRESIDENT
DAVID O.

D0355380

Published by
The Church of Jesus Christ of Latter-day Saints
Salt Lake City, Utah

Your comments and suggestions about this book would be appreciated. Please submit them to Curriculum Planning, 50 East North Temple Street, Room 2420, Salt Lake City, UT 84150-3220 USA.

E-mail: cur-development@ldschurch.org

Please list your name, address, ward, and stake. Be sure to give the title of the book. Then offer your comments and suggestions about the book's strengths and areas of potential improvement.

Faurtella Hollaher
Ivan, ut.

Contents

David O. McKay

David O. McKay was ordained an Apostle in 1906 and sustained as President of the Church in 1951.

Introduction

The First Presidency and Quorum of the Twelve Apostles have established the *Teachings of Presidents of the Church* series to help Church members deepen their understanding of gospel doctrine and draw closer to Jesus Christ through the teachings of the prophets in this dispensation. This book features the teachings of President David O. McKay, who served as President of The Church of Jesus Christ of Latter-day Saints from April 1951 to January 1970.

How to Use This Book

Each chapter in this book includes four sections: (1) an opening quotation that briefly introduces the focus of the chapter; (2) an "Introduction," which illustrates the messages of the chapter with a story or counsel from President McKay; (3) "Teachings of David O. McKay," which presents doctrines from his many messages and sermons; and (4) "Suggestions for Study and Discussion," which contains questions to encourage personal review and inquiry, application of gospel principles, and discussion at home and at church. Reviewing the questions before studying President McKay's words may give additional insight into his teachings. Also, as part of the resources for additional study and discussion, each chapter includes a brief list of related scriptures.

This book is to be used in the following settings:

For personal or family study. Through prayerful reading and thoughtful study, individuals can receive a personal witness of the truths taught by President McKay. This volume will add to each member's gospel library and will serve as an important resource for family instruction and study in the home.

For discussion in Sunday meetings. This book is the text for Sunday meetings in high priests groups, elders quorums, and the Relief Society, usually on the second and third Sundays of each month. These Sunday meetings should be discussions that concentrate on gospel doctrines and principles. Teachers should focus on the content of the text and related scriptures and should apply these teachings to circumstances with which class members will be familiar. They may draw from the questions at the end of each chapter to encourage class discussion. As appropriate, members should bear testimony and share personal examples that relate to the lessons. When teachers humbly seek the Spirit in preparing and directing the lessons, all who participate will be strengthened in their knowledge of the truth.

Leaders and teachers are to encourage members to read the chapters in preparation for Sunday meetings and to bring the book to church. They should honor such preparation by teaching from President McKay's words. When members have read a chapter in advance, they will be prepared to teach and edify each other.

It is not necessary or recommended that members purchase additional commentaries or reference texts to supplement the material in this book. For further study of the doctrine, members are encouraged to turn to the related scriptures that are included at the end of the "Suggestions for Study and Discussion" section.

Since this book is designed for personal study and gospel reference, many chapters contain more material than can be fully addressed in Sunday meetings. Therefore, study at home becomes essential to more thoroughly benefit from President McKay's teachings.

Teaching Lessons from the Chapters in This Book

The chapters in this book contain more information than most teachers will be able to teach in one class period. Teachers should pray for help, seek the guidance of the Holy Ghost, and work diligently as they select the quotations, scripture references, and questions that will best meet the needs of class members.

Preparing a Lesson

The following suggestions illustrate one possible approach to help teachers prepare and present lessons from this book (these guidelines can also be used by parents in preparing family home evening lessons):

1. Prayerfully study the chapter. Consider marking passages that are particularly inspiring to you.

2. Determine what should happen in the lives of those you teach as a result of the teachings in the chapter. Seek the guidance of the Holy Ghost as you ponder the needs of those you teach.

3. Decide what to teach. Read the chapter again, selecting the passages that will be most helpful for those you teach.

4. Decide how to teach. Plan ways to teach the passages you have selected. Some suggestions follow.

- Conduct discussions based on the questions in "Suggestions for Study and Discussion" at the end of each chapter.

- Discuss selected scripture passages from the related scriptures listed at the end of each chapter.

- Plan a way to get members' attention at the beginning of the lesson. For example, you may share a story from the chapter's introduction, write a thought-provoking question on the chalkboard, or use an object lesson.

- Use hymns and Primary songs to help members prepare to feel the Spirit.

- Bear testimony whenever the Spirit prompts you, not just at the end of the lesson.

- Invite one or two members to come to class prepared to bear brief testimony of the principles in the chapter.

- As appropriate, share experiences relating to the principles in the chapter. Invite others to do the same.

For suggestions on how to use these and other teaching methods, refer to *Teaching, No Greater Call* (36123); the *Teaching Guidebook* (34595); and "Gospel Teaching and Leadership," section 16 of the *Church Handbook of Instructions, Book 2: Priesthood and Auxiliary Leaders* (35903). Also, to help you succeed in your calling, you are encouraged to participate in the 12-week Teaching the Gospel course in your ward or branch, as well as the quarterly teacher improvement meetings.

5. Organize your ideas. You may want to write an outline to guide you during the presentation of the lesson.

Conducting Meaningful Discussions

Whether in a family or classroom setting, the chapters in this book provide a wonderful opportunity for individuals to strengthen each other by participating in gospel discussions. The following guidelines may help you conduct meaningful discussions:

- Ask questions that require thought and discussion rather than questions that can be answered *yes* or *no.* Questions that begin with *what, how, why, who,* or *where* are usually most effective for encouraging discussion.

- Encourage others to share experiences that show how gospel principles apply in everyday life. Also encourage them to share their feelings about what they are learning. Listen sincerely and show appreciation for their contributions.

- Be sensitive to the influence of the Holy Ghost. He will help you know what to ask, who to call on, or how to include others in the discussion. If you feel that comments are straying from the topic, politely redirect the discussion.

- Be careful not to end a good discussion too soon in an attempt to cover all the material you have prepared. What matters most is that participants feel the Spirit, increase their understanding of the gospel, apply gospel principles in their lives, and strengthen their commitment to live the gospel.

Information on the Sources
Quoted in This Book

The teachings of President McKay in this book have been collected from a variety of sources. The quotations have retained the punctuation, spelling, and capitalization of the original sources unless editorial or typographic changes have been necessary to improve readability. For this reason, readers may notice minor inconsistencies in the text.

President McKay often used terms such as *men, man,* or *mankind* to refer to all people, both male and female. He also commonly used the pronoun *he* to refer to both genders. This was common in the language of his era. Despite the differences between these language conventions and more current usage, readers will find that President McKay's teachings are equally applicable and valuable to both women and men.

Also, President McKay was very well read, and he often quoted other authors as he taught. In most of the original sources, quotation marks indicate when President McKay is quoting someone else, but the name of the author is seldom given. Rather than disrupt the chapters of this book with numerous instances of "[author unknown]," the book has simply retained original quotation marks to indicate when President McKay is presenting someone else's words.

Historical Summary

This book is not a history, but rather a compilation of gospel principles as taught by President David O. McKay. However, in order to put his teachings in a historical framework, the following chronology is provided. This summary omits some important events in his personal life, such as the births of his children and grandchildren.

1873, September 8:	Born in Huntsville, Utah, to David McKay and Jennette Evans McKay.
1881:	David McKay leaves on a mission to the British Isles. David O. and his mother assume responsibility for the farm and family (7; numbers in parentheses show David O. McKay's age).
1887:	Receives patriarchal blessing from John Smith (13).
1889:	Sustained as secretary of the Huntsville Ward Sunday School (15).
1893–94:	Serves as a teacher and principal at the Huntsville grade school; sustained as a Sunday School teacher in the Huntsville Ward (19–20).
1894–97:	Attends the University of Utah and graduates as valedictorian (20–23).
1897–99:	Fulfills a two-year mission to Great Britain. In addition to his proselyting duties, serves as a leader of all the missionaries in Scotland (23–25).
1899–1900:	Teaches at Weber Stake Academy in Ogden, Utah (25–26).

1900:	Appointed to Weber Stake Sunday School Board (27).
1901, January 2:	Marries Emma Ray Riggs in the Salt Lake Temple (27).
1902:	Appointed as principal of the Weber Stake Academy (28).
1906:	Ordained an Apostle by President Joseph F. Smith (32).
1914–18:	World War I is fought (40–44).
1918:	Appointed general superintendent of the Deseret Sunday School Union. Publishes *Ancient Apostles* (45).
1919–21:	Serves as Church commissioner of education (45–47).
1920, December:	On an assignment from the First Presidency, leaves on a one-year tour with Elder Hugh J. Cannon to visit Church missions around the world (47).
1922–24:	Serves as president of the European Mission (49–51).
1934:	Sustained and set apart as second counselor to President Heber J. Grant (61).
1939–45:	World War II is fought (65–71).
1945:	Sustained and set apart as second counselor to President George Albert Smith (71).
1950:	Sustained and set apart as President of the Quorum of the Twelve Apostles (77).
1951, April 9:	Sustained and set apart as the ninth President of the Church, with Stephen L Richards as first counselor and J. Reuben Clark Jr. as second counselor. At this time,

	the Church had approximately one million members (77).
1952, June:	Leaves on nine-week tour of Europe, during which time he visits Church members in nine countries (78).
1953:	Receives the Boy Scouts' highest honor, the Silver Buffalo (79).
1954:	Begins 32,000-mile mission tour; first Church President to visit Central American and South American missions; first General Authority to visit the South African mission (80).
1955, August:	Visits Europe with the Mormon Tabernacle Choir (81).
1955, September:	Dedicates the Bern Switzerland Temple (82).
1956, March:	Dedicates the Los Angeles California Temple (82).
1956, October:	Dedicates the Relief Society Building (83).
1958, April:	Dedicates the Hamilton New Zealand Temple (84).
1958, September:	Dedicates the London England Temple (85).
1964, November:	Dedicates the Oakland California Temple (91).
1970, January 18:	At age 96, dies in Salt Lake City, Utah. By the end of his administration, Church membership had reached approximately three million.

The Life and Ministry of David O. McKay

In April of 1951, at the age of 77, David Oman McKay became the ninth President of The Church of Jesus Christ of Latter-day Saints. During the nearly 20 years he served as President, he was revered by Church members and many others worldwide as a prophet of God. As he urged Church members to develop Christlike character and to share the gospel through both teaching and example, the Church experienced rapid growth throughout the world. In addition to his teachings, his physical appearance made a powerful impression. Upon meeting him, many people commented that he not only spoke and acted like a prophet, but that he looked like one. Even in his later years, he had a tall, impressive physique and thick, wavy white hair. His countenance radiated the righteous life that he led.

A Heritage and Childhood of High Ideals

In his teachings as a General Authority, David O. McKay often referred with gratitude to the heritage and example he received from his parents. The family of his father, David McKay, had joined the Church in Thurso, Scotland, in 1850. In 1856, the family traveled to America and, after working and saving money for three years, crossed the plains to Utah, arriving in Salt Lake City in August 1859.[1]

In the same year that the McKays joined the Church in Scotland (1850), the family of David O. McKay's mother, Jennette Evans, embraced the restored gospel near Merthyr Tydfil in South Wales. Like the McKay family, the Evans family sailed for America in 1856 and arrived in Utah in 1859. Both families soon settled in Ogden, Utah, where David McKay and Jennette Evans met and fell in love. They were married on 9 April 1867 in the Endowment House by Elder Wilford Woodruff.[2]

On 8 September 1873 in the small Utah town of Huntsville, David O. McKay was born—the third child and first son of David and Jennette Evans McKay. His childhood was happy but not without trials. In 1880, a series of events tested and proved the family's faith and brought early maturity to young David O. McKay. His two older sisters, Margaret and Ellena, died within days of each other, one of rheumatic fever and the other of pneumonia. Approximately one year later, his father received a mission call to Scotland. David McKay was somewhat concerned about accepting the call because it would mean leaving his wife (who was expecting another child) alone with the responsibilities of the family and the farm. However, when hearing of the call, Jennette was firm in her response: "Of course you must accept; you need not worry about me. David O. and I will manage things nicely!"³ With this encouragement and the assurance of help from neighbors and relatives, David McKay accepted the call. His parting words to seven-year-old David O. were to "take care of Mama."⁴

Due to wise management by Jennette McKay, the hard work of many, and the blessings of the Lord, the McKay farm prospered despite David McKay's two-year absence. During this time and, indeed, throughout her life, Jennette McKay was equally vigilant about the spiritual welfare of the children: "Family prayer was an established procedure in the McKay home, and when Jennette was left alone with her small family it seemed an ever more important part of the day's events. David [O.] was taught to take his turn at morning and evening prayers and learned the importance of the blessings of heaven in the home."⁵

President McKay often spoke of his mother as an example worthy of emulation. On one occasion he stated: "I cannot think of a womanly virtue that my mother did not possess. . . . To her children, and all others who knew her well, she was beautiful and dignified. Though high-spirited she was even-tempered and self-possessed. Her dark brown eyes immediately expressed any rising emotion which, however, she always held under perfect control. . . . In tenderness, watchful care, loving patience, loyalty to home and to right, she seemed to me in boyhood, and she seems to me now after these years, to have been supreme."⁶

When David O. McKay was asked to name the greatest man he had ever met, he replied without hesitation, "My father."[7] After returning from his mission, his father served as the bishop of the Eden and Huntsville Wards from 1883 to 1905.[8] David McKay Sr. shared many experiences and his testimony with his young son. President McKay remembered: "As a boy, I sat and heard that testimony from one whom I treasured and honored as you know I treasured no other man in the world, and that assurance was instilled in my youthful soul."[9] The strength of his father's example and testimony sustained him as he grew in his knowledge of the truth.

In everyday life, President McKay's father taught him lessons that strengthened him and found their way into his teachings as an Apostle. He once told of an experience when he was collecting hay with his brothers. The tenth load was to be given as a tithing offering to the Church. David O. McKay's father told the boys to get the tenth load from a better spot than where they had been gathering. His father said, "That is the *tenth* load, and the best is none too good for God." Years later, David O. McKay said that this was the "most effective sermon on tithing I have ever heard in my life."[10] His father also taught him to respect women. President McKay told youth, "I remember my father's admonition when I started in my teens to court a young girl: 'David, you treat that young lady as you would have any young boy treat your sister.' "[11]

Later in life, while serving as President of the Church, he gave the following tribute to his parents: "I am grateful for the wise and careful guardianship and training of noble parents . . . a guardianship which kept me from turning to paths that would have opened to an entirely different kind of life! Every year increases my appreciation and love for an ever watchful, precious mother, and a noble father."[12]

Youth

As a young man, David O. McKay was called to serve in the presidency of the deacons quorum. At that time, the deacons of the ward were responsible to keep the chapel clean, chop wood for the chapel stoves, and make sure that the widows in the ward always had firewood.[13] He told the quorum members that he "felt his inability to fill his position when he could see others that were more capable to occupy it than himself, . . . [but that] he felt to press on with the help of the Lord."[14] This attitude was typical of the humility with which he would accept callings throughout his life.

As the bishop's son, he had the opportunity to meet Church leaders who visited the family home. On one occasion, in July of 1887, Patriarch John Smith visited and gave him his patriarchal blessing (David O. was 13 at the time). After the blessing, Patriarch Smith placed his hands on the young man's shoulders and said, "My boy, you have something to do besides playing marbles." David later went into the kitchen and said to his mother, "If he thinks I'm going to stop playing marbles, he is mistaken." His mother set aside her work and tried to explain what Brother Smith had meant. Although neither David O. McKay nor his mother knew exactly what his future held, the experience showed that the Lord had greater responsibilities in store for the young man.[15]

Throughout his teenage years, he remained active in Church service and continued to gain knowledge and experience. In 1889, at the age of 15, he was called as the Huntsville Ward's Sunday School secretary, a position he held until 1893, when he was called to serve as a Sunday School teacher.[16] His great love for the Sunday School and for teaching would continue throughout his life.

Education, Missionary Service, and Marriage

David O. McKay once wrote, "There are three great epochs in a man's earthly life, upon which his happiness here and in eternity may depend, [namely], his birth, his marriage, and his choice of vocation."[17] Already blessed by birth and upbringing in a righteous family, he continued to benefit from wise decisions relating to his education, profession, and eventual marriage.

After completing his studies through the eighth grade in Huntsville, he attended the Weber Stake Academy in Ogden for two years. Then, during the 1893–94 school year, at the age of 20, he returned to Huntsville and worked as a teacher at the town's grade school. Around this time, his Grandmother Evans made a financial gift to each of her living children of $2,500. Money was scarce for the McKay family, and neighbors suggested that David O. McKay's mother, Jennette, invest the money in stocks. However, she firmly declared, "Every cent of this goes into the education of our children."[18] Therefore, in the fall of 1894, he and three of his siblings (Thomas E., Jeanette, and Annie) journeyed to Salt Lake City by wagon to attend the University of Utah. The wagon was filled with flour and jars of fruit and had a milk cow trailing behind.[19]

Of David O. McKay's university experience, his son Llewelyn wrote: "School was important. The love for learning grew by leaps and bounds; deep friendships were formed; and his fine sense of values was enhanced. He became the president of his class and was selected valedictorian. . . . Participating with enthusiasm in sports, he became right guard on the university's first football team. The greatest event during this time was his acquaintance with Emma Ray Riggs."[20]

During the second year of their university education, the McKay students rented a house from Emma Robbins Riggs, the mother of Emma Ray Riggs. One day, the mother and daughter stood at the window and watched as David O. and Thomas E. McKay arrived with their mother. Emma Ray's mother commented: "There are two young men who will make some lucky girls good husbands. See how considerate they are of their mother." Emma Ray then remarked, "I like the dark one," who was David O. McKay. Although he and Emma Ray Riggs saw each other occasionally, they did not develop a serious relationship until a few years later.[21]

Upon completing his university studies in the spring of 1897, David O. McKay was offered a job as a teacher in Salt Lake County. He was happy for the position and wanted to begin earning money to help the rest of his family. However, around this same time he received and accepted a call to serve a mission in Great Britain.

On 1 August 1897, he was set apart by President Seymour B. Young to serve as a missionary in the British Isles. The first part of his mission was spent in Stirling, Scotland, where the work was slow and difficult. He fulfilled his work diligently and on 9 June

1898, he was called to preside over the missionaries in Scotland. Upon receiving the calling, he turned to the Lord for help. His responsibilities in this calling gave him maturity and experience beyond his years and prepared him for future service.

Another significant experience took place just three months before he went home. As a youth, he had often prayed for a spiritual confirmation regarding his testimony. On 29 May 1899, he attended a memorable missionary meeting. He recounted: "I remember, as if it were but yesterday, the intensity of the inspiration of that occasion. Everybody felt the rich outpouring of the Spirit of the Lord. All present were truly of one heart and one mind. Never before had I experienced such an emotion. It was a manifestation for which as a doubting youth I had secretly prayed most earnestly on hillside and in meadow. It was an assurance to me that sincere prayer is answered 'sometime, somewhere.' During the progress of the meeting, an elder on his own initiative arose and said, 'Brethren, there are angels in this room.' Strange as it may seem, the announcement was not startling; indeed, it seemed wholly proper, though it had not occurred to me there were divine beings present. I only knew that I was overflowing with gratitude for the presence of the Holy Spirit."[22] Elder McKay finished his mission honorably and was released in August of 1899.

During his mission he had corresponded with Emma Ray Riggs, or "Ray," as he affectionately called her (her parents had named her for a ray of sunshine). Their courtship began to blossom through the mail between Scotland and Salt Lake City. He found in her a person who was his equal in every way, including intelligence, social graces, and spiritual qualities.

She had continued her schooling while David O. McKay was on his mission, and after graduating with a B.A. in education, she took a position at the Madison School in Ogden, Utah.[23] At the same time, the fall of 1899, he joined the faculty of the Weber Stake Academy. During that school year, the two of them often met in a park between their schools. It was there, in December 1900, that he asked her to marry him. She asked, "Are you sure I'm the right one?" He said he was sure.[24] On 2 January 1901,

The relationship between President McKay and his wife, Emma Ray Riggs McKay (shown above), served as a model for Church members to follow.

Emma Ray Riggs and David O. McKay became the first couple in the 20th century to be married in the Salt Lake Temple.

A Legendary Educator

In 1902, at the age of 28, he became the principal of the Weber Stake Academy. In spite of many administrative responsibilities, he continued to take an active part in the education of the students. He remained committed to education throughout his life, believing that "true education seeks to make men and women not only good mathematicians, proficient linguists, profound scientists, or brilliant literary lights, but also, honest men, with virtue, temperance, and brotherly love. It seeks to make men and women who prize truth, justice, wisdom, benevolence, and self-control as the choicest acquisitions of a successful life." [25]

He believed that education was important for everyone. He served as a principal during an era when very few women received a secondary education. In discussing the important role of women, he wrote the following: "Not much emphasis has been placed upon the part that women played in the settlement of the Western Empire. In this we are but following the general practice of men throughout the ages. Women bear the burdens of the household, carry most of the responsibility of rearing a family, inspire their husbands and sons to achieve success; and while the latter are being given the applause of public acclaim, the wives and mothers who really merit recognition and commendation remain smilingly content in unheralded achievement." [26] While working at the Weber Stake Academy, he emphasized the importance of education for both sexes, and female student enrollment greatly increased during his tenure.

During the years he served as a professional educator and administrator at the Weber Stake Academy, he also served in the Weber Stake Sunday School presidency, where he developed new programs. At the time he was called to the Sunday School presidency, the organization received little formal direction from general Church leadership. As the second assistant superintendent—assigned to classwork—David O. McKay immediately began working to improve classroom teaching and learning by using the methods he had learned as a professional educator. One Sunday School leader described his work as follows:

"He first called for weekly meetings of the stake board members. He drilled the members in outlining lessons and in selecting an aim (now called objective) for each lesson. He drilled them in organizing and illustrating the aim. He stressed lesson presentation and application of the aim in each child's life. This was followed by a monthly . . . meeting to which all the ward Sunday School teachers and officers were asked to come, having previously read the lessons to be considered. . . . As a result of these . . . meetings, teachers went home with a 'bundle of notes' on each of four lessons for the month ahead. . . . [These] meetings became very popular with 90 per cent to 100 per cent attendance at each."[27]

News spread quickly of the great success of the Weber Stake Sunday School. President Joseph F. Smith, who at that time also served as the general superintendent of the Sunday Schools, was impressed with David O. McKay's innovative ideas regarding teaching and invited him to write an article for the *Juvenile Instructor,* a Sunday School magazine.[28]

Apostle of the Lord

Emphasis on Teaching and Learning

On 9 April 1906, after having served six years in the Weber Stake Sunday School, he was ordained an Apostle at the age of 32. Soon thereafter, he was also sustained as the second assistant in the General Sunday School superintendency. He then became first assistant in 1909, and general superintendent from 1918 to 1934. The same innovations he used in the Weber Stake Sunday School were quickly put into practice by the entire Church. Seeing a need for uniform lessons, he wrote the book *Ancient Apostles,* which was prepared as one of the first Sunday School lesson manuals.

Elder McKay's name became synonymous with the Sunday School in the years he served in the Quorum of the Twelve, and he was still writing lessons for the Sunday School when he became President of the Church. In working to improve gospel instruction, his emphasis often focused on children. In his words, children come "from the Father pure and undefiled, without inherent taints or weakness. . . . Their souls are as stainless white paper on which are to be written the aspirations or achievements of a lifetime."[29] He saw the Sunday School as playing a key role in teaching and building character in children and youth.

World Tour and European Mission President

Other experiences prepared David O. McKay to eventually lead a worldwide Church. In December 1920, he and Elder

Hugh J. Cannon, editor of the *Improvement Era,* were set apart by President Heber J. Grant and his first counselor, President Anthon H. Lund, to tour all Church missions and schools throughout the world. During the tour, which lasted a year, they traveled approximately 60,000 miles (more than twice the circumference of the earth), teaching and blessing Church members worldwide. Despite difficulties such as seasickness, homesickness, and other challenges in traveling, they had a successful mission and arrived home on Christmas Eve, 1921. In the days following their arrival, they made a full report to President Grant and were honorably released.[30] In the first general conference after their return, President Grant declared:

"I rejoice in the fact that Brother McKay is with us today. Brother McKay has circled the globe since he was last at a conference—has visited our missions in nearly every part of the world, and has returned, as every missionary does return who goes out to proclaim this gospel and comes in contact with the people of the world and with all the varieties of faiths of the world, with increased light, knowledge and testimony regarding the divinity of the work in which we are engaged."[31]

When it was Elder McKay's turn to speak in conference, he summarized his travels with a strong testimony: "When we left home, . . . we looked forward with no little misgiving and anxiety to the trip ahead of us. . . . The keen sense of our responsibility, adequately to fulfil the desires of President Grant and his counselors and the Twelve, who had honored us with that call, made us seek the Lord as I had never sought him before in my life, and I wish to say this afternoon that the promise made by Moses to the children of Israel just before they crossed the Jordan River into the Promised land, has been fulfilled in our experiences. As we sought the Lord with all our souls He came to our guidance and assistance."[32]

Shortly after his return from the world tour, he was called to be the president of the European Mission. He left for Liverpool in November of 1922. It was during this calling that he began to teach the concept of "every member a missionary," an emphasis he would later continue as Church President. As a mission president, he reorganized missionaries into groups, with several missionaries acting as traveling elders to help train the other missionaries in better teaching methods. One of his greatest challenges was to defuse negative press. His method was to personally contact the editors and reason with them, asking for equal opportunity to present the truth about the Church. A few editors refused his requests, but many were very receptive to him.[33] His public relations skills proved to be a great blessing to the Church during his mission presidency and throughout his ministry.

Sustained to the First Presidency

In the fall of 1934, he was sustained as second counselor to President Heber J. Grant. President J. Reuben Clark Jr., who had been serving as President Grant's second counselor, became first counselor. Although President McKay came into the First Presidency with a strong Church background, on the day he was sustained he still felt humbled by the calling. He stated: "Needless to say I am overwhelmed. During the past few days I have had difficulty in keeping my thoughts and feelings under control. The light heart, the buoyancy of spirit that should accompany the high appointment that has come to me has been somewhat counterbalanced by a heaviness incident to the realization of the great responsibility that comes with the call to the First Presidency."[34] Even after many years of service as a General Authority, he admitted that it was "always more or less an ordeal for me to face an audience," knowing the magnitude of his responsibilities.[35]

During President McKay's early years in the First Presidency, Church members were facing the Great Depression. In 1936, the First Presidency officially announced the Church Security Program, which would later become the Church Welfare Program. As a strong supporter of welfare, President McKay emphasized that spirituality and welfare were synonymous: "It is something to supply clothing to the scantily clad, to furnish ample food to those whose table is thinly spread, to give activity to those who are fighting desperately the despair that comes from enforced idleness, but after all is said and done, the greatest blessings that will accrue from the Church Security Plan are spiritual. There is more spirituality expressed in giving than in receiving. The greatest spiritual blessing comes from helping another."[36]

Following the death of President Grant in 1945, George Albert Smith became President of the Church and called President McKay to serve as his second counselor. His duties continued much as they had before, with new opportunities and challenges constantly arising. One of the most demanding projects he undertook was an appointment as the chairman of Utah's centennial celebration, which involved many months of planning amid his already heavy workload. The statewide celebration, which culminated in July 1947, was hailed as a great success. A local newspaper reported the following:

"Rodney C. Richardson, Coordinator of California centennial affairs, came to Salt Lake City to study Utah's Centennial, which, he said, was conceded to have 'the best planning in the nation. Lack of commercialism is one of the outstanding features of the Utah Centennial. It has been a true historical celebration.' " In addition to the praise from California, several other states wrote, requesting plans and other literature associated with the celebration.[37]

As President George Albert Smith's health began to decline, the responsibilities of his two counselors increased. In the spring of 1951, President McKay and his wife, Emma Ray, decided to drive from Salt Lake City to California for a much-needed vacation. Stopping in St. George, Utah, the first night, President McKay awoke with a distinct impression that he should return to Salt Lake City. A few days later President George Albert Smith suffered a stroke and passed away on 4 April 1951.

Prophet of a Worldwide Church

Missionary Work and Church Growth

After having served for 45 years as an Apostle, David O. McKay became the ninth President of the Church on 9 April 1951, with Stephen L Richards and J. Reuben Clark Jr. as counselors. In 1952, the First Presidency introduced the first official proselyting plan for full-time missionaries. The program was designed to increase the effectiveness of full-time missionaries by providing a standard outline of the discussions to be used in teaching investigators. The outline included five discussions entitled "The Book of Mormon," "Historical Basis for the Restoration," "Distinctive Doctrines of the Church," "Responsibilities of Church Membership," and "Becoming a Member of the Church."[38]

Nine years later, in 1961, he convened the first seminar for all mission presidents, who were taught to encourage families to fellowship their friends and neighbors and then have these people taught by missionaries in their homes.[39] Emphasizing the concept of "every member a missionary," he urged every member to make a commitment to bring at least one new member into the Church each year. A language training institute for newly called missionaries was also established that year. With these new initiatives, Church membership and the number of full-time missionaries grew rapidly. Under his direction, the number of stakes more than doubled (to approximately 500) as new stakes were formed around the world in such countries as Argentina, Australia, Brazil, England, Germany, Guatemala, Mexico, the Netherlands, Samoa, Scotland, Switzerland, Tonga, and Uruguay. Also in 1961, to accommodate this tremendous growth, members of the First Quorum of the Seventy were made high priests so that they could preside at stake conferences, and the new office of regional representatives of the Twelve was established in 1967.

Travels as President

President McKay traveled more miles than all of his predecessors combined. In 1952, he began the first of several important trips—a nine-week trip to Europe, where he visited nine countries and several missions. At the first stop in Scotland, he dedicated that country's first chapel, which was located in Glasgow. Throughout the remainder of the trip, he held approximately 50 meetings with Church members, gave numerous interviews, and visited with dignitaries from many countries.[40] In 1954, he traveled to the isolated mission in South Africa, being the first General Authority to visit that area. In the second leg of his journey, he visited Church members in South America. In 1955, he visited the South Pacific, and later in the summer of that same year, he returned to Europe with the Tabernacle Choir.

He felt that his travels brought "a keener realization on the part of members of the Church that they are not detached entities but are in reality part of the Church as a whole."[41] For the first time the Church was truly becoming global. President McKay declared: "God bless the Church. It is worldwide. Its influence should be felt by all nations. May his spirit influence men everywhere and incline their hearts toward good will and peace."[42]

Increase in Temples

While in Europe in 1952, he made arrangements to construct new temples, the first that would be built outside the United States and Canada. The Bern Switzerland Temple was dedicated in 1955, and the London England Temple was dedicated in 1958. Also dedicated during his presidency were the Los Angeles California Temple (1956), the Hamilton New Zealand Temple (1958), and the Oakland California Temple (1964). Under his direction, films were used for the temple endowment, making it possible for the ordinance to be received in various languages.

Coordination and Consolidation

In 1960, the First Presidency assigned Elder Harold B. Lee to establish Church Correlation, with the intent of coordinating and consolidating Church programs, reducing overlap, and increasing efficiency and effectiveness. In a general conference address announcing this initiative, Elder Lee stated: "This is a move, which . . . has lain close to President McKay's mind and now as the President of the Church he is instructing us to move forward, that we consolidate to make more efficient, and more effective the work of the priesthood, the auxiliaries, and the other units in order that we may conserve our time, our energy, and our efforts toward the prime purpose for which the Church itself has been organized."[43]

Ambassador for the Church

Among people of other faiths, President McKay was regarded as an important spiritual leader. He met with world leaders and local government officials regularly. He was also visited by United States presidents, including Harry S Truman, John F.

Kennedy, and Dwight D. Eisenhower. On one occasion, U.S. President Lyndon B. Johnson, who called President McKay often, invited him to Washington, D.C., for personal counsel on several issues that were troubling him. During the visit, President McKay told him: "Let your conscience be your guide. Let the people know that you are sincere, and they will follow you."[44]

Beloved Speaker and Leader

Beginning in youth and throughout his life, President McKay studied the words of great authors and frequently taught from the passages he had memorized. For instance, he told Church members: "Wordsworth's heart leaped up when he beheld a rainbow in the sky. Burns' heart wept when his plowshare overturned a daisy. Tennyson could pluck the flower from the 'crannied wall,' and see, if he could read in it the mystery, 'all that God and man is.' All these, and other great men, have shown to us, in the works of nature, the handiwork of God."[45]

Church members loved to hear President McKay speak. His discourses often included inspiring stories from his many experiences, and he always appreciated good humor. He enjoyed telling the story of a newspaper delivery boy who shook hands with him before he got on an elevator. The boy then ran upstairs to greet the aged prophet as he exited on the floor above. The boy said, "I just wanted to shake hands with you once more before you die."[46]

His general conference addresses emphasized the importance of the home and family as the source of happiness and the surest defense against trials and temptations. The axiom "no other success can compensate for failure in the home" was often repeated as he called on parents to spend more time with their children and teach them about character and integrity. He taught, "Pure hearts in a pure home are always in whispering distance of heaven."[47] He called the home the "cell-unit of society" and declared that "parenthood is next to Godhood."[48]

He spoke of the sanctity of marriage and referred often to the love he felt for his family and his wife, Emma Ray. Their marriage of over 60 years became the model union for future generations of Latter-day Saints. He admonished, "Let us teach youth that the marriage relation is one of the most sacred obligations known to man, or that man can make."[49]

As his health began to decline in the mid-1960s, he soon spent much of his time in a wheelchair and called additional counselors into the First Presidency. Despite his weakening physical condition, he continued to conduct the business of the Church and to teach, lead, and inspire. Not long before his death, he spoke at a meeting in the Salt Lake Temple with the General Authorities of the Church. Elder Boyd K. Packer, who was present at the meeting, recalled the experience as follows:

"[President McKay] talked of the temple ordinances and quoted at length from the ceremonies. He explained them to us. (That was not inappropriate, considering that we were in the temple.) After he had spoken for some time, he paused and stood gazing up to the ceiling in deep thought.

"I remember that his big hands were in front of him with his fingers interlocked. He stood gazing as people sometimes do when pondering a deep question. Then he spoke: 'Brethren, I think I am finally beginning to understand.'

"Here he was, the prophet—an Apostle for over half a century and even then he was learning, he was growing. His expression 'I think I am finally beginning to understand,' was greatly comforting to me."[50] Even with his extensive understanding of the gospel and his experience in the Church, President McKay was humble enough to realize that he could still learn and discover deeper levels of meaning.

After serving as the Lord's prophet for almost 20 years, President David O. McKay passed away on 18 January 1970 in Salt Lake City, Utah, with his wife, Emma Ray, and five of his children at his bedside. In a tribute to him, President Harold B. Lee stated that he had "left the world richer and heaven more glorious by the rich treasures he has brought to each."[51] Of David O. McKay's legacy, his successor, President Joseph Fielding Smith, declared: "He was a man of great spiritual strength, a natural-born leader of men, and a man beloved by his people and honored by the world. For all time to come men shall rise up and call his name blessed."[52]

Notes

1. See Jeanette McKay Morrell, *Highlights in the Life of President David O. McKay* (1966), 6–8.

2. See *Highlights in the Life of President David O. McKay,* 8–10.

3. Llewelyn R. McKay, *Home Memories of President David O. McKay* (1956), 6.

4. See *Highlights in the Life of President David O. McKay,* 22–23.

5. See *Highlights in the Life of President David O. McKay,* 24–25.

6. Bryant S. Hinckley, "Greatness in Men: David O. McKay," *Improvement Era,* May 1932, 391; paragraphing altered.

7. Jay M. Todd and Albert L. Zobell Jr., "David O. McKay, 1873–1970," *Improvement Era,* Feb. 1970, 12.

8. See Francis M. Gibbons, *David O. McKay: Apostle to the World, Prophet of God* (1986), 12–13.

9. "Peace through the Gospel of Christ," *Improvement Era,* Mar. 1921, 405–6.

10. See *Cherished Experiences from the Writings of President David O. McKay,* comp. Clare Middlemiss, rev. ed. (1976), 8–9.

11. *Gospel Ideals* (1953), 459.

12. "Expressions of Gratitude and the Importance and Necessity for the Conservation and Training of Youth," *The Instructor,* Nov. 1966, 413.

13. See *Highlights in the Life of President David O. McKay,* 28.

14. Leland H. Monson, "David O. McKay Was a Deacon, Too," *Instructor,* Sept. 1962, 299.

15. See *Highlights in the Life of President David O. McKay,* 26.

16. See *Highlights in the Life of President David O. McKay,* 28.

17. David Lawrence McKay, *My Father, David O. McKay* (1989), 120.

18. See *Highlights in the Life of President David O. McKay,* 31.

19. See *Home Memories of President David O. McKay,* 8–9.

20. *Home Memories of President David O. McKay,* 9.

21. See *My Father, David O. McKay,* 1–2.

22. See *Cherished Experiences from the Writings of President David O. McKay,* 4–5; paragraphing altered.

23. See *Home Memories of President David O. McKay,* 171.

24. See *My Father, David O. McKay,* 4–6.

25. *Treasures of Life,* comp. Clare Middlemiss (1962), 472.

26. "Pioneer Women, Heroines of the World," *Instructor,* July 1961, 217.

27. George R. Hill, "President David O. McKay . . . Father of the Modern Sunday School," *Instructor,* Sept. 1960, 314; paragraphing altered.

28. See *Instructor,* Sept. 1960, 314; see also "The Lesson Aim: How to Select It; How to Develop It; How to Apply It," *Juvenile Instructor,* Apr. 1905, 242–45.

29. "The Sunday School Looks Forward," *Improvement Era,* Dec. 1949, 804.

30. See *Highlights in the Life of President David O. McKay,* 66–72.

31. In Conference Report, Apr. 1922, 16.

32. In Conference Report, Apr. 1922, 63.

33. See Keith Terry, *David O. McKay: Prophet of Love* (1980), 89–93.

34. In Conference Report, Oct. 1934, 89–90.

35. In Conference Report, Oct. 1949, 116.

36. *Pathways to Happiness,* comp. Llewelyn R. McKay (1957), 377; paragraphing altered.

37. See *Highlights in the Life of President David O. McKay,* 95–96.

38. See *Deseret News,* Church section, 9 Apr. 1952, 9.

39. See "Every Member a Missionary," *Improvement Era,* Oct. 1961, 709–11, 730–31.

40. See *My Father, David O. McKay,* 217–37.

41. *Gospel Ideals* (1953), 579.

42. In Conference Report, Oct. 1952, 12.

43. In Conference Report, Oct. 1961, 81.

44. See *Highlights in the Life of President David O. McKay,* 262–66.

45. In Conference Report, Oct. 1908, 108.

46. See *David O. McKay: Apostle to the World, Prophet of God,* 232–33.

47. In Conference Report, Apr. 1964, 5.

48. *Pathways to Happiness,* 117.

49. *Pathways to Happiness,* 113.

50. *The Holy Temple* (1980), 263.

51. *Stand Ye in Holy Places: Selected Sermons and Writings of President Harold B. Lee* (1975), 178.

52. In Conference Report, Apr. 1970, 4.

"Let men and women everywhere keep their eyes upon him who ever shines
as a Light to all the world—for Christ is the Way, the Truth, the Life."

Jesus Christ: "The Way, the Truth, and the Life"

If he would seek the real purpose of life,
the individual must live for something higher than self.
He hears the Savior's voice saying, "I am the way,
the truth, and the life. . . ." (John 14:6.)[1]

Introduction

On 4 December 1920, Elder David O. McKay and his traveling companion, Hugh J. Cannon, a stake president and editor of the Church magazine the *Improvement Era,* began an assignment from the First Presidency to visit and strengthen Church members throughout the world. Their trip lasted one year and took them approximately 60,000 miles, over half that distance traveled on water. On the evening of 10 May 1921, as they sailed toward what is now Western Samoa, Elder McKay had the following experience:

"Toward evening, the reflection of the afterglow of a beautiful sunset was most splendid! . . . Pondering still upon this beautiful scene, I lay in my [bed] at ten o'clock that night. . . . I then fell asleep, and beheld in vision something infinitely sublime. In the distance I beheld a beautiful white city. Though it was far away, yet I seemed to realize that trees with luscious fruit, shrubbery with gorgeously tinted leaves, and flowers in perfect bloom abounded everywhere. The clear sky above seemed to reflect these beautiful shades of color. I then saw a great concourse of people approaching the city. Each one wore a white flowing robe and a white headdress. Instantly my attention seemed centered upon their leader, and though I could see only the profile of his features and his body, I recognized him at once as my Savior! The tint and radiance of his countenance were glorious to behold. There was a peace about him which seemed sublime—it was divine!

"The city, I understood, was his. It was the City Eternal; and the people following him were to abide there in peace and eternal happiness.

"But who were they?

"As if the Savior read my thoughts, he answered by pointing to a semicircle that then appeared above them, and on which were written in gold the words:

*"These Are They Who Have Overcome the World—
Who Have Truly Been Born Again!"²*

In his first general conference address as President of the Church, President McKay reaffirmed his testimony of the Savior and of the blessings that come to those who follow Him:

"No one can preside over this Church without first being in tune with the head of the Church, our Lord and Savior, Jesus Christ. He is our head. This is his Church. Without his divine guidance and constant inspiration, we cannot succeed. With his guidance, with his inspiration, we cannot fail. . . .

". . . I know the reality of his existence, of his willingness to guide and direct all who serve him."³

Teachings of David O. McKay

Christ is the Light to humanity.

Christ is the light to humanity. In that light man sees his way clearly; when it is rejected, the soul of man stumbles in darkness. No person, no group, no nation can achieve true success without following him who said:

"I am the light of the world: he that followeth me shall not walk in darkness, but shall have the light of life." (John 8:12.)

It is a sad thing when individuals and nations extinguish that light—when Christ and his gospel are supplanted by the law of the jungle and the strength of the sword. The chief tragedy in the world at the present time is its disbelief in God's goodness and its lack of faith in the teachings and doctrines of the gospel.⁴

2

The Church of Jesus Christ of Latter-day Saints believes that in his life and teachings Jesus Christ reveals a standard of personal living and of social relations that, if fully embodied in individual lives and in human institutions, would not only ameliorate the present ills of society, but would also bring happiness and peace to mankind.

If it be said that . . . so-called Christian nations have failed to achieve such a goal, we answer that all failure to do so may be found in the fact that they have failed to apply the principles and teachings of true Christianity. . . .

. . . The human family has suffered from unrestrained expressions and manifestations of selfishness, hatred, envy, greed—animal passions that have led to war, devastation, pestilence, and death. If even the simplest principles of the Savior's teachings had been observed, history would have been changed.[5]

When Christians throughout the world have this faith [in Christ] coursing in their blood, when they feel a loyalty in their hearts to the resurrected Christ, and to the principles connoted thereby, mankind will have taken the first great step toward the perpetual peace for which we daily are praying: Reject Him and the world will be filled with hatred, and drenched in blood by recurring wars.[6]

The gospel of Jesus Christ is the crucible in which hate, envy, and greed are consumed, and good will, kindness, and love remain as inner aspirations by which man truly lives and builds.

Let men and women everywhere keep their eyes upon him who ever shines as a Light to all the world—for Christ is the Way, the Truth, the Life, the only safe Guide to that haven of peace for which people the wide world over are earnestly praying.[7]

Christ taught and exemplified the way to the ideal life among our fellowmen.

"How can we know the way?" asked Thomas, as he sat with his fellow apostles and their Lord at the table after the supper on the memorable night of the betrayal; and Christ's divine answer was: "I am the way, the truth, and the life. . . ." (John 14:5–6.)

And so he is! He is the source of our comfort, the inspiration of our life, the author of our salvation. If we want to know our relationship to God, we go to Jesus Christ. If we would know the truth of the immortality of the soul, we have it exemplified in the Savior's resurrection.

If we desire to learn the ideal life to lead among our fellowmen, we can find a perfect example in the life of Jesus. Whatsoever our noble desires, our lofty aspirations, our ideals in any phase of life, we can look to Christ and find perfection. So, in seeking a standard for moral manhood, we need only to go to the Man of Nazareth and in him find embodied all virtues that go to make the perfect man.

The virtues that combined to make this perfect character are truth, justice, wisdom, benevolence, and self-control. His every thought, word, and deed were in harmony with divine law and, therefore, true. The channel of communication between him and the Father was constantly open, so that truth, which rests upon revelation, was always known to him.[8]

The Church of Jesus Christ of Latter-day Saints accepts as literally true the words of Jesus: "I am come that they might have life, and that they might have it more abundantly." (John 10:10.) We believe, however, that this abundant life is obtained not only from spiritual exaltation, but also by the application to daily life of the principles that Jesus taught.

These principles are few and simple and may, if desired, be applied by every normal person. The first of these, and the foundation upon which a true Christian society is built, is: "And thou shalt love the Lord thy God with all thy heart, and with all thy soul, and with all thy mind, and with all thy strength. . . ." (Mark 12:30.) A belief in a Supreme Being who lives and loves his children—a belief that gives power and vigor to the soul. An assurance that he can be approached for guidance, and that he will manifest himself to those who seek him.

Another is the acceptance of the truth that life is a gift of God and therefore divine. The proper use of this gift impels man to become the master, not the slave, of nature. His appetites are to be controlled and used for the benefit of his health and the prolongation of life. His passions are to be mastered and controlled for the happiness and blessings of others and the perpetuity of the race.

A third principle is personal integrity. By this I mean plain, everyday honesty, sobriety, and respect for others' rights, such as will win the confidence of one's fellows. This recognition applies to nations as well as to individuals. It is as wrong for a nation, because it is powerful, to steal from another and oppress it as it is for an individual to rob and kill his neighbor.

A fourth essential is social consciousness that awakens in each individual the realization that it is his duty to make the world better for his having been in it.[9]

The Savior's life was guided principally by . . . *Individual Purity* and *Service.* He kept himself wholly unspotted from the sins of the world, and devoted his life to the consideration of others, to salvation for the human family. He was always looking out for the oppressed, comforting the sick, healing the maimed and disabled, giving his life for the world.[10]

There is imperative need of a drastic change in men's dealings with one another. Never has there been a time in the history of the world when a change for the better was more imperative. And since rejection of Christ's teachings has resulted in repeated disaster, with only intermittent periods of respite and peace and progress, why in the name of reason should people not be willing to substitute for selfish aggrandizement Christ's principle of brotherly consideration, of fair dealing, of the value and sacredness of human life, of the virtue of forgiveness, of the condemnation of the sin of hypocrisy and of covetousness, of the saving power of love.[11]

Members of the Church of Christ are under obligation to make the sinless Son of Man their ideal. He is the one Perfect Being who ever walked the earth; the sublimest example of nobility; Godlike in nature; perfect in his love; our Redeemer; our Savior; the immaculate Son of our Eternal Father; the Light, the Life, the Way.[12]

I accept Jesus Christ as the personification of human perfection.[13]

Christ's teachings are applicable to everyday life.

I believe in every word that Jesus spoke, and to me the teaching is applicable in my life and yours. Keeping in mind the fact that we are the children of our Father in heaven, when we seek the kingdom of God, first, we become conscious of a new aim in life. . . . Only in the complete surrender of our inner life may we rise above the selfish, sordid pull of nature. . . .

For two thousand years, practically, men have considered [Christ's teachings] as impractical—too ideal, they say, but if we sincerely believe in Christ's divinity, that he is "the way, the truth, and the life" (see John 14:6), we cannot consistently doubt the applicability of his teachings to everyday life.

True, there are weighty problems to solve—evils of the slums, the ever-recurring conflicts between labor and capital, drunkenness, prostitution, international hatreds, and a hundred other current questions. But if heeded, Christ's appeal for personal integrity, honor, fair-dealing, and love is basic in the proper solution of all these social and economic difficulties.

Most certainly before the world even approaches these ideals, men's hearts must be changed. Christ came into the world for that very purpose. The principal reason for preaching the gospel is to change men's hearts and lives. . . . Those who have been converted . . . can testify how the conversion has changed their lives. . . . By such conversion they bring peace and good will to the world instead of strife [and] suffering.[14]

As a first step, . . . make truly applicable the simple injunction of putting one's self in the other fellow's place, the surest of all means of eliminating the bitterness that characterizes misunderstandings.

No thinking person can say truthfully that the application of this one simple act if practiced among individuals and nations would not bring about a better world!

Equally effective and applicable are His teachings regarding the value and sacredness of human life, the virtue of forgiveness, the necessity of fair dealing, His condemnation of the sin of hypocrisy, and of covetousness, His teachings regarding the saving power of love, and of the immortality of the soul.[15]

Living the teachings of Christ leads to true greatness and happiness.

No man can sincerely resolve to apply in his daily life the teachings of Jesus of Nazareth without sensing a change in his nature. The phrase "born again" has a deeper significance than what many people attach to it. This changed feeling may be indescribable, but it is real.

Happy the person who has truly sensed the uplifting, transforming power that comes from this nearness to the Savior, this kinship to the living Christ. I am thankful that I know that Christ is my Redeemer.[16]

The highest of all ideals are the teachings and particularly the life of Jesus of Nazareth, and that man is most truly great who is most Christlike.

What you sincerely in your heart think of Christ will determine what you are, will largely determine what your acts will be. No person can study this divine personality, can accept his teachings without becoming conscious of an uplifting and refining influence within himself.[17]

By choosing him as our ideal, we create within ourselves a desire to be like him, to have fellowship with him. We perceive life as it should be and as it may be.[18]

He promised no material rewards, but he did promise perfected, divine manhood. . . . "Be ye perfect, even as your Father which is in heaven is perfect." [See Matthew 5:48.] And with that divine manhood comes the resultant happiness, true happiness.[19]

The gospel, the glad tidings of great joy, is the true guide to mankind; and that man or woman is happiest and most content who lives nearest to its teachings, which are the antitheses of hatred, persecution, tyranny, domination, injustice—things which foster tribulation, destruction, and death throughout the world. What the sun in the heavenly blue is to the earth struggling to get free from winter's grip, so the gospel of Jesus Christ is to the sorrowing souls yearning for something higher and better than mankind has yet found on earth.

What a glorious condition will be in this old world when it can truthfully be said to Christ, the Redeemer of mankind, "All men seek for thee." (Mark 1:37.) Selfishness, envy, hatred, lying, stealing, cheating, disobedience, quarreling, and fighting among nations will then be no more![20]

We celebrate his birth in whose mission on earth (1) God is glorified; (2) earth is promised peace; (3) all men [are] given the assurance of God's good will toward them!

If every man born into the world would have as the beacon of his life these three glorious ideals—how much sweeter and happier life would be! With such an aim, everyone would seek all that is pure, just, honorable, virtuous, and true—all that leads to perfection. . . . He would eschew that which is impure, dishonorable, or vile. If every man *desired* to show good will toward his fellow men and strove to express that desire in a thousand kind sayings and little deeds that would reflect unselfishness and self-sacrifice, what a contribution each would make toward universal peace on earth and the happiness of mankind![21]

What a more delightful world this would be if, for example, man earnestly strove to apply Christ's advice: "If ye have aught against a brother, go to him." [See Matthew 5:23–24.] Or, again, His admonition: "seek first the kingdom of God and His righteousness" [see Matthew 6:33], which means, simply, be not so anxious about worldly things as to make them of superior worth to spiritual attainment.[22]

I feel, and know, that through him and through him only, and by obedience to the gospel of Jesus Christ, can we find happiness and salvation in this world and eternal life in the world to come.[23]

Suggestions for Study and Discussion

- What are some of the major problems facing mankind today? What specific principles taught by Jesus Christ would help resolve these problems? How would they help resolve them?

- Why is faith in Jesus Christ essential to improve conditions in the world today? What does it mean to you that Jesus Christ is "the way, the truth, and the life"?

- What prevents people today from applying the Savior's teachings in their lives? In what ways can we as a Church and as individuals promote His standards in the world?

- Jesus Christ said that He came into the world that we "might have life, and that [we] might have it more abundantly" (John 10:10; see page 4). In what ways has the Savior helped you have a more abundant life?

- President McKay testified of Jesus Christ as the "personification of human perfection" (page 5). What are some of the characteristics of Jesus Christ that make Him the example of perfection? (See pages 4–5.) To what extent are these characteristics realistically attainable in our lives? What can we do to make our individual lives more Christlike?

- President McKay taught that those who apply the Savior's teachings will sense a change in themselves (see page 7). How have you seen this to be true in your life or the lives of others? What is the significance of President McKay's use of the words "born again"? (See pages 7–8.)

Related Scriptures: Matthew 11:28–30; John 13:15–17; 3 Nephi 27:21–22, 27; D&C 84:49–54

Notes

1. In Conference Report, Oct. 1969, 8.
2. *Cherished Experiences from the Writings of President David O. McKay,* comp. Clare Middlemiss, rev. ed. (1976), 59–60; paragraphing altered.
3. In Conference Report, Apr. 1951, 157, 159.
4. *Treasures of Life,* comp. Clare Middlemiss (1962), 203–4.
5. "What Doth It Profit?" *Improvement Era,* Jan. 1970, 2.
6. In Conference Report, Apr. 1944, 124–25.
7. "Walk in the Light," *Improvement Era,* Apr. 1954, 222.
8. In Conference Report, Apr. 1968, 6–7.
9. "What Doth It Profit?" *Improvement Era,* Jan. 1970, 3.
10. In Conference Report, Apr. 1918, 81.
11. "Walk in the Light," *Improvement Era,* Apr. 1954, 221–22.
12. *Treasures of Life,* 210.
13. In Conference Report, Oct. 1965, 144.
14. In Conference Report, Oct. 1953, 10–11; paragraphing altered.
15. In Conference Report, Oct. 1942, 69–70.
16. In Conference Report, Apr. 1944, 124.
17. In Conference Report, Apr. 1951, 93.
18. In Conference Report, Apr. 1951, 98.
19. In Conference Report, Apr. 1953, 137–38.
20. In Conference Report, Apr. 1968, 9.
21. *Gospel Ideals* (1953), 36–37.
22. In Conference Report, Apr. 1944, 124.
23. In Conference Report, Oct. 1953, 9.

President McKay taught that our "earthly existence is but a test" to see whether we choose to follow and develop our carnal nature or our spiritual nature.

10

The Dual Nature of Man

*The question, then, is: Which will give the
more abundant life—pampering our physical
nature or developing our spiritual selves?
Is not that the real problem?*[1]

Introduction

In a general conference address in 1949, President McKay related the following story:

"There is an old story . . . which told of the experience of a great artist who was engaged to paint a mural for the cathedral in a Sicilian town. The subject was the life of Christ. For many years the artist labored diligently, and finally the painting was finished except for the two most important figures, the Christ Child and Judas Iscariot. He searched far and wide for models for those two figures.

" 'One day while walking in an old part of the city he came upon some children playing in the street. Among them was a twelve-year-old boy whose face stirred the painter's heart. It was the face of an angel—a very dirty one, perhaps, but the face he needed.

" 'The artist took the child home with him, and day after day the boy sat patiently until the face of the Christ Child was finished.

" 'But the painter failed to find a model for Judas. For years, haunted by the fear that his masterpiece would remain unfinished, he continued his search.

" 'One afternoon, in a tavern, the painter saw a gaunt and tattered figure stagger across the threshold and fall to the floor, begging for a glass of wine. The painter lifted him up and looked into a face that startled him. It seemed to bear the marks of every sin of mankind.

" ' "Come with me," the painter said, "I will give you wine, food, and clothing."

" 'Here at last was his model for Judas. For many days and parts of many nights the painter worked feverishly to complete his masterpiece.

" 'As the work went on, a change came over the model. A strange tension replaced the stuporous languor, and his blood-shot eyes were fixed with horror on the painted likeness of himself. One day, perceiving his subject's agitation, the painter paused in his work, saying, "My son, I'd like to help you. What troubles you so?"

" 'The model sobbed and buried his face in his hands. After a long moment he lifted pleading eyes to the old painter's face.

" ' "Do you not then remember me? Years ago I was your model for the Christ Child!" ' "

After relating the story, President McKay said, "Well, the story may be fact or fiction, but the lesson it teaches is true to life. The dissipated man made a wrong choice in his youth, and in seeking gratification in indulgence sank ever lower and lower until he wallowed in the gutter." [2]

Teachings of David O. McKay

Each of us has two contrasting natures: the physical and the spiritual.

Man is a dual being, and his life a plan of God. That is the first fundamental fact to keep in mind. Man has a *natural* body and a *spiritual* body. In declaring this fact the scriptures are very explicit:

"And the Gods formed man from the dust of the ground, and took his spirit (that is, the man's spirit), and put it into him; and breathed into his nostrils the breath of life, and man became a living soul." [Abraham 5:7.]

Man's body, therefore, is but the tabernacle in which his spirit dwells. Too many, far too many, are prone to regard the body as the man, and consequently to direct their efforts to the gratifying of the body's pleasures, its appetites, its desires, its passions. Too few recognize that the real man is an immortal spirit, which [is] "intelligence or the light of truth," [see D&C 93:29] animated as an individual entity before the body was begotten, and that this spiritual entity with all its distinguishing traits will continue after the body ceases to respond to its earthly environment. Said the Savior:

"I came forth from the Father, and am come into the world: again, I leave the world, and go to the Father." (John 16:28.)

As Christ's pre-existent Spirit animated a body of flesh and bones, so does the pre-existent spirit of every human being born into this world. Will you keep that in mind as the first basic truth of life?

The question, then, is: Which will give the more abundant life—pampering our physical nature or developing our spiritual selves? Is not that the real problem?[3]

Indulgence in appetites and desires of the physical man satisfy but for the moment and may lead to unhappiness, misery, and possible degradation; spiritual achievements give "joy not to be repented of."

In his epistle to the Galatians, Paul specifically enumerates the "works of the flesh," as he calls them, and the "fruits of the Spirit." Note this classification: The works of the flesh are manifest as these:

". . . Adultery, fornication, uncleanness, lasciviousness,

"Idolatry, witchcraft, hatred, variance, emulations, wrath, strife, seditions, heresies,

"Envyings, murders, drunkenness, revellings, and such like: of the which I tell you before, as I have also told you in time past, that they which do such things shall not inherit the kingdom of God.

"But the fruit of the Spirit is love, joy, peace, longsuffering, gentleness, goodness, faith,

"Meekness, temperance: against such there is no law.

"And they that are Christ's have crucified the flesh with the affections and lusts.

"If we live in the Spirit, let us also walk in the Spirit." (Gal. 5:19–25.)[4]

There is something higher than the animal life; namely, the spiritual realm where there is love, the divinest attribute of the human soul. There are also sympathy, kindness and other attributes.[5]

There is something within [man] which urges him to rise above himself, to control his environment, to master the body and all things physical and live in a higher and more beautiful world.[6]

Man has a greater destiny than just a mere animal life. That is a touch of the spirit! Every man who has sensed that has a testimony himself and every woman also has a testimony herself, that man is a dual being. He has a body, just as all other animals have. But he has something that comes only from his Father in heaven, and he is entitled, is susceptible to whisperings, susceptible to influences from his Divine Parent, through the Holy Ghost, the medium between us and God the Father and his Son Jesus Christ.[7]

Life is a test to see which of our two natures we will follow and develop.

Man's earthly existence is but a test as to whether he will concentrate his efforts, his mind, his soul, upon things which contribute to the comfort and gratification of his physical nature, or whether he will make as his life's pursuit the acquisition of spiritual qualities.

"Every noble impulse, every unselfish expression of love; every brave suffering for the right; every surrender of self to something higher than self; every loyalty to an ideal; every unselfish devotion to principle; every helpfulness to humanity; every act of self-control; every fine courage of the soul, undefeated by pretense or policy, but by being, doing, and living of good for the very good's sake—that is spirituality."[8]

Generally there is in man a divinity which strives to push him onward and upward. We believe that this power within him is the spirit that comes from God. Man lived before he came to this earth, and he is here now to strive to perfect the spirit within. At sometime in his life, every man is conscious of a desire to come

14

in touch with the Infinite. His spirit reaches out for God. This sense of feeling is universal, and all men ought to be, in deepest truth, engaged in the same great work—the search for and the development of spiritual peace and freedom.[9]

The choice is given, whether we live in the physical world as animals, or whether we use what earth offers us as a means of living in the spiritual world that will lead us back into the presence of God.

This means specifically:

Whether we choose selfishness or whether we will deny ourselves for the good of others;

Whether we will cherish indulgence of appetite [and] passion, or whether we will develop restraint and self-control.

Whether we choose licentiousness or chastity;

Whether we will encourage hate or develop love;

Whether [we] practice cruelty or kindness;

Whether [we] be cynical or sanguine—hopeful;

Whether we be traitorous—disloyal to those who love us, to our country, to the Church or to God—or whether we will be loyal;

Whether we be deceitful, or honest, our word our bond;

Whether [we have] a slanderous or a controlled tongue.[10]

Whether a man remains satisfied within what we designate the animal world, satisfied with what the animal world will give him, yielding without effort to the whim of his appetites and passions and slipping farther and farther into the realm of indulgence, or whether, through self-mastery, he rises toward intellectual, moral, and spiritual enjoyments depends upon the kind of choice he makes every day, nay, every hour of his life.[11]

What a travesty on human nature when a person or a group of persons, though endowed with a consciousness of being able to rise in human dignity to realms indiscernible by lower creatures, yet will still be content to obey animal instincts, without putting forth efforts to experience the joy of goodness, purity, self-mastery, and faith that spring from compliance to moral rules! How tragic it is when man, made a "little lower than the angels and crowned with glory and honour" (Psalm 8:5), will content himself to grovel on the animal plane.[12]

Earth in all its majesty and wonder is not the end and purpose of creation. ". . . *[My] glory," says the Lord himself, "(is) to bring to pass the immortality and eternal life of man."* (Moses 1:39.) And man in exercising the divine gift of free agency should feel in duty bound, should sense the *obligation* to assist the Creator in the accomplishment of this divine purpose.

The true end of life is not mere existence, not pleasure, not fame, not wealth. *The true purpose of life is the perfection of humanity through individual effort, under the guidance of God's inspiration.*

Real life is response to the best within us. To be alive only to appetite, pleasure, pride, money-making, and not to goodness and kindness, purity and love, poetry, music, flowers, stars, God and eternal hopes, is to deprive one's self of the real joy of living.[13]

Spirituality requires self-mastery and communion with God.

Spirituality, our true aim, is the consciousness of victory over self and of communion with the Infinite.[14]

Spirituality impels one to conquer difficulties and acquire more and more strength. To feel one's faculties unfolding and truth expanding the soul is one of life's sublimest experiences. Being true to self and being loyal to high ideals develops spirituality. The real test of any religion is the kind of man it makes. Being "honest, true, chaste, benevolent, virtuous, and in doing good to all men" [see Articles of Faith 1:13] are virtues which contribute to the highest acquisition of the soul. It is the "divine in man, the supreme, crowning gift that makes him king of all created things."[15]

The man who . . . [has] in mind making better the world in which he lives, desiring to contribute to the happiness of his family and his fellows, and who does all things for the glory of God, will, to the extent that he denies himself for these ideals, develop his spirituality. Indeed, only to the extent that he does this will he rise above the plane of the animal world.[16]

Spirituality and morality as taught by the Latter-day Saints are firmly anchored in fundamental principles, principles from which the world can never escape even if it would, and the first fundamental is a belief—with Latter-day Saints a knowledge—in the existence of a personal God. Latter-day Saint children have been taught to recognize him, and to pray to him as one who can listen and hear and feel just as an earthly father can listen, hear and feel, and they have absorbed into their very beings, from their mothers and their fathers, the real testimony that this personal God has spoken in this dispensation. There is a reality about it.[17]

I bear testimony that the channel of communication is open, and the Lord is ready to guide and does guide his people. Isn't that worth resisting a temptation, to seek an opportunity to gratify your appetite or your vanity as some others do, and when they do, merit excommunication from the church, just for the gratification of a whim or a passion? It's open to you—two ways are open. One leading to the spirit, the testimony of the spirit that is in harmony with the spirit of creation, the Holy Ghost. The spirit of the Lord animates and enlivens every spirit, in the church or out of it. By Him we live and move and have our being, but the testimony of the Holy Ghost is a special privilege. It's like tuning in your radio and hearing a voice on the other side of the world. Men who are not within that radiation can't hear it, but you hear it, you hear that voice and you are entitled to that voice and the guidance of it and it will come to you if you do your part. But if you yield to your own instincts, your own desires, your own passions, and pride yourself into thinking and planning and scheming, and think you are getting away with it, things will become dark. You have accomplished your gratification and passion and appetite, but you deny the spirit; you cut off the communication between your spirit and the spirit of the Holy Ghost.[18]

I cannot think of any higher and more blessed ideal than so to live in the Spirit that we might commune with the Eternal.[19]

When God becomes the center of our being, we become conscious of a new aim in life—spiritual attainment. Physical possessions are no longer the chief goal in life. To indulge, nourish, and delight the body as any animal may do is no longer the chief end of mortal existence. God is *not* viewed from the standpoint of what we may get from him, but rather from what we may *give* him.

Only in the complete surrender of our inner life may we rise above the selfish, sordid pull of nature. What the spirit is to the body, God is to the spirit. When the spirit leaves the body, it is lifeless, and when we eliminate God from our lives, spirituality languishes. . . .

. . . Let us resolve that from now on we are going to be men and women of higher and more sterling character, more conscious of our weaknesses, more kind and charitable toward the failings of others. Let us resolve that we shall practice more self-control in our homes; that we shall control our tempers, our feelings, and our tongues that they may not wander beyond the bounds of right and purity; that we shall do more seeking to develop the spiritual side of our lives, and realize how dependent we are upon God for success in this life.[20]

The reality of God the Father, the reality of Jesus Christ, the risen Lord, is a truth which should possess every human soul. God is the center of the human mind as surely as the sun is the center of this universe, and once we feel his Fatherhood, once we feel his nearness, sense the divinity of the deity of the Savior, the truths of the gospel of Jesus Christ follow as naturally as the day the night, and as night the day.[21]

Suggestions for Study and Discussion

- Why is it necessary that we have both a physical and a spiritual nature? How can our appetites and passions be used for good or evil?

- President McKay taught that life is a test to see which nature we will follow (see pages 14–16). In what ways do we experience conflict between our physical and spiritual natures? What choices can we make each day to enjoy such great spiritual gifts as love, joy, and peace? (See pages 13–18.)

- What is the "natural man"? (Mosiah 3:19). Why is the natural man an enemy to God? What must be done to "put off" the natural man? (See pages 16–18.)

- What influences cause many people to focus their lives on gratifying only their physical nature? Why is it sometimes difficult to focus on spiritual things?

- What are some seemingly minor faults that can hamper our spirituality? How can developing self-mastery help us increase our spirituality? (See pages 16–18.)

- How does your relationship with God influence your spirituality? (See pages 16–18.) What can you do to center your life in God the Father and Jesus Christ?

Related Scriptures: Job 32:8; 2 Nephi 2:27–29; Mosiah 16:1–5; Abraham 3:24–25

Notes

1. *Gospel Ideals* (1953), 395.
2. In Conference Report, Apr. 1949, 12–13; paragraphing altered.
3. *Gospel Ideals,* 395.
4. *Gospel Ideals,* 395–96.
5. *Pathways to Happiness,* comp. Llewelyn R. McKay (1957), 288.
6. In Conference Report, Oct. 1928, 37.
7. In Conference Report, Apr. 1960, 122.
8. In Conference Report, Oct. 1963, 89–90.
9. In Conference Report, Oct. 1963, 7.
10. *Gospel Ideals,* 346.
11. In Conference Report, Apr. 1949, 13.
12. In Conference Report, Oct. 1963, 5.
13. In Conference Report, Oct. 1963, 7.
14. In Conference Report, Oct. 1969, 8.
15. In Conference Report, Oct. 1963, 8–9.
16. In Conference Report, Apr. 1958, 7.
17. In Conference Report, Apr. 1934, 22–23.
18. "Talk by President David O. McKay Given to the North British Mission 1 March 1961," Family and Church History Department Archives, The Church of Jesus Christ of Latter-day Saints, 6–7.
19. *Gospel Ideals,* 393–94.
20. In Conference Report, Apr. 1967, 134.
21. In Conference Report, Oct. 1925, 106–7.

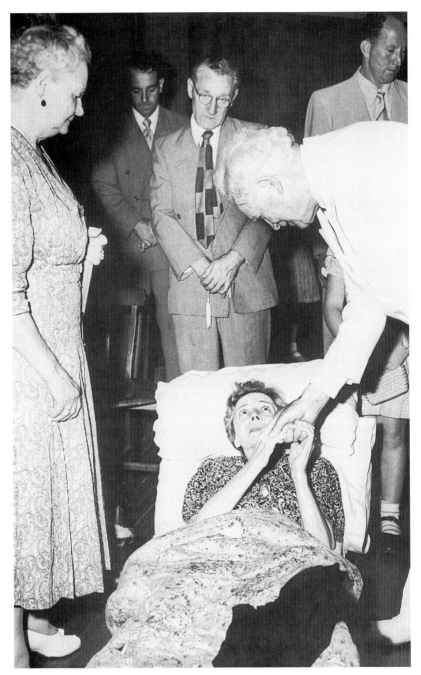

*"The . . . purpose of the organization of this great Church,
so complete, so perfect, is to bless the individual."*

20

The Purpose
of the Church

The Church, with its complete organization,
offers service and inspiration to all.[1]

Introduction

President David O. McKay had a great love for the Church and a strong testimony of its mission to prepare for the final establishment of the kingdom of God. While serving in the Quorum of the Twelve Apostles, he recalled the following experience:

"Just above the pulpit in the meetinghouse where as a boy I attended Sunday services, there hung for many years a large photograph of the late President John Taylor, and under it, in what I thought were gold letters, this phrase:

" 'The Kingdom of God or Nothing'

"The sentiment impressed me as a mere child years before I understood its real significance. I seemed to realize at that early date that there is no other church or organization that approaches the perfection or possesses the divinity that characterizes the church of Jesus Christ. As a child I felt this intuitively; in youth, I became thoroughly convinced of it; and today I treasure it as a firm conviction of my soul. . . .

"The divinity of The Church of Jesus Christ of Latter-day Saints is shown in its organization as well as in its teachings. Godhood, brotherhood, service—these three guiding principles . . . permeate all our Church activity."[2]

President McKay's leadership reflected his firm conviction. During his ministry as President, the Church experienced significant growth and progress worldwide, with membership increasing from approximately one million to almost three million.

Describing President McKay's role in this growth, two historians noted the following:

"Early in his administration President David O. McKay, the first to travel so extensively as Church President, toured missions in Europe, Latin America, Africa, and the South Pacific, dedicating two temple sites in Europe and announcing that a temple would be built in New Zealand. In 1955 he declared that the Church must 'put forth every effort within reason and practicability to place within reach of Church members in these distant missions every . . . spiritual privilege that the Church has to offer' [in Conference Report, Apr. 1955, 25]. Building temples, increasing the number of missions, organizing stakes worldwide, persuading the Saints to build up Zion in their homelands rather than emigrate to America, and eventually putting Church leadership into the hands of each country's native people were all significant steps toward fulfilling that goal."[3]

President McKay's faith in the divine mission and destiny of the Church continued to the end of his life. In a general conference address less than a year before his death, he taught: "God has established his Church never to be thrown down nor given to another people. And as God lives, and his people are true to him and to one another, we need not worry about the ultimate triumph of truth."[4]

Teachings of David O. McKay

The Church's mission is to prepare for the final establishment of the kingdom of God.

The mission of the Church is to prepare the way for the final establishment of the Kingdom of God on earth. Its purpose is, first, to develop in men's lives Christ-like attributes; and, second, to transform society so that the world may be a better and more peaceful place in which to live.[5]

What was the [emphasis] of Christ's teaching when he came among men? The first great proclamation was the announcement that the kingdom of God is at hand. "Repent for the kingdom of God is at hand." [See Mark 1:15.] The fore-runner, John the

Baptist, preached that. He preached the coming of the Lord. He showed the position which the Lord would hold in that kingdom and the Savior bore witness to it and preached the same. And what was the kingdom? Not a mythical, but a real kingdom; not only a feeling within, but also an outward expression of righteousness. *It was divine government among men.* That was what the Savior had in mind, the establishing of a divine government among men.[6]

The term [kingdom of God] implies divine rule in the hearts and wills of men and in society. Man acknowledges a power and authority superior to his own. "It is not the arbitrary rule of a despotic Deity, but is based upon man's voluntary submission of his will to that of God's." On one occasion Jesus said, "The kingdom of God is within you." [Luke 17:21.] That is true, for it is in the heart of man that membership in the outward kingdom has its origin. . . . Only such a group looking as one mind to heaven for guidance can eventually transform human society.

The Kingdom of God implies also a universal brotherhood in which all men acknowledge God as their Supreme Ruler and cherish the desire to obey His divine will.[7]

There are those in the world who say that jealousy, enmity, [and] selfishness in men's hearts will always preclude the establishing of the ideal society known as the Kingdom of God. No matter what doubters and scoffers say, the mission of the Church of Christ is to eliminate sin and wickedness from the hearts of men, and so to transform society that peace and good-will will prevail on this earth.[8]

Priesthood quorums and auxiliary organizations are designed to help accomplish the Church's mission.

Consider the priesthood of the Church. Picture therein the men and boys organized in working sections or groups, from the father ninety years old, down to the boy twelve years of age. In these groups you find exemplified all that human society seeks in social groups and in societies. There is opportunity in these quorum groups for fellowship, brotherhood, and organized service. . . .

Those who are active are working in an organized way for the betterment of one another, for the personal welfare of the membership and for the good of society as a whole. If we considered no further than the quorums, is not that a sublime picture, where men and boys may congregate, associate, affiliate in service for humanity, in which every man considers everyone a brother? In that quorum the doctor sits by the side of a carpenter, each interested in the most ennobling of aspirations— worship of God and helpful service to humanity![9]

The responsibility of the Relief Society is to aid the priesthood in establishing the kingdom of God, in relieving the suffering and giving succor to the poor, and in many ways in contributing to the peace and happiness of the world. . . .

One of the most encouraging promises ever given to people who love service is that made by the Savior in these words, "Inasmuch as ye have done it unto one of the least of these my brethren, ye have done it unto me." (Matt. 25:40.) . . . I grew to manhood before I realized the significance of the service that is rendered by our sisters in this Church.[10]

The Church, recognizing the potency of other influences besides the home in the growing child's life before he reaches self-determination, offers a religious environment almost from the time of birth. The Sunday School, the Primary, the [Young Men and Young Women organizations] arrange suitable instruction, entertainment, and proper guidance from the cradle roll to maturity.[11]

The Latter-day Saints are truly a people who aid one another in the productive life, a life that tends towards the salvation of the human being. By that salvation I do not mean just a place in the hereafter where all our cares and worries may cease, but a salvation that applies to the individual, to the family and to society here and now. Through the Gospel of Jesus Christ, and the perfect organization of the Church as revealed in this dispensation to the Prophet Joseph Smith, we are aiding one another *spiritually* by taking advantage of the many opportunities for service in the Church. We are fostering *brotherhood* by activity and association in priesthood quorums, in auxiliary associations and in our social gatherings.[12]

As the Church fulfills its mission, it blesses and perfects individuals.

To members of The Church of Jesus Christ of Latter-day Saints, the worth of the individual has a special meaning. Quorums, auxiliaries, wards, stakes, even the Church itself are all organized to further the welfare of man. All are but means to an end, and that end is the happiness and eternal welfare of every child of God. I therefore appeal to all members of the Church, and particularly to presidents of quorums and to officers of all auxiliaries, to put forth a unified effort to make sweeter the lives of men.[13]

There is in man not only an instinct, but also a divinity that strives to push him onward and upward. The sense is universal, and at some time in his life every man is conscious of possessing it.

Associated with this spiritual urge are three great needs that remain unchanged throughout the centuries: (1) Every normal person yearns to know something of God. What is he like? Is he interested in the human family, or does he disregard it entirely? (2) What is the best life to live in this world in order to be most successful and to get the most happiness? (3) What is that inevitable thing called death? What is beyond it?

If you want your answers to these longings of the human soul, you must come to the Church to get it. Only true religion can satisfy the yearning soul.[14]

Why do we hold these conference meetings and all other meetings in the Church? They are held for the good of the individual—for your son and my son, your daughter and mine. The Lord has said, ". . . if it so be that you should labor all your days in crying repentance unto this people, and bring, save it be one soul unto me, how great shall be your joy with him in the kingdom of my Father!" [D&C 18:15.] . . .

The . . . purpose of the organization of this great Church, so complete, so perfect, is to bless the individual.[15]

This Church was established in the only way in which the Church of Christ can be established, by direct authority from God. Thus founded it invites the whole world to come to a

Church recognized by God himself, and which offers every advantage that the human mind, the emotions and desires may contemplate in the fulfilling of the individual mission on this earth. "It is an ever-broadening wave of direct personal influence, destined ultimately to touch and transform all men, so that they like Jesus shall become Godlike." "Mormonism," as true Christianity, "subdues selfishness, regulates the passions, subordinates the appetites, quickens the intellect, exalts the affections. It promotes industry, honesty, truth, purity, kindness. It humbles the proud, exalts the lowly, upholds the law, favors liberty, is essential to it, and would unite men in one great brotherhood."[16]

As the Church fulfills its mission, it contributes to the welfare of humanity.

Many citizens are deeply troubled over the increase in crime, the high divorce and illegitimacy rates, the increasing incidents of venereal diseases, the scandals in high office, and other symptoms of private and public dishonesty.

Is there a moral breakdown? Is there cause for alarm? The world is all about us, and the statistics we read about are frightening indeed, and they are a necessary warning. . . .

The mission of the Church is to minimize and, if possible, eliminate these evils from the world. It is evident that we are in need of a unifying force to eliminate these evils. Such a uniting force, such an ideal is the gospel of Jesus Christ, as restored through the Prophet Joseph Smith. It explains man's life and its purpose and has within it the vital saving elements, noble ideals, and spiritual uplift for which the heart of man is yearning.

Right-thinking, upright men and women everywhere are desirous of eliminating from our communities evil elements that are constantly disintegrating society—the liquor problem with its drunkenness, the narcotic habit with all its attendant evils, immorality, poverty, etc. The Church is seeking to make both home and community environment better and brighter.[17]

Let us here and now express gratitude for the Church of Jesus Christ with quorums and auxiliaries specially organized to combat these evils. It was established by divine revelation of

God the Father and his Son Jesus Christ. Its glorious mission is to proclaim the truth of the restored gospel; to uplift society that people may mingle more amicably one with another; to create in our communities a wholesome environment in which our children may find strength to resist temptation and encouragement to strive for cultural and spiritual attainment.[18]

The Church, established by divine inspiration to an unlearned youth, offers to the world the solution of all its social problems. It has stood the test of the first century successfully. In the midst of brilliant concepts of men in this twentieth century, who seek conscientiously for social reforms and who peer blindly into the future to read the destiny of man, the Church shines forth as the sun in the heavens, around which other luminaries revolve as satellites of minor importance. Truly it is the creator and preserver of man's highest values. Its real task, the redemption of our human world. "It is the light of truth radiating everywhere in the world, and this light cannot fail to reveal to man, sooner or later, the divine ideals by which man should live."[19]

The Church, with its complete organization, offers service and inspiration to all. . . . Instead of taking men out of the world, it seeks to develop perfect, Godlike men in the midst of society, and through them to solve the problems of society.[20]

Suggestions for Study and Discussion

- Based on President McKay's teachings, how would you describe the purpose of the Church? (See pages 22–23.) Why do we hold Church meetings and conferences? (See pages 25–26.)

- How does the Church help prepare for the final establishment of the kingdom of God? (See pages 23–27.) In what ways does the Church resemble and exemplify the kingdom of God that is yet to be established? (See pages 22–23.)

- What does the Church provide that will lead faithful members to eternal life? (See pages 23–27.) How have you seen that the organization of the Church, with its quorums and auxiliaries, helps to perfect individuals? (See also Ephesians 4:11–13.)

- What are some of the problems facing society today? (See page 26.) In what ways can applying gospel principles help resolve these problems? (See pages 26–27.)

- In what ways has membership in the Church blessed your life? What can you and your family do to more fully benefit from what the Church offers?

- What can we do to help the Church carry out its responsibilities in these latter days?

Related Scriptures: Ephesians 2:19–22; 4:11–15; Moroni 6:4–9; D&C 10:67–69; 65:1–6

Notes

1. *Gospel Ideals* (1953), 109.
2. *Cherished Experiences from the Writings of President David O. McKay,* comp. Clare Middlemiss, rev. ed. (1976), 15–16.
3. James B. Allen and Richard O. Cowan, "History of the Church: C. 1945–1990, Post–World War II International Era Period," *Encyclopedia of Mormonism,* 4 vols. (1992), 2:639.
4. In Conference Report, Apr. 1969, 152.
5. In Conference Report, Apr. 1941, 106.
6. In Conference Report, Oct. 1919, 76.
7. In Conference Report, Apr. 1941, 106.
8. In Conference Report, Apr. 1941, 109.
9. In Conference Report, Apr. 1963, 97.
10. *Gospel Ideals,* 255–56.
11. In Conference Report, Apr. 1941, 107.
12. In Conference Report, Apr. 1915, 103.
13. In Conference Report, Oct. 1969, 8.
14. In Conference Report, Apr. 1968, 91–92.
15. In Conference Report, Apr. 1965, 137.
16. In Conference Report, Apr. 1927, 105.
17. In Conference Report, Apr. 1967, 5–6.
18. In Conference Report, Oct. 1948, 122.
19. In Conference Report, Apr. 1930, 83.
20. *Gospel Ideals,* 109–110.

Elements
of Worship

*I pray we may have the strength so to live
that we may merit divine guidance and inspiration;
that through worship, meditation, communion,
and reverence we may sense the reality of being able
to have a close relationship with our Father in
heaven. I bear you my testimony that it is real;
that we can commune with our Heavenly Father.* [1]

Introduction

Early in his life, David O. McKay experienced the peace that comes through communion with God. "I remember lying [in bed] one night," he recalled, "trembling with fear. As a child I was naturally, or unnaturally afraid of the darkness, and would frequently lie wondering about burglars, 'bug-a-boos,' and unseen influences. So I lay this night completely unnerved; but I had been taught that God would answer prayer. Summoning strength I arose from the bed, knelt down in the darkness, and prayed to God to remove that feeling of fear; and I heard as plainly as you hear my voice this afternoon, 'Don't be afraid; nothing will hurt you.' Oh, yes, some may say—'simply the imagination.' Say what you will, I know that to my soul came the sweet peace of a child's prayer answered. That is the faith which is inculcated into the minds of the [children] in every Latter-day Saint home throughout the land. I submit that where children are brought up in close communion with our Eternal Father that there can not be much sin or much evil in that home." [2]

In addition to seeking "communion with the infinite" [3] when he was alone, President McKay rejoiced in worshiping with other

Latter-day Saints. He told of a memorable experience he once had at a Church meeting:

"One of the most impressive services I have ever attended was in a group of over eight hundred people to whom the sacrament was administered, and during that administration not a sound could be heard excepting the ticking of the clock—eight hundred souls, each of whom at least had the opportunity of communion with the Lord. There was no distraction, no orchestra, no singing, no speaking. Each one had an opportunity to search himself introspectively and to consider his worthiness or unworthiness to partake of the sacrament. His was the privilege of getting closer to his Father in heaven. That is ideal!"[4]

President McKay encouraged all Latter-day Saints to pursue this ideal in their worship services and in their personal lives. He said, "To have communion with God, through his Holy Spirit, is one of the noblest aspirations of life."[5]

Teachings of David O. McKay

Reverence is profound respect mingled with love.

Inseparable from the acceptance of the existence of God is an attitude of reverence, to which I wish now to call attention most earnestly to the entire Church. The greatest manifestation of spirituality is reverence; indeed, reverence is spirituality. Reverence is profound respect mingled with love. It is "a complex emotion made up of mingled feelings of the soul." [One writer] says it is "the highest of human feelings." I have said elsewhere that if reverence is the highest, then irreverence is the lowest state in which a man can live in the world. . . .

Reverence embraces regard, deference, honor, and esteem. Without some degree of it, therefore, there would be no courtesy, no gentility, no consideration of others' feelings, or of others' rights. Reverence is the fundamental virtue in religion. It is "one of the signs of strength; irreverence, one of the surest indications of weakness. No man will rise high," says one man, "who jeers at sacred things. The fine loyalties of life," he continues, "must be reverenced or they will be foresworn [or rejected] in the day of trial."

Parents, *Reverence,* as charity, begins at home. In early childhood children should be trained to be respectful, deferential—respectful to one another, to strangers and visitors—deferential to the aged and infirm—reverential to things sacred, to parents and parental love.

Three influences in home life awaken reverence in children and contribute to its development in their souls. These are: *first,* firm but *Gentle Guidance; second, Courtesy* shown by parents to each other, and to children; and *third, Prayer* in which children participate. In every home in this Church parents should strive to act intelligently in impressing children with those three fundamentals.[6]

Reverence directs thought toward God. Without it there is no religion.[7]

I look upon reverence as one of the highest qualities of the soul. An irreverent man is not a believing man. . . .

Reverence indicates high culture, and true faith in deity and in his righteousness.[8]

I am prompted to place reverence next to love. Jesus mentioned it first in the Lord's prayer: "Our Father which art in heaven, hallowed be thy name. . . ." [Matthew 6:9.] *Hallow*—to make holy—to hold in reverence.[9]

If there were more reverence in human hearts, there would be less room for sin and sorrow and more increased capacity for joy and gladness. To make more cherished, more adaptable, more attractive, this gem among brilliant virtues is a project worthy of the most united and prayerful efforts of every officer, every parent, and every member of the Church.[10]

Meditation leads to spiritual communion with God through the Holy Spirit.

We pay too little attention to the value of meditation, a principle of devotion. In our worship there are two elements: One is spiritual communion arising from our own meditation; the other, instruction from others, particularly from those who have authority to guide and instruct us. Of the two, the more profitable introspectively is the meditation. Meditation is the language of the soul. It is defined as "a form of private devotion, or spiritual exercise, consisting in deep, continued reflection on some religious theme." Meditation is a form of prayer. . . .

Meditation is one of the most secret, most sacred doors through which we pass into the presence of the Lord. Jesus set the example for us. As soon as he was baptized and received the Father's approval, "This is my Beloved Son, in whom I am well pleased," [Matthew 3:17] Jesus [went] to what is now known as the mount of temptation. I like to think of it as the mount of meditation where, during the forty days of fasting, he communed with himself and his Father, and contemplated upon the responsibility of his great mission. One result of this spiritual communion was such strength as enabled him to say to the tempter:

". . . Get thee hence, Satan: for it is written, Thou shalt worship the Lord thy God, and him only shalt thou serve." (Matt. 4:10.)

Before he gave . . . the beautiful sermon on the mount, he was in solitude, in communion. He did the same thing after that busy Sabbath day, when he arose early in the morning, after having been the guest of Peter. Peter undoubtedly found the guest chamber empty, and when they sought [Jesus] they found him alone. It was on that morning that Peter said:

". . . All men seek for thee." (Mark 1:37.)

Again, after Jesus had fed the five thousand he told the Twelve to dismiss the multitude, but Jesus went to the mountain for solitude. The historian says, "when the evening was come, he was there alone." (Matt. 14:23.) Meditation! Prayer![11]

Let us make God the center of our lives. . . . To have communion with God, through his Holy Spirit, is one of the noblest aspirations of life. It is when the peace and love of God have entered the soul, when serving him becomes the motivating factor in one's life and existence.[12]

We go to the Lord's house to commune with Him in spirit.

We enter a chapel to worship the Lord. We want to partake of his Spirit, and by partaking of his Spirit we build up our own spiritual strength.[13]

Churches are dedicated and set apart as houses of worship. This means, of course, that all who enter do so, or at least pretend to do so, with an intent to get nearer the presence of the Lord than they can in the street or amidst the worries of a workaday life. In other words, we go to the Lord's house to meet him and to commune with him in spirit. Such a meeting place, then, should first of all be fitting and appropriate in all respects, whether God is considered as the invited guest, or the worshipers as his guests.

Whether the place of meeting is a humble chapel or a "poem in architecture" built of white marble and inlaid with precious stones makes little or no difference in our approach and attitude toward the Infinite Presence. To know God is there should be sufficient to impel us to conduct ourselves orderly, reverently.

In this regard, as members of the Church in our worshiping assemblies, we have much room for improvement. Presiding authorities in stake, ward, and quorum meetings, and especially teachers in classes, should make special effort to maintain better order and more reverence during hours of worship and of study. Less talking behind the pulpit will have a salutary effect upon those who face it. By example and precept, children should be impressed with the inappropriateness of confusion and disorder in a worshiping congregation. They should be impressed in childhood, and have it emphasized in youth, that it is disrespectful to talk or even to whisper during a sermon, and that it is the height of rudeness, except in an emergency, to leave a worshiping assembly before dismissal.[14]

There are two purposes for which each chapel is constructed: first, that it might be the place where all may be trained in the ways of God, and second, that in it all might glorify our Father in heaven, who asks for nothing more of his children than that they might be men and women of such noble character as to come back into his presence.[15]

When you enter a church building, you are coming into the presence of our Father in heaven; and that thought should be sufficient incentive for you to prepare your hearts, your minds, and even your attire, that you might appropriately and properly sit in his presence.[16]

Let us not make Sunday a holiday. It is a holy day, and on that day we should go to the house of worship and seek our God. If we seek him on the Sabbath day, get into his presence on that day, we shall find it less difficult to be in his presence the following days of the week.[17]

The sacrament provides an opportunity to commune with the Lord.

The greatest comfort in this life is the assurance of having close relationship with God. . . . The sacrament period should be a factor in awakening this sense of relationship.

". . . the Lord Jesus the same night in which he was betrayed took bread:

"And when he had given thanks, he brake it, and said, Take eat: this is my body, which is broken for you: this do in remembrance of me.

"After the same manner also he took the cup, when he had supped, saying, This cup is the new testament in my blood: this do ye, as oft as ye drink it, in remembrance of me.

"For as often as ye eat this bread, and drink this cup, ye do shew the Lord's death till he come.

"Wherefore whosoever shall eat this bread, and drink this cup of the Lord, unworthily, shall be guilty of the body and blood of the Lord.

"But let a man examine himself, and so let him eat of that bread and drink of that cup." [1 Corinthians 11:23–28.]

No more sacred ordinance is administered in the Church of Christ than the administration of the sacrament. . . .

There are three things fundamentally important associated with the administration of the sacrament. The first is self-discernment. It is introspection. "This do in remembrance of me," but we should partake *worthily*, each one examining himself with respect to his worthiness.

Secondly, there is a covenant made; a *covenant* even more than a promise. . . . There is nothing more important in life than that. . . . A covenant, a promise, should be as sacred as life. That

*"I believe the short period of administering the sacrament is one
of the best opportunities we have for . . . meditation."*

principle is involved every Sunday when we partake of the
sacrament.

Thirdly, there is another blessing, and that is a sense of close
relationship with the Lord. There is an opportunity to commune
with oneself and to commune with the Lord. We meet in the
house that is dedicated to him; we have turned it over to him;
we call it his house. Well, you may rest assured that he will be
there to inspire us if we come in proper attune to meet him. We
are not prepared to meet him if we bring into that room our
thoughts regarding our business affairs, and especially if we
bring into the house of worship feelings of hatred toward our
neighbor, or enmity and jealousy towards the Authorities of the
Church. Most certainly no individual can hope to come into
communion with the Father if that individual entertain any such
feelings. They are so foreign to worship, and so foreign, particularly, to the partaking of the sacrament. . . .

I believe the short period of administering the sacrament is
one of the best opportunities we have for . . . meditation, and

there should be nothing during that sacred period to distract our attention from the purpose of that ordinance. . . .

. . . We [must] surround this sacred ordinance with more reverence, with perfect order, that each one who comes to the house of God may meditate upon his goodness and silently and prayerfully express appreciation for God's goodness. Let the sacrament hour be one experience of the day in which the worshiper tries at least to realize within himself that it is possible for him to commune with his God.

Great events have happened in this Church because of such communion, because of the responsiveness of the soul to the inspiration of the Almighty. I know it is real. President Wilford Woodruff had that gift to a great extent. He could respond; he knew the "still small voice" to which some are still strangers. You will find that when these most inspirational moments come to you that you are alone with yourself and your God. They come to you probably when you are facing a great trial, when the wall is across your pathway, and it seems that you are facing an insurmountable obstacle, or when your heart is heavy because of some tragedy in your life. I repeat, the greatest comfort that can come to us in this life is to sense the realization of communion with God. Great testimonies have come in those moments. . . .

. . . When you stop to consider the matter, you realize that there is nothing during the administration of the sacrament of an extraneous nature so important as *remembering* our Lord and Savior, nothing so worthy of attention as considering the value of the promise we are making. Why should anything distract us? Is there anything more sublime? We are witnessing there, in the presence of one another, and before him, our Father, that we are willing to take upon ourselves the name of Christ, that we will always remember him, *always,* that we will keep his commandments that he has given us. Can you, can anybody living, who thinks for a moment, place before us anything which is more sacred or more far-reaching in our lives? If we partake of it mechanically, we are not honest, or let us say, we are permitting our thoughts to be distracted from a very sacred ordinance. . . .

. . . Let us make that sacrament hour one of the most impressive means of coming in contact with God's spirit. Let the Holy

Ghost, to which we are entitled, lead us into his presence, and may we sense that nearness, and have a prayer offered in our hearts which he will hear.[18]

Suggestions for Study and Discussion

- What does it mean to have "an attitude of reverence"? (See pages 30–31.) In what ways is reverence more than just being quiet? How can we develop this "profound respect mingled with love"?
- How can we teach the principle of reverence in our homes and at church? (See pages 31, 33.)
- Why is it sometimes difficult to find time to meditate upon the things of God? What can we do to make time for meditation? What blessings can we receive as a result of our meditation? (See pages 31–32, 35–36.)
- What can we do to prepare ourselves to "go to the Lord's house . . . [and] commune with him in spirit"? (See pages 32–36.) How can we prepare ourselves to partake of the sacrament? (See pages 32–36.)
- In what ways can we help our children and others be more reverent in the temple, during sacrament meeting, and in other Church meetings? (See pages 31, 33.) How does coming to a meeting late or leaving early disrupt reverence?
- What is the significance of the sacrament in your life?

Related Scriptures: Psalm 89:5–7; D&C 20:75–79; 63:64; 76:19–24; 109:21; 138:1–11

Notes

1. In Conference Report, Apr. 1967, 88.
2. In Conference Report, Apr. 1912, 52.
3. In Conference Report, Oct. 1936, 103.
4. In Conference Report, Apr. 1946, 114.
5. In Conference Report, Apr. 1967, 133.
6. In Conference Report, Oct. 1956, 6–7.
7. In Conference Report, Apr. 1929, 102.
8. In Conference Report, Oct. 1951, 179–80.
9. In Conference Report, Oct. 1950, 163.
10. In Conference Report, Oct. 1955, 5–6.
11. In Conference Report, Apr. 1946, 113.
12. In Conference Report, Apr. 1967, 133.
13. "Reverence," *Improvement Era,* July 1962, 508.
14. In Conference Report, Oct. 1956, 7.
15. "Our Places of Worship," *Improvement Era,* Sept. 1969, 2.
16. "Reverence," *Improvement Era,* July 1962, 509.
17. In Conference Report, Apr. 1929, 102.
18. In Conference Report, Apr. 1946, 111–12, 114–16; paragraphing altered.

President McKay with his counselors, President Stephen L Richards (left) and President J. Reuben Clark Jr. (right). President McKay said he wished Church members could have "glimpsed the unity of the First Presidency."

The Blessings of Unity

Unity and its synonyms—harmony, goodwill, peace,
concord, mutual understanding—express a condition
for which the human heart constantly yearns.[1]

Introduction

From October 1934 to April 1951, Presidents J. Reuben Clark Jr. and David O. McKay served together as counselors in the First Presidency, first to President Heber J. Grant and then to President George Albert Smith. Throughout this time, President Clark served as first counselor and President McKay served as second counselor.

On 9 April 1951, five days after President Smith's death, Latter-day Saints met for general conference and sustained President David O. McKay as President of the Church. There they learned that President Clark, who had served faithfully as first counselor for almost 17 years, had been called to serve as second counselor. President Stephen L Richards had been called as first counselor.

Sensing that Church members would question this change, President McKay took time in general conference to explain the calling of his two counselors. He said that President Richards had been called as first counselor because he had served longer than President Clark in the apostleship. Emphasizing that this practice was not an "established policy," President McKay simply said that "it seemed advisable" in the callings of Presidents Richards and Clark.

As President McKay continued with his address, he spoke of the unity he felt with his counselors: "We do not want any member in this Church, nor any man or woman listening in to harbor the thought for a moment that there has been any rift between the two counselors who sustained President Smith in the

Quorum of the First Presidency, and President Grant for the years that we were together with that inspired leader. Neither should you feel that there is any demotion. President Clark is a wonderful servant. . . .

"You should understand further, that in the counselorship of the Quorum of the First Presidency these two men are coordinate in authority, in love, and confidence, in freedom to make suggestions, and recommendations, and in their responsibility not only to the Quorum but also to the Lord Jesus Christ and to the people generally.

"They are two great men. I love them both, and say God bless them, and give you the assurance that there will be harmony and love and confidence in the Quorum of the First Presidency as you have sustained them today." [2]

Shortly after President McKay made this statement, President Clark spoke to the Saints, expressing his desire to work harmoniously with his fellow servants: "In the service of the Lord, it is not where you serve but how. In the Church of Jesus Christ of Latter-day Saints, one takes the place to which one is duly called, which place one neither seeks nor declines. I pledge to President McKay and to President Richards the full loyal devoted service to the tasks that may come to me to the full measure of my strength and my abilities, and so far as they will enable me to perform them, however inadequate I may be." [3]

In a general conference three years later, President McKay again spoke of the unity he enjoyed with other Church leaders: "I wish that all within the sound of my voice at this moment, all who have any prejudice in their hearts, might have glimpsed the General Authorities in the House of the Lord last Thursday morning, when they met in fasting and prayer to prepare themselves spiritually for the responsibilities awaiting them in this great conference. You would have glimpsed the unity of the First Presidency and through this transmission of heart to heart, soul to soul, you would have known the love I bear for [my] two counselors, for their clear vision and sound judgment and their patience with their leader when necessary. You would have glimpsed the unity and love of these twelve men [the Quorum of the Twelve Apostles], of . . . the Seventy, . . . and the Presiding Bishopric. We pray that the love and unity in that meeting may extend to every stake presidency, mission presidency, every bishopric, every priesthood quorum and auxiliary throughout the Church. With such unity and love there is no power on earth which can stop the progress of this, the work of God."[4]

Teachings of David O. McKay

The Lord desires unity among His followers.

"Holy Father, keep through thine own name those whom thou hast given me, that they may be one, as we are.

"Neither pray I for these alone, but for them also which shall believe on me through their word;

"That they all may be one; as thou, Father, art in me, and I in thee, that they also may be one in us: that the world may believe that thou hast sent me." (John 17:11, 20–21.)

Thus in one of the most sublime prayers ever offered among men, Jesus makes unity pre-eminent among his followers.

Unity and its synonyms—harmony, goodwill, peace, concord, mutual understanding—express a condition for which the human heart constantly yearns. Its opposites are discord, contention, strife, confusion. . . .

May the appeal of our Lord in his intercessory prayer for unity be realized in our homes, our wards and stakes, and in our support of the basic principles of freedom.[5]

Unity of purpose, with all working in harmony, is needed to accomplish God's work. In a revelation given to the Prophet Joseph Smith about one year after the Church was organized, the Lord in a broad sense makes known why his great work, to be accomplished, has been restored for the benefit of mankind and to prepare the way for his second coming. Said he:

"And even so I have sent mine everlasting covenant into the world, to be a light to the world, and to be a standard for my people, and for the Gentiles to seek to it, and to be a messenger before my face to prepare the way before me." (D&C 45:9.)

Herein we learn of the great obligations placed upon this people to assist the Lord in bringing these things to pass among men. It requires unity and dedication to its purposes. Concerning this need, the Lord has given this warning:

". . . Every kingdom divided against itself is brought to desolation; and every city or house divided against itself shall not stand." (Matt. 12:25.)[6]

We must avoid attitudes and actions that lead to disunity.

One of the first conditions that will bring about disunity will be selfishness; another will be envy: "Brother So-and-so passed me by and said nothing to me about the matter." "The bishopric chose Sister So-and-so to be organist, and she can't play half as well as I." "I'm not going to priesthood meeting any more because the bishopric appointed a certain man to act as adviser of the priests." "The Sunday School chose So-and-so as a teacher." . . . "The presidency of the stake has never recognized me, and I feel offended." "The General Authorities do not always see eye to eye." Oh! a hundred and one little things like that may come up—little things, insignificant in themselves when we compare them with the greater and more real things of life. And yet, I know from experience that the adversary can so magnify them that they become mountains in our lives, and we are offended, and our spirituality starves because we entertain those feelings.

There is another element—fault-finding—associated with that spirit of envy. We find fault with a neighbor. We speak ill of each other. When that feeling comes, it is a good thing just to sing that simple little [Church] hymn, "Nay, Speak No Ill."

> *"Nay, speak no ill; a kindly word*
> *Can never leave a sting behind;*
> *And, oh, to breathe each tale we've heard*
> *Is far beneath a noble mind.*
> *Full oft a better seed is sown*
> *By choosing thus the kinder plan,*
> *For, if but little good is known,*
> *Still let us speak the best we can.*

"Then speak no ill, but lenient be
To other's failings as your own.
If you're the first a fault to see,
Be not the first to make it known,
For life is but a passing day;
No lip may tell how brief its span;
Then, O the little time we stay,
Let's speak of all the best we can."
[*Hymns,* no. 233.][7]

May we go forth with greater resolution to defend one another in righteous living, to defend the Church, not to speak against our neighbors, nor against authorities of the Church, local, stake, or general. Let us avoid evil speaking; let us avoid slander and gossip. These are poisons to the soul to those who indulge. Evil speaking injures the reviler more than the reviled.[8]

There are destructive termites of homes, as well as of houses, and some of these are backbiting, evil-speaking, faultfinding on the part either of parents or of children. Slander is poison to the soul. "Slanderers are like flies that pass all over a man's good parts to light only on his sores." In the ideal home, there is no slanderous gossip about . . . schoolteachers, about public officials, or Church officials. I am more grateful now, as years have come and gone, to my father, who with hands lifted said, "Now, no faultfinding about your teacher or anybody else."[9]

Family unity makes the home a place of refuge and protection.

A child has the right to feel that in his home he has a place of refuge, a place of protection from the dangers and evils of the outside world. Family unity and integrity are necessary to supply this need.[10]

I can imagine few, if any, things more objectionable in the home than the absence of unity and harmony. On the other hand, I know that a home in which unity, mutual helpfulness, and love abide is just a bit of heaven on earth. I surmise that nearly all of you can testify to the sweetness of life in a home in which these virtues predominate. Most gratefully and humbly I cherish the remembrance that never once as a lad in the home of my youth did I ever see one instance of discord between father and mother, and that goodwill and mutual understanding has been the uniting bond that has held together a fortunate group of brothers and sisters. Unity, harmony, goodwill are virtues to be fostered and cherished in every home.[11]

Very frequently discords arise in the home because husbands desire to save their own dignity and have their own way, have their own wishes carried out. Wives desire the same. Some exercise their prerogative to have the last word. Husbands are sometimes even more eager to have it than wives. Each really is trying to save himself or herself, and instead of having harmony and peace in the home there arises discord. Instead of saving the life of harmony in the home, you lose it, merely because you are seeking to save your own selfish life, or have your own selfish way. Better to lose that desire. Say nothing, and in losing your desire and that feeling of enmity, of ruling, of governing, you say nothing, and you gain your life in the home.[12]

May God bless you all, and may he guide and help you that righteousness, harmony, and love for one another may dwell in each home.[13]

Unity in the Church leads to progress and spirituality.

The mission of The Church of Jesus Christ of Latter-day Saints is to establish peace. The Living Christ is its head. Under him tens of thousands of men in the Church are divinely authorized to represent him in variously assigned positions. It is the duty of these representatives to manifest brotherly love, first toward one another, then toward all mankind; to seek unity, harmony, and peace in organizations within the Church, and then by precept and example extend these virtues throughout the world.[14]

In branches and wards of the Church, there is no virtue more conducive to progress and spirituality than the presence of this principle. When jealousy, backbiting, [and] evil-speaking supplant mutual confidence, unity, and harmony, the progress of the organization is stifled. . . .

Inner weakness is more dangerous and more fatal than outward opposition. The Church is little if at all injured by persecution and calumnies [or false charges] from ignorant, misinformed, or malicious enemies; a greater hindrance to its progress comes from faultfinders, shirkers, commandment-breakers, and apostate cliques within.[15]

It is the principle of *unity* that has enabled the wards, stakes, branches, and missions of the Church to progress and to accomplish the purposes for which the Church was established. It could not have been done by dissension and hatred. There have been difficulties. Each member of the Church has his own ideas. Sometimes they are not the same as those of the bishopric, and not the same as those of the presidency of the stake, and not the same as the Presidency of the Church; but each has had to submerge his own ideas to the good of the whole, and in that united purpose we have achieved something that is wonderful.

As I think of the future of this Church and of the welfare of the young men and women, as well as of the mothers and fathers, I feel impressed that there is no more important message to give than "to be one," and avoid things that may cause a rift among members. I know that the adversary has no stronger weapon against any group of men or women in this Church than the weapon of thrusting in a wedge of disunity, doubt, and enmity. . . .

The challenge is before us; we cannot fail in the divine commitments given to us as a people. Unity of purpose, with all working in harmony within the structure of Church organization as revealed by the Lord, is to be our objective. Let each member, teacher, and leader feel the importance of the position that each one holds. All are important to the successful accomplishment of God's work, which is our work.[16]

The greatest safeguard we have for unity and strength in the Church is found in the priesthood, by honoring and respecting it. Oh, my brethren—presidents of stakes, bishops of wards, and all who hold the priesthood—God bless you in your leadership, in your responsibility to guide, to bless, to comfort the people whom you have been appointed to preside over and to visit.

Guide them to go to the Lord and seek inspiration so to live that they may rise above the low and the mean, and live in the spiritual realm.

Recognize those who preside over you and, when necessary, seek their advice.[17]

May the [organizations in] the Church be blessed with the spirit of unity and harmony. May there be banished from their hearts the spirit of enmity, backbiting, and evil speaking, and may they keep in their hearts the truth expressed by Jesus when he said, ". . . if ye are not one ye are not mine." (D&C 38:27.)[18]

Let that spirit of unity and oneness for which our Lord and Savior prayed on the night of his betrayal, be characteristic of this his Church: Father, keep them one, as thou and I are one [see John 17:11].[19]

Commitment to gospel ideals is the surest way to unity.

A leading writer . . . [has expressed]: "The world has many good people in it today, more who are ready to believe than ever before, but these people possess no unifying ideals, no organic principles, no coherent view of life, no synthetic program of action. Society is coming to self-consciousness, and is beginning to take note of its troubles and needs, but it has no clear sense of direction, no organizing impulse, no all-inclusive ideals, no mighty impulsion. . . . Is there anything by which our nature can gain its unity; our race acknowledge its brotherhood, our humanity order its affairs as a whole?"

We answer, yes—such a uniting force, such an ideal is the Gospel of Jesus Christ as restored through the Prophet Joseph Smith. It explains man's life and its purpose, and has within it the vital saving elements, noble ideals, and spiritual uplift for which the heart of man today is yearning.[20]

"Good tidings of great joy" [Luke 2:10]—The Gospel of Jesus Christ is that good tidings. The term "Gospel" means, literally, "good news," and such is the news that emanates from above. . . . There have always been, in every dispensation, opportuni-

46

ties for men to receive that good news, and these prophets who were in tune with the Infinite and who heard first and directly that good news, have had imposed upon them the responsibility to convey that good news to others of their fellow-men, that they who are concerned with the things of the world might receive the glad message and be brought back into the environment of peace, harmony, and good will.[21]

Whether in the islands of the sea, in Japan, in Syria, in the Scandinavian countries, in England, Germany, France, Holland— wherever one meets a group of Latter-day Saints whose faith in the gospel of Jesus Christ is unwavering, there one finds the spirit of oneness, the spirit of love, the spirit of willing sacrifice for the good of humanity. God bless the Latter-day Saints all over the world that they may continue in that same spirit.[22]

Suggestions for Study and Discussion

- How are God the Father and Jesus Christ one? What are some specific ways in which we can be united as a Church? as families? as members of the community? (See pages 44–46.) What benefits can come through such unity?

- What are some attitudes and actions that bring disharmony into our homes and wards? (See pages 42–46.) What can we do to increase harmony and unity? How can we apply President Clark's statement ("In the service of the Lord, it is not where you serve but how") as we strive to increase unity in our homes and wards?

- How might children be influenced when their parents speak unkindly of leaders and teachers? Why does evil speaking injure "the reviler more than the reviled"? (See page 43.)

- In what ways can the gospel fulfill people's yearning for unity and harmony? (See pages 46–47.) Why is unity required to bring to pass the Lord's eternal purposes on earth?

Related Scriptures: 1 Corinthians 1:9–10; Mosiah 18:21; 3 Nephi 11:29–30; 4 Nephi 1:2, 15–17; D&C 38:23–27; 105:3–5; Moses 7:18

Notes

1. In Conference Report, Oct. 1967, 7.
2. See Conference Report, Apr. 1951, 150–51.
3. In Conference Report, Apr. 1951, 154.
4. In Conference Report, Oct. 1954, 132–33.
5. "Unity in the Home—the Church—the Nation," *Improvement Era,* Feb. 1954, 77–78.
6. In Conference Report, Oct. 1967, 6.
7. In Conference Report, Oct. 1967, 7.
8. In Conference Report, Apr. 1969, 95–96.
9. In Conference Report, Apr. 1953, 16.
10. In Conference Report, Apr. 1945, 144.
11. In Conference Report, Oct. 1967, 7.
12. In Conference Report, Apr. 1954, 142.
13. In Conference Report, Oct. 1969, 137.
14. In Conference Report, Oct. 1964, 5.
15. "Unity in the Home—the Church—the Nation," *Improvement Era,* Feb. 1954, 77.
16. In Conference Report, Oct. 1967, 5–6.
17. In Conference Report, Oct. 1967, 6.
18. In Conference Report, Apr. 1967, 87–88.
19. In Conference Report, Oct. 1934, 91.
20. In Conference Report, Apr. 1941, 108; paragraphing altered.
21. In Conference Report, Apr. 1910, 106.
22. In Conference Report, Apr. 1925, 11.

"Every Member a Missionary"

The world is hungry to hear the truth. . . .
We have it. Are we equal to the task—to the
responsibility God has placed upon us?[1]

Introduction

Both of President David O. McKay's parents were converts to the Church, the result of proselyting efforts by missionaries called to labor in Great Britain. The family of his father, David McKay, joined the Church in Scotland in 1850 as some of the first converts to the Church in the area. The family of his mother, Jennette Evans, joined the Church in Wales at about that same time in spite of strong opposition from close relatives.

From the righteous heritage given to him by his parents, President McKay had a great testimony of the importance and far-reaching effects of missionary work. In 1953, on a tour of Europe, President McKay visited the humble Scotland home of his father's childhood. President McKay's son Llewelyn, who accompanied him on the trip, recorded the experience as follows:

"[As we approached the home], the sun broke through the clouds and smiled at us as though he were reflecting the joy and happiness in father's heart. As we all gathered in front of the home, tears came to father's eyes as he looked through the door. 'If it had not been for two missionaries knocking on this door about 1850, I shouldn't be here today!' "[2]

Teachings of David O. McKay

Church members have been commissioned to do missionary work.

"Go ye therefore, and teach all nations, baptizing them in the name of the Father, and of the Son, and of the Holy Ghost:

The responsibility to share the gospel rests upon each member of the Church.

"Teaching them to observe all things whatsoever I have commanded you: and, lo, I am with you alway, even unto the end of
the world. . . ." (Matt. 28:19–20.)

Such was the admonition given to the early twelve. Such is the
admonition given to people in this age in the Doctrine and
Covenants to be a light unto the world. "And even so I have sent
mine everlasting covenant into the world, to be a light to the
world, and to be a standard for my people, for the Gentiles to
seek to it, and to be a messenger before my face to prepare the
way before me." [See D&C 45:9.]

The Church of Jesus Christ of Latter-day Saints was scarcely
one year old when that declaration was given by inspiration to
the Prophet Joseph Smith. He himself was in his twenty-sixth
year. It is marvelous to make such a declaration, great in its
potential, comprehensive in its scope. . . .

. . . Mormonism, so-called, has reared an ensign to the nations
and, with words as comprehensive as those I have read in the
revelation, invites the world to peace, to rest, to contentment.[3]

The text . . . "go ye unto all the world" is really the missionary
injunction given by the risen Christ to his Apostles. In effect
he says:

Consider this work unfinished until all nations shall have
accepted the gospel and shall have enlisted themselves as my
disciples. . . .

With the same direct commission from the risen Lord who
with the Father appeared in person in the beginning of the nineteenth century, the proclamation of the gospel is being made by
the Church of Jesus Christ of Latter-day Saints to "every nation,
kindred, tongue and people" as fast as means and personnel can
carry it forward.[4]

Every Latter-day Saint should be involved in missionary work.

If I were to couch in definite terms two of the most potent convictions in the hearts of the Latter-day Saints, I would name: First,
*an abiding assurance that the gospel, as taught by the Redeemer
when he lived among men and which was later modified,*

51

changed and corrupted by men, has been restored by the Redeemer in its purity and fulness; and second, following naturally the first, a conviction in the heart of every member of this Church that the responsibility rests upon the membership of the Church to preach the restored gospel to every nation, kindred, tongue and people.[5]

I am reminded that when Christ was on the earth, He said to some men who also knew of His divinity, that there was an obligation upon all such who possessed the knowledge of the existence of God and of the truths of the gospel of Christ. "He that knew not, and did commit things worthy of stripes, shall be beaten with few stripes. For unto whomsoever much is given, of him shall be much required; and to whom men have committed much, of him they will ask the more." [Luke 12:48.] So with this knowledge that the Latter-day Saints possess there comes a mighty obligation. God's people are spoken of in scripture, ancient and modern, as a chosen people, as a royal priesthood, a peculiar people, as a light set upon a hill. "Ye are the light of the world. A city that is set on a hill cannot be hid. Neither do men light a candle, and put it under a bushel, but on a candlestick; and it giveth light unto all that are in the house. Let your light so shine before men that they may see your good works, and glorify your father which is in heaven." [See Matthew 5:14–16.][6]

What a responsibility . . . of leading good men and good women all over this world to know God, and to know what their mission is on earth! Fathers and mothers, fellow workers, do you fully realize today what it means to assume the responsibility of carrying the message of peace and good will to all men?[7]

The world is hungry to hear the truth as never before in its history. We have it. Are we equal to the task—to the responsibility God has placed upon us?[8]

Every member of the Church should be converted and have a knowledge of the gospel, including a knowledge of the scriptures. How wonderful it would be if every member of the Church could, as Peter of old, "sanctify the Lord God in your hearts: and be ready always to give an answer to every man that asketh you a reason of the hope that is in you. . . ." (1 Pet. 3:15.) . . .

The responsibility of the Church is to preach the gospel of Jesus Christ as restored to the Prophet Joseph Smith, not only to preach it and proclaim it by word, by distribution of literature, but more than anything else by living the gospel in our homes and in our business dealings, having faith and testimony in our hearts, and radiating it wherever we go. . . . There is nothing that can stop the progress of truth excepting only our weaknesses or failure to do our duty.[9]

Every member is a missionary. He or she has the responsibility of bringing somebody: a mother, a father, a neighbor, a fellow worker, an associate, somebody in touch with the messengers of the gospel. If every member will carry that responsibility and if the arrangement to have that mother or that father or somebody meet the authorized representatives of the Church, no power on earth can stop this church from growing. And personal contact is what will influence those investigators. That personal contact, the nature of it, its effect depends upon you. And that's one thing that I wish to emphasize. There's one responsibility which no man can evade, that's the responsibility of personal influence. . . . It's what you are, not what you pretend to be that will bring people to investigate.[10]

Every member of the Church should be a missionary. He is probably not authorized to go from house to house, but he is authorized, by virtue of his membership, to set a proper example as a good neighbor. Neighbors are watching him. Neighbors are watching his children. He is a light, and it is his duty not to have that light hidden under a bushel, but it should be set up on a hill that all men may be guided thereby. . . .

. . . If you will live in accordance with those humble principles under the covenants you made at the water's edge, and since that time in Sacrament meetings, and many of you in the House of God, you will fill a noble mission, and God will reward you.

May every member of the Church experience this transformation in this life, and so live that others, seeing his good deeds, may be led to glorify our Father in heaven.[11]

The Gospel is our anchor. We know what it stands for. If we live it, feel it, and speak well of the Gospel, of the Priesthood, of the authorities in it, speak well even of our enemies, we shall feel happier ourselves, and we shall be preaching the Gospel of Jesus Christ. Everybody can do this. It is possible. God has not asked us to do it and then deprived us of the power of performing it.[12]

Full-time missionaries must be worthy to serve.

In Section 4 of the Doctrine and Covenants, the Prophet Joseph Smith received a revelation that "behold, a marvelous work is about to come forth among the children of men.

"Therefore, O ye that embark in the service of God, see that ye serve him with all your heart, might, mind and strength, that ye may stand blameless before God at the last day." (D&C 4:1–2.) . . .

[A] significant feature of this revelation, and of others given about the same period, is the naming of essential qualifications of those who were to participate in the bringing about of this marvelous work. These qualifications were *not the possession of wealth, not social distinction, not political preferment, not military achievement, not nobility of birth;* but *a desire to serve God with all your "heart, might, mind and strength"*—spiritual qualities that contribute to *nobility of soul.* I repeat: No popularity, no wealth, no theological training in church government—yet "a marvelous work [was] about to come forth among the children of men."[13]

There are certain standards by which [bishops and stake presidents] should be guided in calling our missionaries. First, call no [missionary] for the purpose of saving him or her. The young man is getting wayward and you think a mission would do him good. It would. But that is not why you are sending him out. Choose [missionaries] who are worthy to represent the Church, see that they are sufficiently mature, and, above all, that they have character.[14]

It is well for us to have in mind not so much the benefit to those representatives as their preparation and fitness to carry on the responsibilities entailed in a missionary call. In choosing a missionary it is well to keep in mind questions as follows:

Is he worthy to represent the Church?

Has he sufficient will power to resist temptation?

President McKay instructed bishops and stake presidents to "choose [missionaries] who are worthy to represent the Church."

Has he kept himself clean while he has been home and by that standard proved himself capable of resisting possible temptation in the field?

Has he taken active part in Church organizations at home?

Does he at least glimpse what the Church has to offer the world?

Has he glimpsed that the Church is the greatest thing in the world, and the only authorized group to represent the Lord Jesus Christ in the salvation of mankind? . . .

Has he, through prayer, or experience, felt God's nearness to him, so that he can approach the Lord as he would his earthly father?[15]

Every elder therefore who goes abroad to preach this gospel must first live the gospel to the best of his ability, and have a conviction in his heart that he is preaching the truth. True, at first this testimony may be somewhat indefinite; but all our children have it to some extent. . . . Through study, service, humility and prayer, this testimony will increase.

Another qualification is this: Every elder should be a Christian gentleman always. A gentleman—who is he? "Whoever is open"— nothing to hide, no downcast look because of the consciousness of guilt; "whoever is loyal"—loyal to the truth, to virtue, to the Word of Wisdom—"true, of humane and affable demeanor, honorable himself and in his judgment of others, faithful to his word as to law, and faithful alike to God and to man—such a man is a true gentleman," and such a man the elder of this Church should be who goes out to Christianize the world.[16]

Every deacon, teacher, and priest, every elder in the Church understands that to be worthy to be a representative of the Church of Christ, he must be temperate in his habits and morally clean. He is taught that there is no double standard of chastity, that every young man, as well as every young woman, is to keep himself free from sexual impurity. . . .

These young men are instructed that they go out as representatives of the Church, and that a representative of any organization—economic or religious—must possess at least one outstanding quality, and that is: trustworthiness. He was right who said, "To be trusted is a greater compliment than to be loved." And whom do these missionaries represent? First, they represent their parents, carrying the responsibility of keeping their good name unsullied. Second, they represent the Church, specifically the ward in which they live. And third, they represent the Lord Jesus Christ, whose authorized servants they are.

These ambassadors, for such they are, represent these three groups and carry in that representation one of the greatest responsibilities of their lives.[17]

Many blessings result from missionary service.

If you will have your testimonies strengthened, to have it revealed to you now individually that Christ is aiding you in your work, guiding his Church, well the best way to do that is . . . doing your duty, . . . attending to missionary work.[18]

To render service . . . in the mission field is a blessing to anyone. It is recognized as such by thousands of parents throughout the Church who appreciate the value of such labor to their sons and daughters, in whom this experience awakens an appreciation of home and of the gospel. Parents know also that missionary activity brings into the plane of consciousness a knowledge of the truth of the gospel, which the young men have perhaps felt but not expressed.[19]

Many of us fail to realize the value and potent possibilities of this great branch of Church activity [missionary work].

1—As an example of voluntary service in the cause of the Master, it is unexcelled.

2—As an incentive to clean living among youth, as a contributing factor to character building, its influence is immeasurable.

3—As an educative force and uplifting influence upon our communities, its effect is clearly manifest.

4—As a contributing factor to a better understanding among nations, and to the establishing of international friendship, it wields a significant influence.

5—As it is the purpose of the Almighty to save the individual, . . . the missionary service works most harmoniously in the consummation of this eternal plan!

"Remember the worth of souls is great in the sight of God; . . .

"And if it so be that you should labor all your days in crying repentance unto this people, and bring, save it be one soul unto me, how great shall be your joy with him in the kingdom of my Father!

"And now, if your joy will be great with one soul that you have brought unto me into the kingdom of my Father, how great will be your joy if you should bring many souls unto me!" (D&C 18:10, 15–16.)[20]

Men's hearts must be changed. Christ came into the world for that very purpose. The principal reason for preaching the gospel is to change men's hearts and lives, and you brethren who go from stake to stake and hear the evidence and testimony of those who have been converted . . . can testify how the conversion has changed their lives, as they have given their testimonies. By such conversion they bring peace and good will to the world instead of strife [and] suffering.[21]

Our missionaries . . . are now declaring to a troubled world that the message heralded at the birth of Jesus—"peace on earth, good will toward men" [see Luke 2:14]—may become a reality here and now by obedience to the principles of the gospel.[22]

Suggestions for Study and Discussion

- President McKay often expressed gratitude for the efforts of the missionaries who taught his parents. How have you or someone you know been blessed by missionary work?

- Where does the responsibility for missionary work rest today? (See pages 49–54.) What opportunities do we have to follow President McKay's instruction that every member should be a missionary? How can we prepare ourselves to fulfill this responsibility?

- What resources has the Church provided to help us share the gospel? In what ways have we been instructed to assist full-time and ward missionaries in our area?

- What qualifications are required for full-time missionary service? (See pages 54–56.) Why are worthiness and trustworthiness essential to missionary service?

- What can young people do to prepare themselves to serve missions? What can adults do to help youth prepare to serve missions?

- How can individuals with physical or mental limitations advance the cause of missionary work? What alternative means of Church service are available to them?

- In what ways can older couples be a significant resource in the mission field?

Related Scriptures: 3 Nephi 12:14–16; D&C 4:1–7; 18:15–18; 75:2–5; 88:81; 90:11

Notes

1. In Conference Report, Oct. 1945, 113–14.
2. Llewelyn R. McKay, *Home Memories of President David O. McKay* (1956), 15; paragraphing altered.
3. "Every Member a Missionary," *Improvement Era,* Oct. 1961, 710–11.
4. In Conference Report, Oct. 1949, 118.
5. In Conference Report, Apr. 1927, 102.
6. In Conference Report, Oct. 1910, 47.
7. In Conference Report, Apr. 1927, 106.
8. In Conference Report, Oct. 1945, 113–14.
9. In Conference Report, Oct. 1969, 88–89; paragraphing altered.
10. "Talk by President David O. McKay Given to the North British Mission 1 March 1961," Family and Church History Department Archives, The Church of Jesus Christ of Latter-day Saints, 2–3.
11. In Conference Report, Oct. 1958, 93–94.
12. In Conference Report, Apr. 1910, 110.
13. In Conference Report, Oct. 1966, 86.
14. In Conference Report, Apr. 1950, 176.
15. In Conference Report, Apr. 1961, 96.
16. In Conference Report, Apr. 1927, 106.
17. In Conference Report, Oct. 1949, 119–20.
18. In Conference Report, Oct. 1959, 89.
19. In Conference Report, Apr. 1961, 96.
20. In Conference Report, Oct. 1949, 117.
21. In Conference Report, Oct. 1953, 11.
22. In Conference Report, Oct. 1966, 87.

"The literal resurrection from the grave was a reality to the disciples who knew Christ intimately. . . . They were witnesses of the fact."

The Significance of the Resurrection

*As Christ lives after death, so shall
all men, each taking that place in the next
world for which he is best fitted.*[1]

Introduction

In 1912, Elder David O. McKay, then a member of the Twelve, and his wife, Emma Ray, experienced their first great sorrow in parenthood when their two-and-a-half-year-old son, Royle, passed away. Elder McKay's account of the event shows the heartache he felt but also demonstrates his faith in a future resurrection:

"Mon., 8 April 1912. O what a night of suffering for our darling boy! Every breath he drew seemed agony to him! The doctors examined him this morning, and discovered that his pain was due to pleurisy [inflammation of the lung] on both sides. At this we almost lost hope; but later when [the doctor] told us that by an examination he knew what germ had caused the infection and that he had the anti-toxin, we again took courage.

"But Royle was too weak and the complications of diseases too many. He battled bravely all day, taking the little stimulant given him at intervals as willingly as a grown person would. At 9:30 P.M., Papa, Thomas E. [McKay] and I again administered to him. Ray felt very hopeful, and lay down on the cot beside him for a little rest. Soon his little pulse weakened, and we knew that our baby would soon leave us. 'Mama' was the last word on his precious lips. Just before the end came, he stretched out his little hands, and as I stooped to caress him, he encircled my neck, and gave me the last of many of the most loving caresses ever a father received from a darling child. It seemed he realized that he was going, and wanted to say, 'Goodbye, Papa,' but his little voice was already stilled by weakness and pain. I am sure he recognized his Mama a moment later. She had rested only a few minutes; and noticing that the nurses were somewhat agitated, she was bending over her darling baby in a second and did not leave him until we gently led her from the room from which Death had taken our baby boy.

"The end came at 1:50 A.M., without even a twitch of a muscle. 'He is not dead but sleepeth' was never more applicable to any soul, for he truly went to sleep. He did not die."[2]

Teachings of David O. McKay

Jesus' Apostles became witnesses of the reality of His Resurrection.

About two thousand years ago . . . there were some pretty gloomy apostles. Peter was heavy-hearted; John was grieving; as was Mary, Christ's Mother. The other apostles had fled. Judas had realized what a crime he had committed. What a gloomy night!

Next morning Christ arose. . . . That being true, this event establishes the immortality of the soul, the existence of loved ones who are on the other side, their personality persisting. They are as real in that spiritual realm as Christ's spirit when He preached to the spirits in prison.[3]

Nearness to the event [of Jesus' Resurrection] gives increased value to the evidence given by the Apostles. A deeper value of their testimony lies in the fact that with Jesus' death the Apostles were stricken with discouragement and gloom. For two and a half years they had been upheld and inspired by Christ's presence. But now he was gone. They were left alone, and they seemed confused and helpless. . . .

"What was it that suddenly changed these disciples to confident, fearless, heroic preachers of the Gospel of Jesus Christ? It was the revelation that Christ had risen from the grave. His promises had been kept, his Messianic mission fulfilled." . . .

Mark does not himself recount any appearance of the risen Lord; but he testifies that the angel at the tomb announced the resurrection, and promised that the Lord would meet his disciples. From Mark we hear the glorious proclamation of the first empty tomb in all the world. For the first time in the history of man the words "Here lies" were supplanted by the divine message "He is risen." No one can doubt that Mark was not convinced in his soul of the reality of the empty tomb. To him the resurrection was not questionable—it was real; and the appearance of his Lord and Master among men was a fact established in his mind beyond the shadow of a doubt. To the proclaiming of this truth he devoted his life, and if tradition can be relied upon, he sealed his testimony with his blood.

Another who records the testimony of eye witnesses was Luke, a Gentile, or, as some think, a proselyte of Antioch in Syria, where he followed the profession of physician. (Col. 4:14.) Even some of his most severe modern critics have placed him in the first rank of an historian, and his personal contact with early apostles makes his statements of inestimable value.

What he wrote was the result of personal inquiry and investigation, and was drawn from all available sources. Particularly he interviewed and recorded the declarations of those "who from the beginning were [eye] witnesses and ministers of the Word." He avers that he "accurately traced all things from the very first," so that he might "write them in order." [See Luke 1:1–4.] This means that Luke obtained the testimony of these "eye witnesses" directly from themselves and not from previous narratives.

According to all trustworthy testimony, we have the Gospel of Luke as it came from his hand. In chapter 24, Luke testifies to the divine message: "Why seek ye the living among the dead? He is not here, but is risen." [Luke 24:5–6.]

With equal assurance as to their accuracy we can accept his statements and witness in regard to Peter's and Paul's and other apostles' testimony regarding the resurrection. "To whom also Christ showed himself alive after his passion by many infallible proofs, being seen of them forty days, and speaking of the things pertaining to the kingdom of God." [See Acts 1:3.] Who can doubt Luke's absolute confidence in the reality of the resurrection?

It is true that neither Mark nor Luke testifies to having personally seen the risen Lord, and therefore, some urge that their recorded testimonies cannot be taken as first hand evidence. That they do not so testify, and yet were convinced that others did see Him, shows how incontrovertible was the evidence among the apostles and other disciples that the resurrection was a reality.

Fortunately, however, there is a document which does give the personal testimony of an eye witness to an appearance of Jesus after his death and burial. This personal witness also corroborates the testimony not only of the two men whom I have quoted but of others also. I refer to Saul, a Jew of Tarsus, educated at the feet of Gamaliel, a strict Pharisee, and before his conversion a bitter persecutor of all who believed in Jesus of Nazareth as having risen from the dead. And now in the oldest authentic document in existence relating or testifying to the resurrection of Christ, we find Paul saying this to the Corinthians:

"For I delivered unto you first of all that which I also received, how that Christ died for our sins according to the scriptures, and that he was buried, and that he rose again the third day according to the scriptures; and that he was seen of Cephas, then of the Twelve. After that he was seen of above five hundred brethren at once, of whom the greater part remain unto this present, but some are fallen asleep. After that he was seen of James; then of all the apostles. And last of all he was seen of me also, as of one born out of due time." [1 Corinthians 15:3–8.][4]

Worldly skepticism cannot negate the testimony of eyewitnesses.

Too many today are like the men on Mars' Hill two thousand years ago who erected an altar to "The Unknown God," but who knew little or nothing about him. We read that on his way to the Areopagus, Paul had beheld magnificent statues erected to various gods. . . . Here frequently gathered philosophers and judges, the ablest thinkers, the wisest sages of the ancient world, considering and discoursing on the mysteries of life and the destiny of the human race.

In the midst of all this worldly wisdom there stood a lonely little brown-eyed man who challenged much of their philosophy as false and their worship of images as gross error—the only man in that great city of intellectuals who knew by actual experience that a man may pass through the portals of death and live. . . . As Paul discoursed eloquently on the personality of God, the philosophers listened curiously though attentively until he testified that God had raised Jesus from the dead.

When they heard of the resurrection, some mocked and all but a few turned away, leaving him who had declared the truth even more lonely than ever. [See Acts 17:22–33.] Today, as on Mars' Hill, when we speak of the resurrection of the dead, there are some who mock and others who doubt and turn away. Today, as then, too many men and women have other gods to which they give more thought than to the resurrected Lord. . . .

Establish it as a fact that Christ did take up His body and appeared as a glorified, resurrected Being, and you answer the question of the ages—"If a man dies, shall he live again?" [See Job 14:14.]

That the literal resurrection from the grave was a reality to the disciples who knew Christ intimately is a certainty. In their minds there was absolutely no doubt. They were witnesses of the fact. They knew because their eyes beheld, their ears heard, their hands felt the corporal presence of the risen Redeemer.[5]

That the spirit of man passes triumphantly through the portals of death into everlasting life is one of the glorious messages given by Christ, our Redeemer. To him this earthly career is but a day and its closing but the setting of life's sun. Death, but a sleep, is followed by a glorious awakening in the morning of an eternal realm. When Mary and Martha saw their brother only as a corpse in the dark and silent tomb, Christ saw him still a living being. This fact he expressed in two words: ". . . Lazarus sleepeth. . . ." (John 11:11.) If everyone . . . knew that the crucified Christ actually rose on the third day—that after having greeted others and mingled with others in the spirit world, his spirit did again reanimate his pierced body, and after sojourning among men for the space of forty days, he ascended a glorified soul to his Father—what benign peace would come to souls now troubled with doubt and uncertainty!

The Church of Jesus Christ of Latter-day Saints stands with Peter, with Paul, with James, and with all the other early apostles who accepted the resurrection not only as being literally true, but as the consummation of Christ's divine mission on earth.[6]

The latest and greatest confirmation that Jesus rose from the grave is the appearance of the Father and the Son to the Prophet Joseph Smith, nineteen hundred years after the event. . . . This miracle of life is significant not only in itself, but in its connotation of all the basic principles of true Christianity.[7]

Christ's Resurrection affirms the omnipotence of God and the immortality of man.

For over four thousand years, man had looked into the grave and had seen only the end of life. Of all the millions who had entered therein, not one person had ever returned as a resurrected, immortal being. "There was in all earth's area, not one empty grave. No human heart believed; no human voice declared that there was such a grave—a grave robbed by the power of a Victor stronger than man's great enemy, Death."

It was, therefore, a new and glorious message that the angel gave to the women who fearfully and lovingly had approached the sepulcher in which Jesus had been buried: ". . . Ye seek Jesus of Nazareth, which was crucified: he is risen; he is not here: behold the place where they laid him." (Mark 16:6.)

If a miracle is a supernatural event whose antecedent forces are beyond man's finite wisdom, then the resurrection of Jesus Christ is the most stupendous miracle of all time. In it stand revealed the omnipotence of God and the immortality of man.

The resurrection is a miracle, however, only in the sense that it is beyond man's comprehension and understanding. To all who accept it as fact, it is but a manifestation of a uniform law of life. Because man does not understand the law, he calls it a miracle.[8]

Resurrection and Spring are happily associated, not that there is anything in nature exactly analogous to the resurrection, but there is so much which suggests an AWAKENING thought. Like the stillness of death Old Winter has held all vegetable life in his grasp, but as Spring approaches the tender life-giving power of heat and light compels him to relinquish his grip, and what seems to have been dead comes forth in newness of life, refreshed, invigorated, strengthened after a peaceful sleep.

So it is with man. What we call death Jesus referred to as sleep. "Lazarus sleeps," he said to his disciples [see John 11:11]. "The damsel sleepeth," were his comforting words to the bereaved and sorrowing parents of a little girl [see Mark 5:39]. Indeed, to the Savior of the world there is no such thing as death—only life—eternal life. Truly he could say, "I am the Resurrection and the Life. He that believeth in me though he were dead, yet shall he live." [John 11:25.]

With this assurance, obedience to eternal law should be a joy, not a burden, for life is joy, life is love. . . . Obedience to Christ and his laws brings life. May each recurring Easter emphasize this truth, and fill our souls with the divine assurance that Christ is truly risen, and through him man's immortality secured.[9]

The faithful receive the comforting testimony of the Resurrection.

There is no cause to fear death; it is but an incident in life. It is as natural as birth. Why should we fear it? Some fear it because they think it is the end of life, and life often is the dearest thing we have. Eternal life is man's greatest blessing.

If only men would "do his will" [see John 7:17], instead of looking hopelessly at the dark and gloomy tomb, they would turn their eyes heavenward and know that Christ is risen!

No man can accept the resurrection and be consistent in his belief without accepting also the existence of a personal God. Through the resurrection Christ conquered death and became an immortal soul. "My Lord and my God" (John 20:28) was not merely an idle exclamation of Thomas when he beheld his risen Lord. Once we accept Christ as divine, it is easy to visualize his Father as being just as personal as he; for, said Jesus, ". . . he that hath seen me hath seen the Father. . . ." (John 14:9.)[10]

As Christ lived after death so shall all men, each taking his place in the next world for which he has best fitted himself. The message of the resurrection, therefore, is the most comforting, the most glorious ever given to man, for when death takes a loved one from us, our sorrowing hearts are assuaged by the hope and the divine assurance expressed in the words:

"He is not here: he is risen." [See Matthew 28:6.] Because our Redeemer lives so shall we. I bear you witness that He does live. I know it, as I hope you know that divine truth.[11]

Jesus passed through all the experiences of mortality just as you and I. He knew happiness, he experienced pain. He rejoiced as well as sorrowed with others. He knew friendship. He experienced, also, the sadness that comes through traitors and false accusers. He died a mortal death even as you will. Since Christ lived after death, so shall you, and so shall I. . . .

Jesus was the one perfect man who ever lived. In rising from the dead, he conquered death and is now Lord of the earth. How utterly weak, how extremely foolish is he who would willfully reject Christ's way of life, especially in the light of the fact that such rejection leads only to unhappiness, misery, and even to death! . . .

When Christians throughout the world have this faith [in Jesus Christ] coursing in their veins, when they feel a loyalty in their hearts to the Resurrected Christ and to the principles connoted thereby, mankind will have taken the first great step toward the perpetual peace for which we are daily praying.[12]

There are many so-called Christians who do not believe in the literal resurrection, and upon your shoulders and the shoulders of . . . others in this Church rests the responsibility of declaring to the world his divine Son-ship, his literal resurrection from the grave, and his appearance in person in the presence of the Father to the prophet Joseph Smith.[13]

Suggestions for Study and Discussion

- What evidence exists of the literal Resurrection of Jesus Christ? (See pages 62–64, 66.) How has your testimony of Jesus' Resurrection been strengthened by the witness of His ancient and modern-day Apostles?

- In what ways does "worldly wisdom" attempt to dispute the reality of Jesus' Resurrection? (See pages 64–65.)

- How is the doctrine of the Resurrection a fundamental part of the plan of salvation?

- President McKay taught that the Resurrection is a "manifestation of a uniform law of life" and that "Resurrection and Spring are happily associated." In what ways is the Resurrection similar to spring? (See pages 66–67.) How might you use this analogy to help children understand the Resurrection?

- How can we gain or strengthen a testimony of the Resurrection? (See pages 67–68.) How does your testimony of the Resurrection influence the decisions you make? What other gospel principles are more easily understood after we have a testimony of the Resurrection?

- How does a knowledge of the Resurrection lessen the sorrow associated with death and help comfort those who mourn? (See pages 67–68.) What examples have you seen of people being strengthened in trials by their testimony of the Resurrection?

- Why is the existence of a resurrected God so important to mankind?

Related Scriptures: Job 19:25–27; Mark 16:1–6; Acts 2:22–32; 4:33; 1 Corinthians 15:3–8; 3 Nephi 11:15; D&C 76:22–24

Notes

1. In Conference Report, Apr. 1966, 59.
2. Quoted in David Lawrence McKay, *My Father, David O. McKay* (1989), 84–85.
3. In Conference Report, Apr. 1950, 178.
4. In Conference Report, Apr. 1939, 112–14; paragraphing altered.
5. In Conference Report, Apr. 1944, 120–22; paragraphing altered.
6. In Conference Report, Apr. 1966, 57; paragraphing altered.
7. In Conference Report, Apr. 1944, 120; paragraphing altered.
8. In Conference Report, Apr. 1966, 56.
9. In Conference Report, Apr. 1939, 115.
10. In Conference Report, Apr. 1966, 58–59.
11. In Conference Report, Apr. 1944, 125.
12. In Conference Report, Apr. 1966, 59.
13. In Conference Report, Apr. 1950, 179.

"I cherish as one of the dearest experiences of life the knowledge that God hears the prayer of faith."

The Power of Prayer

God will be there to guide and direct
him who "will seek Him in faith with all
his might and with all his soul."[1]

Introduction

In the spring of 1921, Elder David O. McKay and Brother Hugh J. Cannon visited New Zealand as part of their worldwide tour of the missions of the Church. One Sunday, Elder McKay was scheduled to speak to a conference of Saints in the afternoon. However, when he awoke that morning he was ill and so hoarse he could barely speak above a whisper. Nevertheless, he attended the conference with faith he would be able to deliver his message. He later recorded:

"A thousand people . . . assembled for the afternoon service. They came with curiosity and high expectations. It was my duty to give them a message, but I was not only too hoarse to speak and be heard by that crowd, but I was also ill.

"However, with a most appealing prayer in my heart for divine help and guidance, I arose to perform my duty. My voice was tight and husky. . . .

"Then happened what had never before happened to me. I entered into my theme with all the earnestness and vehemence I could command and spoke as loud as possible. Feeling my voice getting clearer and more resonant, I soon forgot I had a voice and thought only of the truth I wanted my hearers to understand and accept. For forty minutes I continued with my address, and when I concluded, my voice was as resonant and clear as it ever was. . . .

"When I told Brother Cannon and some other brethren how earnestly I had prayed for the very blessing I had received, he

71

said, 'I too, was praying—never prayed more fervently for a speaker in my life.' "[2]

Teachings of David O. McKay

God is a personal Being whom we can approach in prayer.

I have cherished from childhood the truth that God is a personal being, and is, indeed, our Father whom we can approach in prayer and receive answers thereto. I cherish as one of the dearest experiences of life the knowledge that God hears the prayer of faith. It is true that the answers to our prayers may not always come as direct and at the time, nor in the manner, we anticipate; but they do come, and at a time and in a manner best for the interests of him who offers the supplication.

There have been occasions, however, when I have received direct and immediate assurance that my petition was granted. At one time, particularly, the answer came as distinctly as though my Heavenly Father stood by my side and spoke the words. These experiences are part of my very being and must remain so long as memory and intelligence last. Just as real and just as close to me seems the Savior of the world.

I feel as I have never felt before that God is my Father. He is not just an intangible power, a moral force in the world, but a personal God with creative power, the governor of the world, the director of our souls. I would have all men, and especially the young people of the Church, feel so close to our Father in heaven that they will approach Him daily—not in public alone, but in private. If our people will have this faith, great blessings will come to them. Their souls will be filled with thanksgiving for what God has done for them; they will find themselves rich in favors bestowed. It is not imagination that we can approach God and receive light and guidance from him, and that our minds will be enlightened and our souls thrilled by his Spirit.[3]

When you kneel down to pray at night, do you feel his nearness, his personality hearing you, do you feel a power that operates perhaps as the radio or a greater power so that you feel that you are communing with him?[4]

I would like to have the young men of Israel feel so close to [God] that they will approach Him daily, not in public alone, but in private. I would have them have the trust in Him which the little blind girl had in her father. She was sitting on his lap in the train, and a friend sitting by said: "Let me rest you," and he reached over and took the little child on his lap. The father said to her: "Do you know who is holding you?" "No," she replied, "but you do." Oh, the trust of that child in her father. . . . Just so real should be the trust which the Latter-day Saint boys and girls have in their Father in heaven.[5]

It is a good thing for boys and girls to learn that they can go to God in prayer. You students in the university will learn, as students in every school should learn, when you have difficulties that you can receive help and guidance if you seek it in sincerity. Perhaps you will arise as some of us did in youth and feel that your prayers are not answered, but some day you will realize the fact that God did answer your prayers just as a wise parent would have done. That is one of the greatest possessions of youth to feel that you can go to our Father and pour out your heart to him.[6]

Prayer is more than words; it requires faith, effort, and a proper attitude.

Prayer is the pulsation of a yearning, loving heart in tune with the Infinite. It is a message of the soul sent directly to a loving Father. The language is not mere words. . . .

The first and most fundamental virtue in effective prayer is faith. A belief in God brings peace to the soul. An assurance that God is our Father, into whose presence we can go for comfort and guidance, is a never-failing source of comfort.

Another essential virtue is reverence. This virtue is exemplified in the model prayer given by the Savior in the words "Hallowed be thy name." [Matthew 6:9.] This principle should be exemplified in classrooms, and particularly in our houses of worship.

The third essential element is sincerity. Prayer is the yearning of the spirit. Sincere praying implies that when we ask for any virtue or blessing we should work for the blessing and cultivate the virtue.

The next essential virtue is loyalty. Why pray for the Kingdom of God to come unless you have in your heart a desire and a willingness to aid in its establishment? Praying for His will to be done and then not trying to live it, gives you a negative answer at once. You would not grant something to a child who showed that attitude towards a request he is making of you. If we pray for the success of some cause or enterprise, manifestly we are in sympathy with it. It is the height of disloyalty to pray for God's will to be done, and then fail to conform our lives to that will.

A final essential virtue is humility. . . . The principle of humility and prayer leads one to feel a need of divine guidance. Self-reliance is a virtue, but with it should go a consciousness of the need of superior help—a consciousness that as you walk firmly in the pathway of duty, there is a possibility of your making a misstep; and with that consciousness is a prayer, a pleading that God will inspire you to avoid that false step.[7]

Prayer in the home teaches children faith in God.

If you ask me where I first received my unwavering faith in the existence of a God, I would answer you: in the home of my childhood—when Father and Mother invariably called their children around them in the morning and at night and invoked God's blessing upon the household and upon mankind. There was a sincerity in that good patriarch's voice that left an undying impression in the souls of his children, and Mother's prayers were equally impressive. I ask tonight that every father in the Church see to it that in all sincerity he impress his children with the reality of the existence of God and with the reality that God will guide and protect his children. You carry that responsibility. Home is one of the units—the fundamental unit—of society. Before I heard my father testify that he had heard a divine voice, I knew that he lived near to his Maker.[8]

Latter-day Saint children have been taught to recognize [God], and to pray to him as one who can listen and hear and feel just as an earthly father can listen, hear and feel, and they have absorbed into their very beings, from their mothers and their fathers, the real testimony that this personal God has spoken in this dispensation. There is a reality about it.[9]

I submit that where children are brought up in close communion with our Eternal Father that there can not be much sin or much evil in that home. When a little suffering child burning with fever, will look up to his father and in simple faith say, "Papa, bless me," I want to tell you that from such homes arise the strength and the glory of any nation. Such are the homes of Latter-day Saints.[10]

"Lord, teach us how to pray" was the reverent plea of the disciples of the Master [see Luke 11:1]. Humble as children they sought proper guidance, and their appeal was not in vain.

Just as keenly as did the disciples, so at times may children sense the need of divine guidance and comfort, yet not express their yearning in spoken request. Hence the Lord placed upon parents the duty to "teach their children to pray." [D&C 68:28.]

Worries, perplexities, and sorrows are as real in the life of a little child as in the adult world, and children are entitled to the comfort, consolation, and guidance obtained from God through prayer.

Not only that, but from the standpoint of faith, sincerity, and abiding trust, the prayer of an innocent child will surely receive most ready response from a loving Father.[11]

The inspiration of God is seen in requiring the Latter-day Saints to keep their homes intact, and to teach their children the principles of the gospel of Jesus Christ. Now, I do not mean by that that we should make such teaching formal or in any way distasteful. I mean that the gospel of Jesus Christ should radiate in every home; that the prayer night and morning should be offered up in sincerity; that the children daily would realize that we desire in our home the presence of God. If we can invite the Savior there, we may know that the angels will be not only willing but eager to protect our boys and girls. I believe that in most homes boys and girls are taught to pray before retiring for the night. I believe, however, that, too generally, the morning prayers are neglected. When we come to think of it, though, it is during the waking hours that our boys and girls need the protection of God, and the guidance of his Holy Spirit, more even than when they are asleep.[12]

Are you following Christ's admonition to pray to the Father and teach your children to pray, that godliness, reverence for God and his work, every day may be impressed upon the hearts of your children? That should be in every home. Pray not only for yourselves, but pray even for your enemies.[13]

Parents, if you do not do anything else, kneel down in the morning with your children. I know your mornings are usually busy, . . . but have some time when you can kneel and invite God into your home. Prayer is a potent force.[14]

Through family prayer let parents and children come into the presence of God.[15]

"Are you following Christ's admonition to pray to the Father and teach your children to pray?"

Prayer brings many great blessings.

The potency of . . . prayers throughout the Church came to me yesterday when I received a letter from a neighbor in my old home town. He was milking his cows when the word came over his radio which he has in his barn that President [George Albert] Smith had passed. He sensed what that would mean to his former fellow-townsman, and he left his barn and went to the house and told his wife. Immediately they called their little children, and there in that humble home, suspending their activities, they knelt down as a family and offered prayer. The significance of that scene I leave for you to understand. Multiply that by a hundred thousand, two hundred thousand, half a million homes, and see the power in the unity and prayers, and the sustaining influence in the body of the Church.[16]

If we can get our young people to have . . . faith and so to approach their God in secret, there are at least four great blessings that will come to them here and now. The first is gratitude—gratitude for blessings before unrealized. Their souls will be filled with thanksgiving for what God has done for them. They will find themselves rich in favors bestowed. The young man who closes the door behind him, who draws the curtains, and there in silence prepares to plead with God for help, should first pour out his soul in gratitude for health, for friends, for loved ones, for the gospel, for the manifestations of God's existence, as seen in the rocks and the trees and the stones and the flowers, and all things about him. He should first count his many blessings, name them one by one, and it will surprise him what the Lord has done [see "Count Your Blessings," *Hymns,* no. 241].

The second blessing of prayer is guidance. I cannot conceive of a young man's going astray who will kneel down by his bedside in the morning and pray to God to help him keep himself unspotted from the sins of the world. I think that a young girl will not go far wrong who will kneel down in the morning and pray that she might be kept pure and spotless during the coming day. I cannot think that a Latter-day Saint will hold enmity in his heart if he will sincerely, in secret, pray God to remove from his heart all feelings of envy and malice toward any of his fellowmen. Guidance? Yes, God will be there to guide and direct him who "will seek Him in faith with all his might and with all his soul."

The third blessing is confidence. All over this land there are thousands and tens of thousands of students who are struggling to get an education. Let us teach these students that if they want to succeed in their lessons, they should seek their God, that the greatest teacher known to the world stands near them to guide them. Once the student feels that he can approach the Lord through prayer, the student will receive confidence that he can get his lessons, that he can write his speech, that he can stand up before his fellow students and deliver his message without fear of failure. Confidence comes through sincere prayer.

Finally he will get inspiration. It is not imagination, that we can approach God and can receive light and guidance from Him, that our minds will be enlightened, our souls thrilled by His Spirit. . . . Joseph Smith knew it; and the testimony, the evidence of the Prophet Joseph's inspiration is manifest to all who will but open their eyes to see and their hearts to understand.[17]

Suggestions for Study and Discussion

- How has prayer strengthened your relationship with God? Why is it important to know that you are praying to your Father in Heaven, in whose image you were created? (See pages 72–73.)

- What are some ways that God answers prayers? (See pages 72–73.) Why does it seem that some prayers are not answered immediately? What blessings have you had with prayers being answered?

- What attributes or attitudes can we adopt that will help our prayers become more sincere and meaningful? (See pages 73–74.) How can we prepare ourselves spiritually before offering prayer?

- How can parents teach children to pray? (See pages 74–76.) In what ways can individual and family prayer in the home influence the lives of children? (See pages 74–76.) Why is daily prayer such a significant part of strengthening and unifying families?

- What are some blessings that come from regular prayer? (See pages 77–78.) What can we do to make our prayers more meaningful and less repetitive or mechanical?

- How can sincere and earnest prayer help to cleanse our souls of unkindness or feelings of ill will toward others?

Related Scriptures: Matthew 21:22; James 5:16; 2 Nephi 32:8–9; Alma 17:3; 34:17–28; 3 Nephi 18:18–21; D&C 19:38

Notes

1. In Conference Report, Apr. 1922, 65.
2. *Cherished Experiences from the Writings of President David O. McKay,* comp. Clare Middlemiss, rev. ed. (1976), 58–59.
3. In Conference Report, Apr. 1969, 152–53; paragraphing altered.
4. In Conference Report, Oct. 1954, 84.
5. In Conference Report, Apr. 1922, 64; paragraphing altered.
6. *Stepping Stones to an Abundant Life,* comp. Llewelyn R. McKay (1971), 42.
7. *Pathways to Happiness,* comp. Llewelyn R. McKay (1957), 225–26.
8. In Conference Report, Apr. 1966, 107.
9. In Conference Report, Apr. 1934, 23.
10. In Conference Report, Apr. 1912, 52–53.
11. *True to the Faith: From the Sermons and Discourses of David O. McKay,* comp. Llewelyn R. McKay (1966), 210–11.
12. In Conference Report, Oct. 1917, 57–58.
13. In Conference Report, Oct. 1919, 78.
14. *Man May Know for Himself: Teachings of President David O. McKay,* comp. Clare Middlemiss (1967), 300.
15. *Stepping Stones to an Abundant Life,* 281.
16. In Conference Report, Apr. 1951, 158.
17. In Conference Report, Apr. 1922, 64–65.

"You are in the midst of temptation, but you, as Christ on the Mount of Temptation, can rise above it."

Overcoming Temptation

Resist the devil, and he will flee from you.
Court him, and you will soon have shackles,
not on your wrists, but on your soul.[1]

Introduction

As a young missionary in Scotland, David O. McKay attended a meeting conducted by James L. McMurrin, a counselor in the European Mission presidency. During the course of the meeting, those in attendance witnessed several manifestations of the gifts of the Spirit. About 70 years later, in a priesthood meeting, President McKay recalled: "I remember, as if it were yesterday, the intensity of the inspiration of that occasion. Everybody felt the rich outpouring of the Spirit of the Lord. All present were truly of one heart and one mind. Never before had I experienced such an emotion. . . .

"Such was the setting in which James L. McMurrin gave what has since proved to be a prophecy. I had learned by intimate association with him that James McMurrin was pure gold. His faith in the gospel was implicit. No truer man, no man more loyal to what he thought was right ever lived. So when he turned to me and gave what I thought then was more of a caution than a promise, his words made an indelible impression upon me. Paraphrasing the words of the Savior to Peter, Brother McMurrin said: 'Let me say to you, Brother David, Satan hath desired you that he may sift you as wheat, but God is mindful of you.' [See Luke 22:31.] . . .

"At that moment there flashed in my mind temptations that had beset my path, and I realized even better than President McMurrin, or any other man, how truly he had spoken when he said, 'Satan hath desired thee.' With the resolve then and there to keep the faith, there was born a desire to be of service to my fellowmen; and with it came a realization, a glimpse at least, of what I owed to the elder who first carried the message of the restored gospel to my grandfather and grandmother, who had accepted the message years before in the north of Scotland and in South Wales."

President McKay concluded this story for the young men of the Church with counsel that is applicable to all: "I ask God to continue to bless you. . . . Do not let temptation lead you astray."[2]

Teachings of David O. McKay

We must guard ourselves and our families against the influence of the adversary.

Trees that can stand in the midst of the hurricane often yield to the destroying pests that we can scarcely see with a microscope. Likewise the greatest foes of humanity today are the subtle and sometimes unseen influences at work in society that are undermining the manhood and womanhood of today. The test, after all, of the faithfulness and effectiveness of God's people is an individual one. What is the individual doing?

Every temptation that comes to you and me comes in one of three forms:

(1)   A temptation of the appetite or passion;

(2)   A yielding to pride, fashion, or vanity;

(3)   A desire for worldly riches or power and dominion over lands or earthly possessions of men.

Such temptations come to us in our social gatherings; they come to us in our political strivings; they come to us in our business relations, on the farm, in the mercantile establishment; in our dealings in all the affairs of life we find these insidious influences working. It is when they manifest themselves to the consciousness of each individual that the defense of truth should exert itself.

The Church teaches that life here is probationary. It is man's duty to become the *master*, not the *slave* of nature. His appetites are to be controlled and used for the benefit of his health and the prolongation of his life—his passions mastered and controlled for the happiness and blessing of others. . . .

If you have lived true to the promptings of the Holy Spirit, and continue to do so, happiness will fill your soul. If you vary from it and become conscious that you have fallen short of what you know is right, you are going to be unhappy even [if] you have the wealth of the world. . . .

In their yearning for a good time, young people are often tempted to indulge in the things which appeal only to the baser side of humanity, five of the most common of which are: *first,* vulgarity and obscenity; *second,* drinking and petting; *third,* unchastity; *fourth,* disloyalty; and, *fifth,* irreverence.

Vulgarity is often the first step down the road to indulgence. To be vulgar is to give offense to good taste or refined feelings.

It is only a step from vulgarity to obscenity. It is right, indeed essential, to the happiness of our young people that they meet in social parties, but it is an indication of low morals when for entertainment they must resort to physical stimulation and debasement. Drinking and petting parties form an environment in which the moral sense becomes dulled, and unbridled passion holds sway. It then becomes easy to take the final step downward in moral disgrace.

When, instead of high moral principles, a life of immoral indulgence is chosen, and man or woman gets far down in the scale of degeneracy, disloyalty is an inevitable part of his or her nature. Loyalty to parents becomes quenched; obedience to their teachings and ideals abandoned; loyalty to wife and children smothered in base gratification; loyalty to Church impossible, and often supplanted by sneers at its teachings.[3]

Temptation often comes in [a] quiet way. Perhaps the yielding to it may not be known by anyone save the individual and his God, but if he does yield to it, he becomes to that extent weakened, and spotted with the evil of the world.[4]

Satan was cast down because he tried to replace the Creator. But his power is still manifest. He is active and is prompting at this moment the denial of God's existence, of the existence of his Beloved Son, and denying the efficacy of the gospel of Jesus Christ.[5]

The enemy is active. He is cunning and wily, and seeks every opportunity to undermine the foundation of the Church, and strikes wherever it is possible to weaken or to destroy. . . . God has given the freedom of choice. Our moral and spiritual progress depends upon the use we make of that freedom.[6]

Satan is still determined to have his way, and his emissaries have power given them today as they have not had throughout the centuries. Be prepared to meet conditions that may be severe, ideological conditions that may seem reasonable but are evil. In order to meet these forces, we must depend upon the whisperings of the Holy Spirit, to which you are entitled. They are real.

God is guiding this church. Be true to it; be loyal to it. Be true to your families, loyal to them. Protect your children. Guide them, not arbitrarily, but through the kind example of a father, and so contribute to the strength of the Church by exercising your priesthood in your home and in your lives.[7]

Membership in the Church of Jesus Christ of Latter-day Saints carries with it the responsibility to overcome temptation, to battle error, to improve the mind, and to develop one's spirit until it comes to the measure of the stature of the fulness of Christ.[8]

The adversary tries to strike at our weakest point, but we gain strength as we resist him.

You cannot tamper with the Evil One. Resist temptation, resist the Devil and he will flee from you. [See James 4:7.]

The Savior on the Mount gave us the greatest example in all the world. . . . Just after the Savior's baptism, he was led up to the mount that is known now as the Mount of Temptation. I do not know whether that is where he stood, where he fasted for forty days, or not. But it was on some mount that he went, and after . . . forty days, the Tempter came to him, so we are told, and as the Tempter always does, he struck at him in what the Tempter thought was his weakest point.

After [Jesus had] fasted, the Tempter thought he would be hungry, and the first temptation, you will remember, was, "If," and he said it sarcastically, "If thou be the Son of God," referring to the testimony of the Father when he said, "This is my beloved Son,"—"If thou be the Son of God, command that these stones be made bread." And there is a stone there in that area which is not unlike a Jewish wheat-loaf, so that would make the temptation of it appeal all the stronger. Christ's answer was: "Man shall not live by bread alone, but by every word that proceedeth out of the mouth of God." (Matt. 4:3–4.)

The next temptation quoted scripture also. It was an appeal to vanity, an appeal to gain ascendancy over our fellows: "If thou be the Son of God, cast thyself down . . ." (from a pinnacle of the temple) ". . . for it is written . . ." (and the Devil can cite scripture for his purpose) ". . . for it is written, He shall give his angels charge concerning thee: and in their hands they shall bear thee up, lest at any time thou dash thy foot against a stone." And the answer was, "Thou shalt not tempt the Lord thy God." (Matt. 4:6–7.)

The third temptation was of love of wealth and power. The tempter took Jesus to a high mountain and showed him the things of the world and the power thereof. He was not sarcastic in this temptation. He was pleading, for the resistance of the Savior had weakened the Tempter's powers. He showed him the things of the world. "All these things will I give thee, if thou wilt fall down and worship me." Rising in the majesty of his divinity, Jesus said: "Get thee hence, Satan: for it is written, Thou shalt worship the Lord thy God, and him only shalt thou serve." And the Tempter slunk away. [See Matthew 4:8–11.] . . .

There is your story. . . . Your weakest point will be the point at which the Devil tries to tempt you, will try to win you, and if you have made it weak before you have undertaken to serve the Lord, he will add to that weakness. Resist him and you will gain in strength. He will tempt you in another point. Resist him and he becomes weaker and you become stronger, until you can say, no matter what your surroundings may be, "Get thee behind me, Satan: for it is written, Thou shalt worship the Lord thy God, and him only shalt thou serve." (Luke 4:8.)[9]

With his disciples just before Gethsemane, . . . [Jesus] said, "And now I am no more in the world, but these are in the world, . . .

"I pray not that thou shouldest take them out of the world, but that thou shouldest keep them from the evil." (John 17:11, 15.)

There is your lesson. . . . You are in the midst of temptation, but you, as Christ on the Mount of Temptation, can rise above it.[10]

As we live the gospel and exercise self-control, we receive joy and peace.

As long as the Adversary to truth is free to exercise dominion in this world, we are going to have attacks, and the only way to meet those attacks is to live the Gospel.[11]

This gospel gives us a chance to live above this old world and its temptations and, through self-control and self-mastery, to live in the spirit, and that is the real life here and hereafter.[12]

May we realize as never before that mastery of one's personal inclinations is the heart of the Christian religion and of all religions. By nature the individual is selfish and inclined to follow his immediate impulses. It requires religion, or something higher than an individual or even a society of individuals, to overcome the selfish impulses of the natural man. . . . Self-mastery comes through self-denial of little things. Christ in these singular words said: ". . . whosoever will save his life shall lose it: and whosoever will lose his life for my sake shall find it." (Matt. 16:25.)

Whenever you forget self and strive for the betterment of others, and for something higher and better, you rise to the spiritual plane. If, in the moment of quarreling, in the moment of temptation to find fault with another, we will lose our self-centered self for the good of the Church of which we are members, for the good of the community, and especially for the progress of the gospel of Jesus Christ, we will be blessed spiritually, and happiness will be our reward.

> *"What though I conquer my enemies,*
> *And lay up store and pelf!*
> *I am a conqueror poor indeed*
> *Till I subdue myself."*
> [Author unknown.][13]

86

A person who indulges his appetites, either secretly or otherwise, has a character that will not serve him when he is tempted to indulge his passions.[14]

What a man continually thinks about determines his actions in times of opportunity and stress. A man's reaction to his appetites and impulses when they are aroused gives the measure of that man's character. In these reactions are revealed the man's power to govern or his forced servility to yield.[15]

Actions in harmony with divine law and the laws of nature will bring happiness, and those in opposition to divine truth, misery. Man is responsible not only for every deed, but also for every idle word and thought. Said the Savior:

". . . every idle word that men shall speak they shall give account thereof in the day of judgment." (Matthew 12:36.)[16]

All good things require effort. That which is worth having will cost part of your physical being, your intellectual power, and your soul power—"Ask, and it shall be given you; seek, and ye shall find; knock, and it shall be opened unto you." (Matt. 7:7.) But you have to seek, you have to knock. On the other hand, sin thrusts itself upon you. It walks beside you, it tempts you, it entices, it allures. You do not have to put forth effort. . . . It is like the billboard advertising attracting you to drink and to smoke. It is like the message that comes into your very homes with the television and radio. . . . Evil seeks you, and it requires effort and fortitude to combat it. But truth and wisdom are gained only by seeking, by prayer, and by effort.[17]

Let us ever keep in mind that life is largely what we make it, and that the Savior of men has marked clearly and plainly just how joy and peace may be obtained. It is in the gospel of Jesus Christ and adherence thereto.[18]

May God grant that as we are seeking the further establishment of the kingdom of God, that we may instruct our young people, and the members of the Church everywhere, to resist temptations that weaken the body, that destroy the soul, that we may stand truly repentant as we were when we entered the waters of baptism; that we may be renewed in the true sense of the word, that we may be born again; that our souls might bask in the light of the Holy Spirit, and go on as true members of the Church of Jesus Christ until our mission on earth is completed.[19]

Suggestions for Study and Discussion

- President McKay used the analogy of strong trees that could withstand great storms but were destroyed by microscopic pests that entered in (see page 82). In what ways can this analogy apply to our battles against temptation? (See pages 84–85.) What can we do to avoid inviting temptation into our lives? How can we strengthen children and youth against the increasing temptations in the world?

- In what ways might temptations differ, depending on our individual situations? What can we do to help each other resist temptation?

- What can we learn from the account of the Savior withstanding Satan's temptations? (See Matthew 4:1–11 and Luke 4:1–13, including the footnotes with excerpts from the Joseph Smith Translation; see also D&C 20:22.)

- In what ways does the pleasure of yielding to temptation differ from the joy of following the Savior?

- How does Satan try to use our weaknesses? (See pages 84–85.) How can we overcome our weaknesses through Jesus Christ? (See also Ether 12:27.)

- What can you do to resist and overcome temptations that often beset you? Why is it essential to establish our values before we find ourselves in tempting situations?

- In our efforts to follow the Savior and resist temptation, how can it help us to remember that "no man can serve two masters"? (Matthew 6:24).

- How do righteous and wholesome thoughts help us overcome temptation? What can we do to develop the self-mastery and self-control of which President McKay often spoke? (See pages 86–88.)

Related Scriptures: 1 Corinthians 10:13; James 1:12–17; 2 Peter 2:9; 1 Nephi 12:17; 15:23–24; Helaman 5:12; 3 Nephi 18:18–19; D&C 10:5

Notes

1. *Gospel Ideals* (1953), 352.
2. In Conference Report, Oct. 1968, 86.
3. In Conference Report, Oct. 1963, 7–8.
4. In Conference Report, Oct. 1911, 59.
5. In Conference Report, Oct. 1965, 9.
6. In Conference Report, Apr. 1967, 6.
7. In Conference Report, Apr. 1969, 97.
8. *Gospel Ideals,* 503.
9. In Conference Report, Oct. 1959, 88.
10. In Conference Report, Oct. 1953, 11.
11. In Conference Report, Oct. 1955, 90.
12. In Conference Report, Apr. 1969, 153.
13. In Conference Report, Apr. 1967, 133; paragraphing altered.
14. In Conference Report, Apr. 1968, 8.
15. In Conference Report, Apr. 1967, 8.
16. In Conference Report, Apr. 1950, 33.
17. In Conference Report, Oct. 1965, 144–45.
18. In Conference Report, Oct. 1963, 9.
19. In Conference Report, Apr. 1960, 29.

"The appearing of the Father and the Son to Joseph Smith is the foundation of this Church. Therein lies the secret of its strength and vitality."

The Divine Calling of the Prophet Joseph Smith

I have an abiding testimony that the Father and the Son appeared to the Prophet Joseph Smith and revealed through him the gospel of Jesus Christ, which is, indeed, "the power of God unto salvation." [Romans 1:16.][1]

Introduction

President David O. McKay said, "Since childhood it has been very easy for me to believe in the reality of the visions of the Prophet Joseph Smith."[2] He said that his testimony of the Prophet Joseph was strengthened when he heard of an experience his father had as a missionary in Scotland:

"When [my father] began preaching in his native land and bore testimony of the restoration of the gospel of Jesus Christ, he noticed that the people turned away from him. They were bitter in their hearts against anything [related to the Church], and the name of Joseph Smith seemed to arouse antagonism in their hearts. One day he concluded that the best way to reach these people would be to preach just the simple principles, the atonement of the Lord Jesus Christ, the first principles of the gospel, and not bear testimony of the restoration. In a month or so he became oppressed with a gloomy, downcast feeling, and he could not enter into the spirit of his work. He did not really know what was the matter, but his mind became obstructed; his spirit became depressed; he was oppressed and hampered; and that feeling of depression continued until it weighed him down with such heaviness that he went to the Lord and said, 'Unless I can get this feeling removed, I shall have to go home. I can't continue having my work thus hampered.'

"The discouragement continued for some time after that, when, one morning before daylight, following a sleepless night,

91

he decided to retire to a cave, near the ocean, where he knew he would be shut off from the world entirely, and there pour out his soul to God and ask why he was oppressed with this feeling, what he had done, and what he could do to throw it off and continue his work. He started out in the dark toward the cave. He became so eager to get to it that he started to run. As he was leaving the town, he was hailed by an officer who wanted to know what was the matter. He gave some noncommittal but satisfactory reply and was permitted to go on. Something just seemed to drive him; he had to get relief. He entered the cave or sheltered opening, and said, 'Oh, Father, what can I do to have this feeling removed? I must have it lifted or I cannot continue in this work'; and he heard a voice, as distinct as the tone I am now uttering, say, 'Testify that Joseph Smith is a prophet of God.' Remembering then what he tacitly had decided six weeks or more before, and becoming overwhelmed with the thought, the whole thing came to him in a realization that he was there for a special mission, and he had not given that special mission the attention it deserved. Then he cried in his heart, 'Lord, it is enough,' and went out from the cave."

President McKay recalled, "As a boy, I sat and heard that testimony from one whom I treasured and honored as you know I treasured no other man in the world, and that assurance was instilled in my youthful soul."[3]

Teachings of David O. McKay

Joseph Smith's First Vision revealed glorious truths about God the Father and Jesus Christ.

So far-reaching and significant were the wonderful discoveries and inventions of the latter half of [the nineteenth] century that they overwhelm us. . . . But none of them has answered man's greatest need and man's most yearning desire. Not one has yet revealed that for which man has sought for ages. That need—that ever-present yearning in man's heart—is to know God, and man's relation to him. . . . Only one event of the nineteenth century claims to give to the human soul this answer. If in that event man finds the truth for which the human race has ever sought, then it truly merits the distinguishing tribute of the greatest event of the nineteenth century!

That event was the appearing of two heavenly Beings to the boy Prophet Joseph Smith, revealing the personal identity respectively of God the Eternal Father and of his Son Jesus Christ.[4]

Eighteen hundred years after Jesus died upon the cross, the Prophet Joseph Smith declared that the risen Lord appeared to him. [He said]: ". . . I saw two Personages, whose brightness and glory defy all description, standing above me in the air. One of them spake unto me, calling me by name and said, pointing to the other—*This is My Beloved Son. Hear Him!*" [Joseph Smith—History 1:17.][5]

His declaration was simple but positive; and he was surprised when men doubted its truth. To him his claim was but the statement of a simple fact; to the Christian world it proved to be a lightning flash that, striking, weakened their religious structure from turret to foundation.

Two important elements in his first message were these: first, that God is a personal Being, who communicates his will to man; and second, that no creed in Christendom had the true plan of salvation.[6]

The appearing of the Father and the Son to Joseph Smith is the foundation of this Church. Therein lies the secret of its strength and vitality. This is true, and I bear witness to it. That one revelation answers all the queries of science regarding God and his divine personality. Don't you see what that means? What God is, is answered. His relation to his children is clear. His interest in humanity through authority delegated to man is apparent. The future of the work is assured. These and other glorious truths are clarified by that glorious first vision.[7]

The world still does not comprehend its significance; but as a contributive factor to man's knowledge of his relationship to Deity and of his place in the universe; as a means of establishing proper relationships between men as individuals and groups of men as nations; as a revelation pointing the way to man's happiness and peace on earth as well as in the eternities to come, the appearing of the Father and the Son to Joseph Smith and the subsequent restoration of the priesthood and the establishing of the Church of Jesus Christ in its fulness, will yet be recognized not only as the greatest event of the nineteenth century, but as one of the greatest of all ages.[8]

The Lord restored gospel truths through the Prophet Joseph Smith.

It is of Joseph Smith not only as a great man, but as an inspired servant of the Lord that I desire to speak. . . . Indeed, Joseph Smith's greatness consists in divine inspiration. . . .

Nobody can study critically and intelligently the restored gospel of Jesus Christ without being deeply impressed with the harmony of the teachings with those given by the Lord and Savior Himself when He was on the earth with His disciples. Consider, for example, the Prophet's revelation concerning the Creator—God as an intelligent Being, one who is, as Jesus taught, "Our Father in heaven." [See Matthew 6:9.] . . .

Joseph Smith's doctrine that Jesus Christ is the only Begotten of the Father, the Savior of the world, is identical with the teachings of Jesus Himself and His apostles.

So also is his doctrine of the persistence of personality after death. . . .

The same harmony is found in the teachings of other principles of the gospel such as faith, repentance, baptism, laying on of hands for the gift of the Holy Ghost, ordination to the priesthood, his teachings on "knowledge, temperance, godliness, brotherly kindness, charity," etc. [See 2 Peter 1:5–7; D&C 4:6.] . . .

. . . The advocates of infant baptism taught regarding little children: "Infants who come into the world are not only destitute of knowledge, righteousness, and holiness, but have a natural inclination to evil and only evil."

. . . Boldly and fearlessly, and speaking as one having assurance that he is right, the Prophet Joseph said: "Little children are holy and are sanctified through the atonement of Jesus Christ." [See D&C 74:7.][9]

Divine inspiration is manifest . . . in [Joseph Smith's] glorious announcement of the eternal nature of covenants and ceremonies and the opportunity of salvation for every human being. The Church is not exclusive but all inclusive to every soul who will accept its principles. . . . All mankind shall be saved by obedience to the laws and ordinances of the gospel. Even they who died without law shall be judged without law. To this end is the ordinance of salvation for the dead revealed.

The eternity of the marriage covenant is a glorious revelation, giving assurance to hearts bound by the golden clasp of love and sealed by authority of the holy Priesthood that their union is eternal.

Other covenants also continue with eternal progress throughout the ages of eternity.

Joseph Smith could not have accomplished all this of his own wisdom, intellect, and influence. He could not have done it.[10]

The Lord has revealed in this day the Plan of Salvation, which is nothing more or less than the way to the spiritual realm by building character worthy of entrance into his kingdom. The Plan is the gospel of Jesus Christ as restored to the Prophet Joseph Smith, and it is ideal and comprehensive.[11]

The restored Church of Jesus Christ is evidence of the Prophet Joseph's divine inspiration.

About 1820, religious excitement led Joseph Smith to seek the right church, the proper mode of worship, the right way to live. The desire to know impelled the youth to seek the Lord in earnest prayer. One result of the answer to his prayer was the organization of the Church in Peter Whitmer's home on . . . April 6, 1830. In that organization may be found the comprehension of the whole plan of man's salvation.

Now I wish to consider that organization as one evidence of his inspiration. . . . [It] has survived financial panics, social upheavals, and religious turmoil; and today stands as a means of supplying the highest needs of mankind. . . .

"The result of [Joseph Smith's] divine guidance was an assurance of the righteousness of what he taught and a fearlessness in proclaiming it."

. . . "The Church of Jesus Christ was organized in accordance with the order of the Church as recorded in the New Testament," said Joseph Smith [see *History of the Church*, 1:79]. The practical and beneficent workings of this organization prove its divine authenticity.[12]

Many years ago Joseph Smith, a mere boy between fourteen and fifteen years of age, declared that, in answer to prayer, he received a revelation from God. . . . The result of this declaration was his immediate ostracism from the religious world. In a very short time he found himself standing alone.

Alone—and unacquainted with the learning and philosophy of his day!

Alone—and unschooled in the arts and sciences!

Alone—with no philosopher to instruct him, no minister to guide him! In simplicity and kindness he had hastened to them with his glorious message; in scorn and derision they had turned from him saying it was all of the devil; that there were no such things as visions or revelations in these days; that all such things had ceased with the Apostles; and that there would never be any more of them [see Joseph Smith—History 1:21].

Thus he was left alone to embark upon the ocean of religious thought, having rejected every known vessel with which to sail and never having built one or even having seen one built himself. Surely if an impostor, the bark [or ship] he could build would be indeed a crude one.

On the other hand, if that which he built possesses an excellence and superiority over that which the learned professors and philosophers had given to the world during the preceding hundreds of years, men will be forced, at least, to say in surprise, whence hath this man his wisdom!

It would appear, then, that though he seemed alone, he was alone only as was Moses on Sinai; as Jesus on the Mount of Olives. As with the Master, so with the prophet, his instructions came not through man-made channels but direct from God, the source of all intelligence. He says: "I am a rough stone. The sound of the hammer and chisel were never heard on me until the Lord took me in hand. I desire the learning and wisdom of heaven alone." [*History of the Church*, 5:423.] . . .

His claim to revelation from God, if established, leaves no doubt as to his authority to organize the Church of Jesus Christ upon earth, and to administer authoritatively the principles and ordinances thereof. Thus at the very inception of this great latter-day work was laid the immovable cornerstone of Christ's Church in this dispensation, [namely], the authority to officiate in the name of Jesus Christ in things pertaining to his Church.[13]

As we consider [Joseph Smith's] outstanding accomplishments during the brief span of fourteen years between the organization of the Church and his martyrdom; as we contemplate the perfect harmony of the restored gospel with that of the primitive church established by Jesus and His apostles; as we note his penetrating insight into principles and ordinances; and as we see the incomparable plan and efficiency of the Church established by the inspiration of the Christ whose name it bears—the answer to the question, whence this man's wisdom? is given in the stirring stanza:

> *Praise to the man who communed with Jehovah!*
> *Jesus anointed "that Prophet and Seer"—*
> *Blessed to open the last dispensation;*
> *Kings shall extol him and nations revere.*
> [See *Hymns,* no. 27][14]

The Prophet Joseph lived and died in defense of the truths revealed to him.

Great men have the ability to see clearly into the heart of things. They discern truth. They think independently. They act nobly. They influence strong men to follow them. Small men sneer at them, ridicule them, persecute them, but the critics die and are forgotten, and the great man lives on forever.

Some of Joseph Smith's contemporaries sneered at him; others admired him; his followers revered him. . . .

No one unbiased in his judgment can study the life of this religious leader without being impressed with the fact that he possessed in a rich degree the qualities of true greatness, the source of which is found in a desire to know God's will, and in a determination, when it is found, to follow it.[15]

Throughout all ages truth has been first perceived by a few heroic leaders who, in defense of it, frequently sacrificed their lives. To the clear perception and the courage of these intrepid leaders of men is due the progress of mankind. At some time or other, they have had to make a choice whether to deny, modify, or defend truth—a choice between personal ease and preferment, or ostracism, punishment, or even death. Such a choice came to Peter and John as they stood prisoners before Annas, the high priest. It took real courage from them to bear witness of Christ in the presence of the very men who had condemned him to death. [See Acts 4.]

It took courage for Paul, a chained prisoner before King Agrippa and his royal company, to bear witness that Christ did suffer, and that he should be the first that should rise from the dead, and should show light unto the people, and to the gentiles. [See Acts 26.]

It took courage for Joseph Smith to testify to an unbelieving and bitter world the truth that God and his Beloved Son had appeared in vision to him.[16]

All men who have moved the world have been men who will stand true to their conscience—such men as Peter, James, and Paul, and their brethren of the ancient apostles, and also others. When the religious leaders of Palmyra, New York, turned against the youthful Joseph Smith for what he had seen and heard in the Sacred Grove, he said, having a testimony of the Lord Jesus in his bosom: "I had seen a vision; I knew it, and I knew that God knew it, and I could not deny it, neither dared I do it. . . ." [Joseph Smith—History 1:25.]

Joseph Smith was true to his testimony to the last.[17]

The result of [Joseph Smith's] divine guidance was an assurance of the righteousness of what he taught and a fearlessness in proclaiming it. When Joseph Smith taught a doctrine, he taught it authoritatively. His was not the question whether it agreed with man's thoughts or not, whether it was in harmony with the teachings of the orthodox churches or whether it was in direct opposition. What was given to him he gave to the world irrespective of its agreement or disagreement, of its harmony or its discord with the belief of the churches, or the prevailing standards of mankind; and today, as we look through the vista of over one hundred years, we have a good opportunity of judging of the virtue of his teachings, and of concluding as to the source of his instruction. . . .

Not only did he receive guidance and instruction from the divine Head, but, once received, defended it with invincible resolution.[18]

Through railings, scoffings, mobbings, arrests, imprisonments, persecutions that led to martyrdom, Joseph Smith as Peter and Paul before him, ever strove to the utmost of his ability to follow the light that had made him a "partaker of the divine nature." [See 2 Peter 1:4.][19]

The best blood of this country was shed in innocence. [The Prophet Joseph] knew he was innocent. He knew his rights. So did his brother Hyrum, John Taylor and Willard Richards who were there with him. But because of lies, black and damnable, the Prophet Joseph and his brother Hyrum were martyred.

. . . In the midst of it all what was the Prophet's attitude? A calm, Christ-like attitude. Said he, when he was going to Carthage that evening:

"I am going like a lamb to the slaughter, but I am calm as a summer's morning. I have a conscience void of offense toward God and all men. If they take my life I shall die an innocent man, and it will yet be said of me, he was murdered in cold blood." [See D&C 135:4.][20]

The lives of the Prophet, of his brother, Hyrum, the patriarch, and of hundreds of thousands of others who accepted the truth of [the First Vision] bear evidence that the plan of salvation, as it is purported Jesus Christ revealed it, most assuredly leads toward Christlike character. So real was the revelation to the Prophet and his brother, Hyrum, that they unflinchingly sealed their testimony with their blood.[21]

Suggestions for Study and Discussion

- President McKay related an experience his father had on his mission concerning the need to testify of Joseph Smith (see pages 91–92). Why is the answer his father received significant for us today?

- Why was it necessary for the Lord to call a prophet in the latter days? (See pages 92–94.) Why is a testimony of Joseph Smith an essential part of a testimony of the gospel? In what way is the appearance of the Father and the Son to Joseph Smith the "foundation of this Church"?

• What are some truths that were revealed through the First Vision? (See pages 92–94.) In what ways has your knowledge of the First Vision influenced your testimony of Heavenly Father and Jesus Christ?

• What are some other doctrines that the Lord revealed through the Prophet Joseph Smith? (See pages 94–95.) How have you been blessed as you have studied and applied these doctrines?

• In what ways are the Church and its teachings a testament that Joseph Smith was a prophet of God? (See pages 95–98.)

• What are some Christlike attributes shown by the Prophet Joseph Smith? (See pages 98–100.) What can you do to follow his example?

• What responsibilities do we have when we have a testimony of Joseph Smith and the restoration of the gospel?

Related Scriptures: Amos 3:7; 2 Nephi 3:6–15; D&C 135; Joseph Smith—History 1:1–75

Notes

1. *Cherished Experiences from the Writings of President David O. McKay,* comp. Clare Middlemiss, rev. ed. (1976), 16.

2. *Gospel Ideals* (1953), 524.

3. *Cherished Experiences,* 11–12.

4. *Gospel Ideals,* 79–80; paragraphing altered.

5. In Conference Report, Apr. 1966, 58.

6. *Gospel Ideals,* 80.

7. *Gospel Ideals,* 85.

8. *Treasures of Life,* comp. Clare Middlemiss (1962), 227.

9. "The Prophet Joseph Smith—On Doctrine and Organization," *Improvement Era,* Jan. 1945, 14–15; paragraphing altered.

10. "Joseph Smith—Prophet, Seer, and Revelator," *Improvement Era,* Jan. 1942, 55.

11. *Treasures of Life,* 420.

12. *Improvement Era,* Jan. 1942, 13, 54.

13. *Gospel Ideals,* 80–82; paragraphing altered.

14. *Improvement Era,* Jan. 1945, 47.

15. *Pathways to Happiness,* comp. Llewelyn R. McKay (1957), 284–85.

16. *Treasures of Life,* 376–77.

17. In Conference Report, Apr. 1969, 151.

18. *Gospel Ideals,* 81–82.

19. In Conference Report, Apr. 1951, 95.

20. In Conference Report, Oct. 1931, 12–13.

21. *Treasures of Life,* 226–27.

*Through his teachings and his example, President McKay demonstrated
the blessings of living the Word of Wisdom.*

Living the Word of Wisdom

The Word of Wisdom is a vital part of the gospel, which is "the power of God unto salvation"—physical salvation as well as spiritual salvation.[1]

Introduction

President McKay taught and testified that the Word of Wisdom was a commandment given by the Lord to bless us both physically and spiritually. In his teachings as well as his actions, he strictly obeyed this commandment. During a visit with the queen of the Netherlands in 1952, President and Sister McKay had an interesting experience. The queen had scheduled 30 minutes for a visit with them. President McKay carefully watched the time, and when the half hour was up, he politely thanked the queen and began to leave. "Mr. McKay," she said, "sit down! I have enjoyed this thirty minutes more than I have enjoyed any thirty minutes in a long time. I just wish you would extend our visit a little longer." He sat down again. Then a coffee table was brought in, and the queen poured three cups of tea, giving one to President McKay, one to Sister McKay, and keeping one for herself. When the queen noticed that neither of her guests drank the tea, she asked, "Won't you have a little tea with the Queen?" President McKay explained, "I must tell you that our people do not believe in drinking stimulants, and we think tea is a stimulant." She said, "I am the Queen of the Netherlands. Do you mean to tell me you won't have a little drink of tea, even with the Queen of the Netherlands?" President McKay responded, "Would the Queen of the Netherlands ask the leader of a million, three hundred thousand people to do something that he teaches his people not to do?" "You are a great man, President McKay," she said. "I wouldn't ask you to do that."[2]

Teachings of David O. McKay

The Word of Wisdom is a clear commandment given by revelation from the Lord.

On the 27th of February, 1833, the Prophet Joseph Smith received the revelation recorded in the 89th section of the Doctrine and Covenants. . . . I want to read a few [verses] from that section:

"Behold, verily, thus saith the Lord unto you, in consequence of evils and designs which do and will exist in the hearts of conspiring men in the last days, I have warned you, and forewarn you, by giving unto you this word of wisdom by revelation.

"That inasmuch as any man drinketh wine or strong drink among you, behold it is not good, neither meet in the sight of your Father, only in assembling yourselves together to offer up your sacraments before him.

"And, behold, this should be wine, yea, pure wine of the grape of the vine, of your own make." [D&C 89:4–6.] . . .

The particular sentence that I wish to call attention to is this: "Inasmuch as any man drinketh wine or strong drink . . . behold *it is not good,* neither meet in the sight of your Father." That is the word of God to the people of this generation. It stands with just as much force as the words of the Savior, "If any man will do His will he shall know of the doctrine, whether it be of God or whether I speak of myself." [John 7:17.] Latter-day Saints, you know this statement of the Savior's is true; we testify that if any man will do the will of God he will get the testimony, in his heart and in his life, that the Gospel of Jesus Christ is true. We accept the words of the Savior, "Except ye repent, ye shall all likewise perish." [Luke 13:3.] Those eternal truths, so tersely expressed, we accept as true. We may not live up to them wholly, but as a people we accept them, because they are the word of God. Just so strong, just so eternal stands this truth . . . , "Strong drink is not good for man." [See D&C 89:7.] Yet [many years] have passed, and during that time this doctrine has been preached every week, if not every day, in some congregation of Israel, and still we find in our midst a few who say, by their acts, it is good for man.

I am glad when I study this passage, to find that the Lord did not say, "Strong drink *to excess* is not good;" nor "Drunkenness is not good." Suppose He had weakened that expression by modifying it and saying, "Strong drink in excess, or when taken in large quantities, is not good," how soon we should have justified ourselves that a little drink is good. But like other eternal truths it stands unqualified; *strong drink is not good.*[3]

I think tobacco is a vice which should be shunned as the bite of a rattlesnake. . . . The Lord has said that tobacco is not good for man. That should be sufficient for Latter-day Saints.[4]

Members of the Church who have formed either the tobacco habit or the tea and coffee habit, or both, are prone to seek justification for their indulgences in things which the Lord has said plainly are not good for man. Whenever they try to do so, they only parade the weakness of their faith in the Lord's words, which were given as admonition and "wisdom," and obedience to which will bring blessing as certain and sure as if he had said, "Thou shalt not."[5]

Disobeying the Word of Wisdom brings harmful physical and spiritual consequences.

There is a substance in tea and coffee which when taken into the human system, tends to increase the beating of the heart; which in turn increases the rapidity of the circulation of the blood and of breathing. This causes the body to become warmer and more exhilarated. After a time, however, this temporary enlivenment passes off, and the body is really in a greater need of rest and recuperation than it was before the beverage was taken. Stimulants are to the body what the lash is to the lagging horse— it causes a spurt forward but gives no permanent strength or natural nourishment. Frequently repetitions of the lash only make the horse more lazy; and the habitual use of strong drink, tobacco, tea, and coffee, only tends to make the body weaker and more dependent upon the stimulants to which it is addicted.

The Lord has said in unmistakable words that these things are not good for man. Science declares the same. God's word alone should be sufficient for every true Latter-day Saint.[6]

A person's reaction to his appetites and impulses when they are aroused gives the measure of that person's character. In such reactions are revealed the man's power to govern, or his forced servility to yield. That phase of the Word of Wisdom, therefore, which refers to intoxicants, drugs, and stimulants, goes deeper than the ill effects upon the body, and strikes at the very root of character building itself. . . .

During the last one hundred years, the marvelous advance of science has made it possible for man to determine by experiments the ill effect of intoxicants and drugs upon the nerves and tissues of the human body. Observation and experiment have demonstrated their effects upon character. All such experiments and observations have proved the truth of the . . . statement: "Strong drinks and tobacco are not good for man."[7]

As I recall the influences upon my young life, I believe the greatest was the memorizing of that important saying: "My spirit will not dwell in an unclean tabernacle."

Then there were . . . others, and they were all in the form of warnings. The first came to me as a boy as I sat on a spring seat by the side of my father as we drove into Ogden. Just before we crossed the bridge across the Ogden River, a man came out from a saloon, which was just on the northern bank of the river. I recognized him. I liked him because I had seen him on the local stage. But on that occasion he was under the influence of liquor, and had been for, I suppose, several days.

I did not know . . . he drank, but as he broke down and cried and asked father for fifty cents to go back into the saloon, I saw him stagger away. As we drove across the bridge my father said: "David, he and I used to go [home] teaching together."

That was all he said, but it was a warning to me that I have never forgotten, about the effect of dissipation [or excessive drinking].

A little later, a teacher [assigned] us to read a story about a group of young people sailing down the St. Lawrence River. . . . I cannot give you the author, I cannot give you the title, but I can give you the memory that has stayed with me, about those young folks who were drinking and carousing and having a good time in the boat sailing down that noted river. But a man on the shore, recognizing, realizing the dangers ahead of them, cried: "Hello, there, the rapids are below you."

But they ignored his warning, defied him. "We are all right," and continued in their jocularity [or joking] and their indulgences. And again he cried out: "The rapids are below you," and again they gave no heed to his warning.

Suddenly they found themselves in the rapids. Then they immediately began to row for the shore, but it was too late. I do not remember but just the words of the last paragraph, but cursing, yelling, over the rapids, over the falls they went.

Negative? Yes. But I will tell you there are many in the stream of life who are rowing just that way. I have never forgotten that story.[8]

We must be watchful against the "evils and designs of conspiring men."

One of the most significant statements in the Doctrine and Covenants, one which carries with it evidence of the inspiration of the Prophet Joseph Smith, is found in the 89th Section . . . :

"In consequence of evils and designs which do and will exist in the hearts of conspiring men in the last days, I have warned you, and forewarn you, by giving unto you this word of wisdom by revelation . . . " (D&C 89:4.)

"Evils and designs which do and will exist in the hearts of conspiring men. . . ." The purport of that impressed me in the twenties, and the thirties of [the 20th] century. I just ask you . . . to recall the methods employed by certain tobacco interests to induce women to smoke cigarettes.

You remember how insidiously they launched their plan. First, by saying that it would reduce weight. They had a slogan: "Take a cigarette instead of a sweet."

Later, some of us who like the theatre, noticed that they would have a young lady light the gentleman's cigarette. Following this a woman's hand would be shown on billboards lighting or taking a cigarette. A year or two passed and soon they were brazen enough to show the lady on the screen or on the billboard smoking the cigarette. . . .

I may be wrong, but I thought I saw an indication recently that *conspiring* men now have evil designs upon our youth. Keep your eyes and ears open.[9]

Members have a duty to themselves and the Church to live and teach the Word of Wisdom.

Every man, every woman, must bear a part of the responsibility of this Church. . . . No matter where we are, . . . wherever circumstances or business affairs may call us, be it in the canyon or elsewhere, and we are tempted, on a cold morning, to break the Word of Wisdom by drinking two or three cups of tea or coffee, let us feel then the responsibility of right.

Let each one say to himself, "The responsibility of membership in the Church is upon me; I will not yield. What though nobody sees me, I know and God knows when I yield, and every time I yield to a weakness I become weaker myself and do not respect myself." If you are in business, and your companions say, "Come, let us go in and have a drink on this bargain, or this sale," let your answer be, No, no! What though your thirsty appetite makes you long for it, be men, be Latter-day Saints, and say, "No; the responsibility of membership in the Church rests upon me."[10]

The Church of Jesus Christ of Latter-day Saints stands committed unequivocally to the doctrine that tea, coffee, tobacco, and intoxicants are not good for man. True Latter-day Saints refrain from indulgence in tobacco and drink, either of stimulants or of intoxicants, and by example and precept, teach others to do the same.[11]

Living the Word of Wisdom strengthens character and brings happiness.

The Church urges men to have self-mastery to control their appetites, their tempers, and their speech. A man is not at his best when he is a slave to some habit. A man is not his best who lives merely to gratify his passions. That is one reason why the Lord has given the Church the revelation of the Word of Wisdom so that, even from boyhood and girlhood, young men and young

President McKay encouraged Latter-day Saints to teach their children and others the Word of Wisdom "by example and precept."

women may learn to control themselves. That is not always easy. The youth today face enemies—false ideologies and immoral practices. . . . Sound preparation is necessary to meet and conquer these enemies.[12]

Every young man throughout Zion, when he comes forth from the waters of baptism, ought to know that it is part of his duty to resist smoking a cigarette, no matter where he may be. Every young person in the Church should be taught, when coming from the waters of baptism, that he should resist intoxicants when passed around at the social gathering. Every young member of this Church should know that tobacco in any form should not be used. He or she should resist all these habits, not only for the blessing that is promised herein by our Father, but also because of the strength so acquired to resist greater temptations.[13]

One of the most practical teachings of the Church regarding [self-control] is the Word of Wisdom. It is true. It deals principally with the appetite. You show me a man who has complete control over his appetite, who can resist all temptations to indulge in stimulants, liquor, tobacco, marijuana, and other vicious drugs, and I will show you a youth or man who has likewise developed power to control his passions and desires.[14]

Neither the Church nor the world at large can hear too much about the Word of Wisdom. It is a doctrine given to man for man's happiness and benefit. It is part of the philosophy of living. . . . He who fails to live it robs himself of strength of body and strength of character to which he is entitled. Truth is loyalty to the right as we see it; it is courageous living of our lives in harmony with our ideals; it is always power.[15]

Suggestions for Study and Discussion

- In what ways was the Word of Wisdom far ahead of its time?

- Why do people sometimes try to justify using the substances prohibited in the Word of Wisdom? What are some dangers in this type of thinking? (See pages 105–7.)

- Why is it important to take care of our bodies? What are some of the negative physical effects of disobeying the Word of Wisdom? (See pages 105–7.) How does disobeying this commandment affect us spiritually? (See pages 105–7.)

- President McKay spoke of tobacco advertising tactics used in the 1930s (see pages 107–8). What examples do we see today of "evil and conspiring men" promoting the use of harmful substances? How can we help youth recognize the benefits of obeying the Word of Wisdom?

- How is the Word of Wisdom both a physical and a spiritual commandment? (See pages 105–7, 109–10.) What blessings are promised to those who obey this commandment? (See D&C 89:18–21.) What are the most important blessings you or your family have received from obeying the Word of Wisdom?

- What can we do to increase our strength to resist temptations to break the Word of Wisdom? How does obeying the Word of

Wisdom help protect and strengthen character? (See pages 109–10.)

• What harmful and addictive substances are available today that are not specifically mentioned in D&C 89? How can the teachings in D&C 89 and the words of latter-day prophets help guide and strengthen us against these substances?

Related Scriptures: Daniel 1:3–20; 1 Corinthians 3:16–17; D&C 89:1–21

Notes

1. *Gospel Ideals* (1953), 379.
2. See Carl W. Buehner, *People of Faith,* Brigham Young University Speeches of the Year (14 Jan. 1953), 2.
3. In Conference Report, Apr. 1911, 61–62; paragraphing altered.
4. In Conference Report, Oct. 1949, 188.
5. *Gospel Ideals,* 375–76.
6. *Gospel Ideals,* 376–77.
7. In Conference Report, Apr. 1964, 4.
8. In Conference Report, Apr. 1949, 180.
9. In Conference Report, Oct. 1949, 185–86.
10. In Conference Report, Oct. 1906, 115; paragraphing altered.
11. *Gospel Ideals,* 379.
12. In Conference Report, Oct. 1969, 7–8.
13. In Conference Report, Apr. 1960, 28.
14. In Conference Report, Apr. 1968, 8.
15. *Gospel Ideals,* 377.

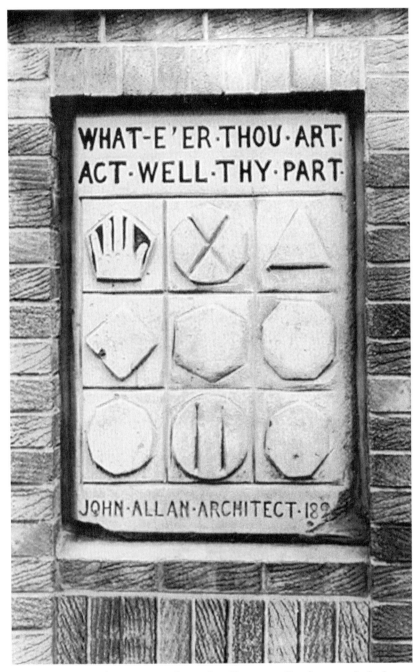

*President McKay often encouraged priesthood bearers to live the motto he had seen
chiseled on a stone in Scotland: "What-E'er Thou Art Act Well Thy Part."*

Priesthood, the Responsibility to Represent God

*The priesthood is an everlasting principle
that has existed with God from the beginning and
will exist throughout all eternity. The keys that
have been given to be used through the priesthood
come from heaven, and this priesthood power
is operative in this Church today as it continues
to expand in the earth.*[1]

Introduction

While addressing a priesthood session of general conference, President McKay told of an experience he had while serving as a missionary in Scotland in 1898. He and his companion, Elder Peter Johnston, walked by a building that caught their attention because it had a stone arch over the front door and an inscription chiseled in the arch. President McKay recalled:

"I said to my companion: 'That's unusual! I am going to see what the inscription is.' When I approached near enough, this message came to me, not only in stone, but as if it came from One in whose service we were engaged:

" 'Whate'er Thou Art, Act Well Thy Part.' . . .

"God help us to follow that motto. It is just another expression of Christ's words: 'He that will do the will of God shall know of the doctrine, whether the work is of God, or whether I speak of myself,' [see John 7:17] and that testimony leads us all to the guidance of the Holy Spirit in life. I humbly pray that the Priesthood assembled this night . . . will take upon themselves the responsibilities which God has placed upon them, and do their duty wherever it may be."[2]

President McKay had been blessed in his life when several priesthood holders righteously exercised priesthood power in his behalf. In March 1916, the Ogden River overflowed and caused the bridge near the mouth of the canyon to become unstable. He recounted: "We [he and his brother Thomas E.] jumped into a little Ford car and dashed through the rain and mud. . . . I saw the pile of rocks there at the bridge, and it seemed to be intact just as it had been the day before. So [jokingly] I said, 'I'm going across the bridge. Can you swim?' With that I stepped on the gas and dashed across the bridge, only to hear Thomas E. say, 'Oh, look out! There's a rope!' The watchman who left at seven o'clock had stretched the derrick rope across the road, and his successor, the day watchman, had not arrived. I reached for the emergency brake but was too late. The rope smashed the window, threw back the top, and caught me in the chin, severing my lip, knocking out my lower teeth, and breaking my upper jaw. Thomas E. ducked his head and escaped uninjured, but I was left partially senseless. . . .

"About nine o'clock that morning I was on the operating table. . . . They sewed my upper jaw in place and took fourteen stitches in my lower lip and lacerated cheek. One of the attendants remarked, 'Too bad; he will be disfigured for life.' Certainly I was most unrecognizable. When I was wheeled back to my room in the hospital, one of the nurses consolingly remarked, 'Well, Brother McKay, you can wear a beard,' meaning that thus I might hide my scars. . . . Three very close friends . . . called and administered to me. In sealing the anointing, [one of them] said, 'We bless you that you shall not be disfigured and that you shall not have pain.' . . .

"Saturday evening Dr. William H. Petty called to see if the teeth that were still remaining in the upper jaw might be saved. It was he who said, 'I suppose you are in great pain.' I answered, 'No, I haven't *any* pain.' . . . Sunday morning President Heber J. Grant came up from Salt Lake City. . . . He entered and said, 'David, don't talk; I'm just going to give you a blessing.' . . .

"The following October, . . . I sat at a table near where President Grant was sitting. I noticed that he was looking at me somewhat intently, and then he said, 'David, from where I am

114

sitting I cannot see a scar on your face!' I answered, 'No, President Grant, there are no scars.' "[3]

Teachings of David O. McKay

The priesthood is the power and authority to represent God.

Whenever the priesthood is delegated to man, it is conferred upon him not as a personal distinction, although it becomes such as he honors it, but as authority to represent Deity and an obligation to assist the Lord in bringing to pass the immortality and eternal life of man [see Moses 1:39].[4]

You are men who hold the priesthood of God, who hold divine authority to represent Deity in whatever position to which you have been assigned. When a man, an ordinary man is set apart in his community as a sheriff, there is something added to him. When a policeman on these streets, at the crossing, holds up his hand, you stop. There is something more about him than just an individual, there is the power that is given him. And so it is throughout life. No man can be given a position without being enhanced. It is a reality. So, too, is the power of the priesthood.[5]

Priesthood is inherent in the Godhead. It is authority and power which has its source only in the Eternal Father and his Son Jesus Christ. . . .

In seeking the source of the priesthood, . . . we can conceive of no condition beyond God himself. In him it centers. From him it must emanate. Priesthood, being thus inherent in the Father, it follows that he alone can give it to another. Priesthood, therefore, as held by man, must ever be delegated by authority. There never has been a human being in the world who had the right to [take] to himself the power and authority of the priesthood. There have been some who would [take] to themselves that right, but the Lord has never recognized it. As an ambassador from any government exercises only that authority which has been given him by his government, so a man who is authorized to represent Deity does so only by virtue of the powers and rights delegated to him. However, when such authority is given, it carries, within limitations, all the privileges of a power of attorney, by which one is empowered by another to act in another's stead. All official action performed in accordance with such power of attorney is as binding as if the person himself had performed it. . . .

Recognizing the fact that the Creator is the eternal and everlasting source of this power, that he alone can direct it, and that to possess it is to have the right, as an authorized representative, of direct communion with God, how reasonable yet sublime are the privileges and blessings made possible of attainment through the possession of the power and authority of the Melchizedek Priesthood—they are the most glorious that the human mind can contemplate.

A man who is thus in communion with his God will find his life sweetened, his discernment sharpened to decide quickly between right and wrong, his feelings tender and compassionate, yet his spirit strong and valiant in defense of right; he will find the priesthood a never failing source of happiness—a well of living water springing up unto eternal life.[6]

Priesthood power finds expression through quorums as well as individuals.

Strictly speaking, priesthood as delegated power is an individual acquirement. However, by divine decree men who are appointed to serve in particular offices in the priesthood unite in quorums. Thus, this power finds expression through groups as well as in individuals. The quorum is the opportunity for men of like aspirations to know, to love, and to aid one another.[7]

If priesthood meant only personal honor, blessing, or individual elevation, there would be no need of groups or quorums. The very existence of such groups established by divine authorization proclaims our dependence upon one another, the indispensable need of mutual help and assistance. We are, by divine right, social beings.[8]

[The Lord] realized that these [priesthood holders] need companionship, fellowship, the strength of the group; and so he

*"Men who are appointed to serve in particular offices
in the priesthood unite in quorums."*

organized quorums and designated the number in each from the deacon to the seventy.

These groups meet together, first, to instruct and to edify, to improve in knowledge generally, and particularly to instruct in moral and religious knowledge, in faith, in holiness, but also to obtain mutual strength, to act uprightly. These groups supply a need that is felt among mankind generally. . . . Priesthood quorums . . . will supply every yearning for fellowship, fraternity, and service if men will but do their duty.[9]

Members in the Aaronic priesthood, and members of the quorums in the Melchizedek priesthood, we have a duty to build up our quorums; let us not tear them down by being absent from [priesthood] meeting, or by non-preparation, or by negligence of duty. Let us feel, every one of us, . . . that it is our duty to do something to build up the Church, as the Church's duty is to build on truth and redeem mankind from sin. Men of the priesthood, let us be one in this upbuilding; let us fall into the class of benefactors; and let no man, from the high priest to the deacon, in this great priesthood movement . . . , fall into the class of malefactors [evil doers] or murmurers.[10]

A priesthood holder must be conscious of his actions and words under all conditions.

Priesthood is authority to represent God. A man who is given the priesthood is an authorized representative of the Lord in any particular field to which the individual is assigned. It is the duty of a representative of any individual group or organization to strive to represent that individual group or organization in honor. The best way to be worthy representatives is so to live that each may be susceptible to the promptings of the Lord whom he represents. Now think what that means as to a virtuous life.

". . . my Spirit shall not always strive with man," (D&C 1:33) says the Lord. Everyone, then, who holds this priesthood should live such a life as will entitle him to the inspiration of the Lord. And let me say in this regard that communion with the Holy Spirit is just as real as your connection through the radio with the unheard voices and music that fill the air. The vibrations are there.

It is so with God's Spirit. He is ever ready to guide and instruct those who tune in by upright living and who sincerely seek him. I repeat, it is the duty of every man authorized to represent him so to live as to be responsive to that Spirit.[11]

To hold the priesthood of God by divine authority is one of the greatest gifts that can come to a man, and worthiness is of first importance. The very essence of priesthood is eternal. He is greatly blessed who feels the responsibility of representing Deity. He should feel it to such an extent that he would be conscious of his actions and words under all conditions. No man who holds the Holy Priesthood should treat his wife disrespectfully. No man who holds that priesthood should fail to ask the blessings on his food or to kneel with his wife and children and ask for God's guidance. A home is transformed because a man holds and honors the priesthood. We are not to use it dictatorially, for the Lord has said that "when we undertake to cover our sins, or to gratify our pride, our vain ambition, or to exercise control or dominion or compulsion upon the souls of the children of men, in any degree of unrighteousness, behold, the heavens withdraw themselves; the Spirit of the Lord is grieved; and when it is withdrawn, Amen to the priesthood or the authority of that man." (D&C 121:37.)

That revelation, given by the Lord to the Prophet Joseph Smith, is one of the most beautiful lessons in pedagogy or psychology and government ever given, and we should read it over and over again in the 121st section of the Doctrine and Covenants.[12]

No member of this Church, no husband or father, has the right to utter an oath in his home, or ever to express a cross word to his wife or to his children. By your ordination and your responsibility, you cannot do it as a man who holds the priesthood and be true to the spirit within you. You contribute to an ideal home by your character, controlling your passion, your temper, guarding your speech, because those things will make your home what it is, and what it will radiate to the neighborhood. You do what you can to produce peace and harmony, no matter what you may suffer.[13]

I pray that we may . . . sense the value of the priesthood, and that every deacon in this Church will realize that when he is given the Aaronic Priesthood he is set apart among his fellows, that he is different from others. He cannot with impunity swear as other boys may swear, he cannot participate in pranks in the neighborhood as other boys may participate, he stands apart. That is what it means to a twelve-year-old boy, and, bishops, that is just what you should explain to them when you choose them to be deacons. Do not just call them up and ordain them, but have a talk with them and let them realize what it means to be given the Aaronic Priesthood. In the boyhood area these boys so chosen and instructed should exert an influence for good. . . .

. . . It is our obligation when we accept the priesthood to set an example worthy of imitation by our fellows. It is not what we say that will influence them. It is what we do. It is what we are.[14]

As long as members of the priesthood merit the guidance of Christ by honest and conscientious dealing with their fellow men, by resisting evil in any of its forms, by the faithful performance of duty, there is no opposing power in this world which can stay the progress of the Church of Jesus Christ.[15]

119

Priesthood power becomes productive when it is used to serve others.

We can conceive of the power of the priesthood as being potentially existent as an impounded reservoir of water. Such power becomes dynamic and productive of good only when the liberated force becomes active in valleys, fields, gardens, and happy homes. So the priesthood, as related to humanity, is a principle of power only as it becomes active in the lives of men, turning their hearts and desires toward God and prompting service to their fellowmen.[16]

Our lives are wrapped up with the lives of others. We are happiest as we contribute to the lives of others. I say that because the priesthood you hold means that you are to serve others. You represent God in the field to which you are assigned. "Whosoever will lose his life for my sake shall find it." (Matt. 16:25.)[17]

You elders perhaps have one of your number sick, and his crop needs harvesting. Get together and harvest it. One of your members has a son on a mission, and his funds are getting low. Just ask if you can be of help to him. Your thoughtfulness he will never forget. Such acts as these are what the Savior had in mind when he said, "Inasmuch as ye do it unto the least of these my brethren, ye do it unto me." (See Matt. 25:40.) There is no other way that you can serve Christ. You can kneel down and pray to him, that is good. You can plead with him to give you his guidance through the Holy Spirit—yes, we do that and must do it. We have to do it. But it is these practical, daily visits in life, it is the controlling of our tongue, in not speaking evil of a brother, but speaking well of him, that the Savior marks as true service.[18]

"What e'er thou art, act well thy part." Are you a deacon, do the duties of a deacon well. Are you a teacher, do your work well. A priest watching over the Church, visiting with them—young men in this Church, if we could just do the duties of the teacher and of the priest, teaching people their duty, what a power for good to young men eighteen years of age, and nineteen. Not incorrigible [unwilling to take correction], not recreants [disloyal cowards], but leaders. Brethren there is nothing in the world so powerful in guiding youth as to have them act well their parts in the priesthood.[19]

Priesthood holders have the responsibility to represent God as home teachers.

It is said in Ephesians, fourth chapter, that Christ gave some apostles and some prophets, some evangelists and some pastors and teachers; "for the perfecting of the Saints, for the work of the ministry, for the edifying of the body of Christ." [Ephesians 4:12.] The [home] teachers, in the Church, holding the holy priesthood, have devolving upon them the great responsibility of *perfecting the Saints,* and of *edifying the body of Christ;* therefore, I think it is not too much to say that it is their duty, their *duty,* to carry into every home just such a divine spirit as we have experienced here in these sessions of conference. No greater responsibility can rest upon any man, than to be a teacher of God's children.

. . . Some of [the home teachers] feel that their calling is of little importance, that there is not much dignity attached to it, when the fact is, that there is no more important work in the Church. We can not say of any one calling in the Church, that it is of more importance than another, because all are devoted to the development, to the instruction, to the salvation of God's children. So it is with the calling of teacher; but if there be any preference given, because of superior advantages in winning these people to salvation, it will go to those men holding the priesthood of God, who come in direct contact with the individual members of the Church. . . .

The first thing to do, my brethren, is to look to yourselves, to see whether or not you are prepared to teach. No man can teach that which he himself does not know. It is your duty to teach that Jesus Christ is the redeemer of the world, that Joseph Smith was a prophet of God, and that to him in this last dispensation there appeared God the Father and his Son in person. Do you believe it? Do you feel it? Does that testimony radiate from your being when you enter into the home? If so, that radiation will give life to the people whom you go to teach. If not, there will be a dearth, a drouth [drought], a lack of that spiritual environment in which the Saints grow. . . .

... Brethren, the message, and particularly the manner of presenting that message might not be the same when given to one who had spent his life in faithful labor in the Church, as when given to those who are newly converted. As each family is different from another . . . , so our messages and our methods, particularly our methods of presentation, might vary. I cite this just to impress us with this thought, that it is our duty to know those whom we are going to teach.[20]

The [home] teacher's duty is not performed when he goes only once a month to each house. I remember when one Bishop made it a duty of the [home] teacher to go at once to a house bereaved of a loved one and see what could be done in order to bring comfort to those who were grieving and to make arrangements for the funeral. It is the [home] teacher's duty to see that there is no want; if there is sickness there, to go and administer—watching over those families always.[21]

I believe that in [home] teaching there is one of the greatest opportunities in all the world to awaken in those who are negligent, discouraged, downhearted, and sad, renewed life and a desire to re-enter into activity in the Church of Jesus Christ. By such activity they will be led back into the spiritual atmosphere which will lift their souls and give them power to overcome weaknesses which are now shackling them.

To give help, encouragement, and inspiration to every individual is the great responsibility and privilege of [home] teachers.[22]

Suggestions for Study and Discussion

- What is priesthood power? (See pages 115–16.) For what purposes did the Lord delegate to man the authority of the priesthood? (See pages 116–17, 120–21.) What is the difference between simply receiving the authority of the priesthood and having power in the priesthood?

- Think of an experience when the power of the priesthood was exercised in your behalf. How did this affect you or the members of your family? How can we use such experiences as "teaching moments" for our children and grandchildren?

122

- Why is it necessary that a priesthood holder live worthy to be guided by the Spirit of the Lord? (See pages 118–19.) What blessings are promised to those who are faithful to priesthood covenants and obligations? (See also D&C 84:33–34.)

- Why is home teaching so vital in the Church? (See pages 121–22.) What can we do to be more effective home teachers? How can President McKay's counsel to home teachers be applied to visiting teachers? What can we do to help our home and visiting teachers feel welcome in our homes and be effective in their callings?

- How do praying, studying the scriptures, and becoming more Christlike help us to honor the priesthood? In what ways can fathers and mothers prepare their sons to receive the priesthood?

- How do women share in the blessings that come from the power of the priesthood?

- What is the purpose of priesthood quorums? (See pages 116–17.) What responsibilities are associated with being a member of a quorum? (See pages 116–17.)

Related Scriptures: 1 Peter 2:9; D&C 84:33–48; 121:34–46

Notes

1. In Conference Report, Oct. 1967, 94.
2. In Conference Report, Oct. 1956, 91.
3. See *Cherished Experiences from the Writings of President David O. McKay,* comp. Clare Middlemiss, rev. ed. (1976), 138–40; paragraphing altered.
4. *Gospel Ideals* (1953), 168.
5. In Conference Report, Oct. 1954, 83.
6. In Conference Report, Oct. 1965, 103–4.
7. In Conference Report, Oct. 1965, 104.
8. *Gospel Ideals,* 168.
9. *Gospel Ideals,* 180–81.
10. In Conference Report, Apr. 1909, 68.
11. *Gospel Ideals,* 180.
12. In Conference Report, Oct. 1967, 97.
13. In Conference Report, Apr. 1969, 150–51.
14. In Conference Report, Oct. 1948, 174.
15. *Gospel Ideals,* 167–68.
16. In Conference Report, Oct. 1965, 103–4.
17. In Conference Report, Oct. 1950, 112.
18. In Conference Report, Oct. 1955, 129.
19. In Conference Report, Oct. 1954, 84.
20. In Conference Report, Oct. 1916, 57–60; paragraphing altered.
21. In Conference Report, Apr. 1956, 86–87.
22. *Gospel Ideals,* 196.

During his ministry, President McKay dedicated five temples around the world, including the London England Temple, shown here.

The Sacred Importance of Temples

*I pray with all my soul that all members of
the Church and their children and their children's
children may realize the great truths presented
in the house of the Lord.[1]*

Introduction

When David O. McKay became President of the Church in 1951, the Church had eight temples in operation. Four were in Utah, with the others in Arizona, Hawaii, Idaho, and Alberta. In the summer of 1952, President McKay traveled to nine European countries. During this trip, he selected the sites for temples in Switzerland and England, opening an era in which the blessings of the temple would become available outside the United States and Canada.[2]

In the process of selecting and acquiring temple sites, President McKay was guided by divine inspiration. When he had selected the site for the London England Temple, engineers were reluctant, saying that the ground was too swampy. However, after closer examination, bedrock was found at the right depth to support the temple's foundation. In Switzerland, when President McKay and other Church leaders were unable to obtain the first site that had been selected, they prayed to the Lord for help. Soon they found another site that was larger but cost only half as much. At about the same time, a highway was unexpectedly constructed through part of the original site, making the discovery of the new site all the more fortunate.[3]

President McKay dedicated the Bern Switzerland Temple in 1955 and the London England Temple in 1958. He also dedicated the Los Angeles California Temple (1956), the Hamilton

New Zealand Temple (1958), and the Oakland California Temple (1964). President McKay's leadership in making temples more widely available throughout the world blessed the lives of countless members, their ancestors, and their posterity. An excerpt from his diary reflects his testimony of the importance of temple work; on the day he dedicated the Bern Switzerland Temple site, he wrote, "I want to bring the temple to the people."[4]

Teachings of David O. McKay

The temple endowment leads us to the kingdom of God.

There is the Temple "endowment," which is . . . an ordinance pertaining to man's eternal journey and limitless possibilities and progress which a just and loving Father has provided for the children whom he made in his own image—for the whole human family. This is why Temples are built.[5]

God help us to appreciate the restored gospel of Jesus Christ, which is all-comprehensive. The philosophy of life is contained in it, and in our temples will be presented the endowment, obedience to which will take the individual (and this is my testimony, for I know it) from the most selfish, envious, antagonistic, hateful characteristics of the animal plane, to the highest spiritual plane and to the kingdom of God.[6]

In temples, couples and families can be sealed for eternity.

One of the principal questions asked by reporters, newsmen and by people generally is, "What is the difference between your Temple and your other church edifices?" As all members of the Church know, the answer is that Temples are built for the performance of sacred ordinances—not secret, but sacred. A Temple is not a public house of worship. It is erected for special purposes. Indeed after a Temple is dedicated only members of the Church in good standing may enter.

One of the distinguishing features of the restored Church of Jesus Christ is the eternal nature of its ordinances and ceremonies.

For example, generally in civil as well as in church ceremonies, couples are married "for time" only, or "until death dost thee part." But love is as eternal as the spirit of man; and if man continues after death, which he does, so will love.

This interests nearly every intelligent inquirer and investigator, especially when he or she realizes the truth, that love—the divinest attribute of the human soul—will be just as eternal as the spirit itself. So whenever any person dies, the virtue of love will persist, and if any inquirer believes in the immortality of the soul, or in the persistence of personality after death, he must admit that love will also persist. . . .

. . . The injunction of the Savior [is] to love our neighbor as ourselves. But if earthly things are typical of heavenly things, in the spirit world we shall recognize our loved ones there and know them as we loved them here. I love my wife more than I can love other people. I love my children. I can have sympathy; I can have a desire to help all mankind, but I love her by whose side I have sat and watched a loved one in illness, or, perhaps, pass away. Those experiences bind heart to heart, and it is a glorious thought to cherish that death cannot separate hearts that are thus bound together; for each of you husbands will recognize your wife in the other world, and you will love her there as you love her here, and will come forth to a newness of everlasting life in the resurrection. Why should death separate you when love will continue after death?

It should not, and it need not, for when Jesus was upon the earth he told his Apostles: "And I will give unto thee the keys of the kingdom of heaven: and whatsoever thou shalt bind on earth shall be bound in heaven: and whatsoever thou shalt loose on earth shall be loosed in heaven." (Matthew 16:19.) And with the restoration to earth of the Holy Priesthood, the Church asserts that this power was again given to chosen men, and that in the house of the Lord where the marriage ceremony is performed by those who are properly authorized to represent our Lord and Savior, Jesus Christ, the union between husband and wife, and between parents and children, is effected for time and all eternity, and that for those thus married the family will continue into the eternities.[7]

Joseph [Smith] the seer . . . revealed the eternity of the marriage covenant, a doctrine so beautiful, so logical, so far-reaching in its significance that if it were adopted in its entirety, many of the present evils of society might be abolished.[8]

Temple work offers salvation for those who have died without the gospel.

A Chinese student, returning to his homeland, having graduated from one of our leading colleges, was in conversation with a Christian minister, also en route to China. When this minister urged the truth that only through acceptance of Christ's teachings can any man be saved, the [student] said: "Then what about my ancestors who never had an opportunity to hear the name of Jesus?" The minister answered: "They are lost." Said the student: "I will have nothing to do with a religion so unjust as to condemn to eternal punishment men and women who are just as noble as we, perhaps nobler, but who never had an opportunity to hear the name of Jesus."

One who understands the truth, as revealed to the Prophet Joseph regarding this doctrine, would have answered: "They will have an opportunity to hear the gospel, and to obey every principle and ordinance by proxy. Every man here or hereafter will be judged and rewarded according to his works."[9]

Since repentance and baptism by water as well as by the Spirit are essential to salvation, how shall the millions who have never heard the Gospel, who have never had an opportunity either to repent or to be baptized, enter into the kingdom of God? Surely a God of love can never be satisfied if the majority of His children are outside His kingdom, dwelling eternally either in ignorance, misery or hell. Such a thought is revolting to intelligent minds. On the other hand, if these millions who died without having heard the Gospel can enter into the kingdom of God without obeying the principles and ordinances of the Gospel, then Christ's words to Nicodemus [see John 3:2–5] were not the statement of a general and eternal truth, and Peter's words on the Day of Pentecost [see Acts 2:38] had not a universal application, even though he said plainly, "This promise is unto you, and to your children, and to all that are afar off, even as many as the Lord our God shall call." [See Acts 2:39.]

Now the Gospel of Jesus Christ teaches that *all* mankind may be saved by obedience to the laws and ordinances thereof. [See Articles of Faith 1:3.] Nor is the term "all" restricted in meaning to include only a chosen few; it means every child of a loving and divine Father. And yet, hundreds of millions have died without ever having heard that there is such a thing as a Gospel plan.

All nations and races have a just claim upon God's mercies. Since there is only one plan of salvation, surely there must be some provision made whereby the "uncounted dead" may hear of it and have the privilege of either accepting or rejecting it. Such a plan is given in the principle of salvation for the dead. . . .

Paul referred to [the] practice of baptism [for the dead] in his argument in favor of the resurrection. He said, "Else what shall they do which are baptized for the dead, if the dead rise not at all?" (1 Cor. 15:29). . . . Not a few commentators have tried to explain away [this passage's] true significance; but its context proves plainly that in the days of the apostles there existed the practice of baptism for the dead; that is, living persons were immersed in water for and in behalf of those who were dead—not who were "dead to sin" but who had "passed to the other side."

In the Kirtland Temple, April 3, 1836, the Prophet Elijah appeared to Joseph Smith and Oliver Cowdery and delivered to them "powers of the priesthood" that authorize the living to do work for the dead. These "keys" were restored in fulfilment of the prophecy of Malachi:

"Behold, I will send you Elijah the prophet, before the coming of the great and dreadful day of the Lord: and he shall turn the heart of the fathers to the children, and the heart of the children to their fathers, lest I come and smite the earth with a curse" (Mal. 4:5–6). The hearts of the fathers and of the children will be turned to one another when the fathers in the spirit world, hearing the Gospel preached and realizing that they must obey the ordinances thereof, know that their children on the earth are performing those ordinances for them.

All such "work for the dead" is performed in temples, dedicated and set apart for such purposes, where proper records are kept, and where everything is considered sacred.

With the responsibility resting upon them to carry out this important phase of Gospel service, the Latter-day Saints have become a temple-building people.[10]

You may have the opportunity of gathering the names of your ancestors, who, being baptized by proxy, may become members of the kingdom of God in the other world as we are members here.

Since the restoration of this principle and practice, Church members have zealously searched the records of the world for the history of their ancestors that their forefathers might receive vicariously the blessings of the gospel of Christ. In connection with this work the Church maintains an extensive genealogical organization.[11]

In this principle of salvation for the dead, is revealed the comprehensiveness of the saving power of the Gospel, and the applicability to all mankind of the Savior's teachings. Truly, "There is none other name under heaven given among men, whereby we must be saved." [Acts 4:12.] All ordinances performed by the Priesthood of the Most High are as eternal as love, as comprehensive and enduring as life, and through obedience to them, all mankind, living and dead, may enter into and abide eternally in the kingdom of God.[12]

We must enter the temple worthily and be faithful to the covenants we make there.

Those who go into the temple will go with recommends that they are true Christians; that they are true members of the Church of Christ; that they are honest with their fellow men; that they live in accordance with the ideals of the gospel of Jesus Christ.[13]

Before [a temple] marriage is performed, it is necessary for the young man and young woman first to obtain a recommend from the bishop. . . . There, in the presence of the priesthood, before taking upon themselves the obligation of marriage, the young people receive instructions upon the sacredness of the duty that is before them; and, furthermore, they determine whether or not they are prepared to go in holiness and purity to the altar of God and there seal their vows and love.[14]

Marriage in the temple is one of the most beautiful things in all the world. A couple is led there by love, the most divine attribute of the human soul. . . . Together they stand in the house of the Lord to testify and covenant before him that they will be true to the covenants they make that day, each keeping himself or herself to the other and no one else. That is the highest ideal of marriage ever given to man. If those covenants are kept as sacred as sacred covenants should be kept, there would be fewer broken hearts among wives and fewer among the husbands. A covenant is a sacred thing. . . . Keep it true, be true to it.[15]

Those who make covenants for their loved ones and participate in the highest ideal of marriage ever given to man will walk in the spirit and not indulge in the flesh. You will be true to the covenants you make in the House of God.[16]

"My spirit shall not always strive with man" (Gen. 6:3), says the Lord. "My spirit will not dwell in an unclean tabernacle." He who tries to live a double life, who does live a double life in violation of his covenants, to quote one author, "is either a knave or a fool." Often he is both, because he himself is using his free agency to gratify his passions, to waste his substance in riotous living, to violate the covenants that he has made in the house of God.[17]

We have a responsibility to help make temple blessings available to others.

Our temples erected for the salvation and exaltation of the human family contribute to the carrying out of the eternal plan of salvation. The same laws of eternal progress are applicable to all of our Father's children whether living in a mortal or a spiritual existence. Such a universal requirement reflects divine justice. . . .

The restored Church of Jesus Christ is the plan given by our Heavenly Father whereby every human being who can think for himself or herself may work with God for the happiness and salvation of his or her soul. *Reason* and *justice* would demand *universal application* of *eternal principles* and *ordinances* to *persons living* in *mortality,* and *to those living in the spirit world.*

Only thus may God's work and glory be consummated through the immortality and eternal life of man.

The eternal plan of salvation is given by direct revelation by the Father and his Son to the Prophet Joseph Smith, and the divine authority to officiate in the principles and ordinances rests upon the men who now guide the destiny of the revealed Church.[18]

One of our greatest responsibilities is to make accessible to faithful members of the Church in foreign lands suitable houses of the Lord. Tens of thousands of them are not able to come where temples are, and where they receive the blessings of the endowment, to have sealed to them their wives and their children for time and all eternity. Ours is the duty to carry the temple to them.[19]

O how glorious is the gospel! How great our responsibility to let the world glimpse its magnificence, its comprehensiveness, its divinity! I pray with all my soul that our temples will radiate further interest and a desire to know God's will in the hearts of thousands and tens of thousands of noble people who want to know the truth. God help us all to increase our ability to spread this truth and to help mankind to know it.[20]

Suggestions for Study and Discussion

- Why is it vital that we receive the ordinances of the temple and make and keep the associated covenants? (See pages 126–28, 130–31.)

- How can the temple endowment lead us to eternal life? (See page 126.) Why is it important to attend the temple often? What blessings have you received from participating in temple ordinances and covenants? Why do you think it is important to receive these ordinances and covenants before serving a mission or starting an eternal family?

- What is required for marriage and family relationships to continue in the eternities? (See pages 126–28.) How should the doctrine of eternal marriage and families influence our relationships with our spouse and children? How would greater obedience to this doctrine help abolish "the present evils of society"?

- What are our responsibilities regarding the salvation of the dead? (See pages 128–30.) What are some ways you can participate in the work for the dead?

- How are temples a great manifestation of God's love for all His children? (See pages 128–30.) How does temple work reflect the universal nature of the plan of salvation? (See pages 128–30.)

- What is the purpose of a temple recommend? (See page 130.) Why is individual worthiness essential to entering the temple? In what ways are we blessed as we remain faithful to our temple covenants? Why is it important to maintain a current temple recommend even if our circumstances do not allow us to attend often or at all?

- What can we do to help make temple blessings available to others? (See pages 131–32.)

Related Scriptures: 1 Corinthians 15:29; D&C 124:37–41; 128:1, 15–24; 131:1–4; 132:19; 138:28–37, 57–60

Notes

1. *Treasures of Life,* comp. Clare Middlemiss (1962), 282.

2. See James B. Allen, "McKay, David O.," in Daniel H. Ludlow, ed., *Encyclopedia of Mormonism* (1992), 4 vols., 2:872–73.

3. See Richard O. Cowan, "Temples: History of Latter-day Saint Temples from 1831 to 1990," in *Encyclopedia of Mormonism,* 4:1453.

4. Francis M. Gibbons, *David O. McKay: Apostle to the World, Prophet of God* (1986), 323.

5. *The Purpose of the Temple* (1976), Church History Library of The Church of Jesus Christ of Latter-day Saints (closed stacks, pamphlet), 11; paragraphing altered.

6. *Treasures of Life,* 282.

7. *The Purpose of the Temple,* 5–7.

8. "The Prophet Joseph Smith—On Doctrine and Organization," *Improvement Era,* Jan. 1945, 45.

9. *Improvement Era,* Jan. 1945, 15, 45.

10. "Salvation for the Dead," *Millennial Star,* 25 Oct. 1923, 680–82.

11. *The Purpose of the Temple,* 10.

12. *Millennial Star,* 25 Oct. 1923, 682.

13. *Treasures of Life,* 282.

14. In Conference Report, Apr. 1969, 9.

15. In Conference Report, Apr. 1969, 94; paragraphing altered.

16. In Conference Report, Apr. 1959, 49–50.

17. In Conference Report, Apr. 1945, 123.

18. *Treasures of Life,* 340–42.

19. In Conference Report, Apr. 1954, 26.

20. *Treasures of Life,* 342.

"Young men and young women who would live the happiest lives
would do well to prepare themselves to be worthy of that form of marriage
which God has ordained."

134

Preparing for an Eternal Marriage and Family

Truly no higher ideal regarding marriage can be cherished by young people than to look upon it as a divine institution.[1]

Introduction

David O. McKay proposed to his future wife, Emma Ray Riggs, in early December 1900, and she asked, "Are you sure I'm the right one?" He answered that he felt sure that she was. In a subsequent letter to Dr. Obadiah H. Riggs, Emma Ray's father, David O. McKay described some of the qualities he valued in her:

"Her sweetness of disposition, her virtue, her intelligence, her unselfish nature, in short, her *perfect* qualities, won my love. When she told me that this affection was reciprocated, my happiness seemed complete. . . . I have asked your daughter to be mine in marriage, and now I ask you, Dr. Riggs, her father, if you will give your consent. She has given hers. . . . In return for this I can give her nothing but a true love and a heart and mind whose one desire is to make her happy."

David O. McKay's letters to Emma Ray during their engagement reflect the noble character of their relationship and the qualities that she inspired in him. In a letter dated 11 December 1900, he wrote: "Do you know that since I *truly loved,* I can better understand why the gallant knights of old always had a lady love to fight for. The very thought of pleasing her would nerve their arms, steel their swords, and make their courage dauntless. Each one would try to develop the best strength and activity that he could possibly reach that he might be the more worthy of the approbation of his lady. Nobility of character, too, the best would

135

prize, that they might merit the companionship of those, who, they thought, possessed the truest and purest of souls."[2]

In another letter written to Emma Ray on 22 December 1900, David O. McKay wrote of the union that he and his fiancée envisioned: "You say our union will be an eternal one. Eternity alone can satisfy the love I long for, and the love I have to give. . . . I am lonesome without you, Ray, and I long for the time to come when you will always be by my side."[3] Because of righteous living and honorable, wise courtship, Brother and Sister McKay were able to realize their goal. During his ministry, President McKay often taught about preparing for an eternal marriage and family.

Although President McKay's teachings in this chapter are directed to youth who are preparing for marriage, these principles are also helpful for people who are married, particularly as they teach and counsel their children and other youth regarding dating and courtship.

Teachings of David O. McKay

Youth must be taught the sacred nature of marriage and parenthood.

Teach the young people that marriage is not merely a man-made institution, but that it is ordained of God, and is a sacred ceremony, and should receive their gravest consideration before they enter upon a contract that involves either happiness or misery for the rest of their lives. Marriage is not something which should be entered into lightly . . . or ended at the first little difficulty that might arise. The least young people can do is to approach it with honest intentions of building a home that will contribute to the bulwark of a noble society.[4]

Young people of both sexes should be taught the responsibilities and ideals of marriage so that they may realize that marriage involves obligation and is not an arrangement to be terminated at pleasure. They should be taught that pure love between the sexes is one of the noblest things on earth and the bearing and rearing of children the highest of all human duties. In this regard, it is the duty of parents to set an example in the home that children may see and absorb the sacredness of family life and the responsibility associated therewith.[5]

[The purpose of marriage] is to bear children and rear a family. Let us keep that in mind. Hundreds are now saying, and hundreds more will say—"How can I marry and support a bride in a manner with which she has been accustomed? How can I get an education and support a family? I cannot even find a place in which to live."

These are practical questions. . . . I am willing to recognize these and other difficulties and meet them, keeping in mind what the Lord has said that "marriage is ordained of God for man." [See D&C 49:15.] And I repeat that the very purpose of marriage is to rear a family and not for the mere gratification of man or woman.[6]

It is said that the best and noblest lives are those which are set toward high ideals. Truly no higher ideal regarding marriage can be cherished by young people than to look upon it as a divine institution. In the minds of the young, such a standard is a protection to them in courtship, an ever-present influence inducing them to refrain from doing anything that may prevent their going to the temple to have their love made perfect in an enduring and eternal union. It will lead them to seek divine guidance in the selection of their companions, upon the wise choice of whom their life's happiness here and hereafter is largely dependent. It makes their hearts pure and good; it lifts them up to their Father in heaven. Such joys are within the reach of most men and women if high ideals of marriage and home [are] properly fostered and cherished.[7]

Youth should prepare for marriage and parenthood by living clean lives.

Often the health of children, if a couple be blessed with such, depends upon the actions of parents before marriage. In the press, from the pulpit, and particularly in the home, there should ring more frequently the message that in their youth boys and girls are laying the foundation for their future happiness or misery. Every young man, particularly, should prepare for the responsibility of fatherhood by keeping himself physically clean, that he might enter into that responsibility not as a coward or deceiver, but as one honorable and fit to found a home. The young man who, in unfitness, takes upon himself the responsibility of fatherhood is worse than a deceiver. The future happiness of his wife and children depends upon his life in youth.

Let us also teach girls that motherhood is divine, for when we touch the creative part of life, we enter into the realm of divinity. It is important, therefore, that young womanhood realize the necessity of keeping their bodies clean and pure. . . . No mother has the right to shackle a child through life for what seems in youth to be a pleasant pastime or her right to indulge in harmful drugs and other sinful practices.[8]

Happiness does not begin at the altar; it begins during the period of youth and courtship. These seeds of happiness are sown by your ability to master your driving passion. Chastity should be the dominant virtue among young people—the ideal which the world has not accepted, and which many in the world will not believe exists or is cherished in the hearts of youth.[9]

A dominant evil of the world today is unchastity. . . . He who is unchaste in young manhood is untrue to a trust given him by the parents of the girl; and she who is unchaste in maidenhood is untrue to her future husband and lays the foundation of unhappiness, suspicion, and discord in the home. . . . Just keep in mind this eternal truth that chastity is a virtue to be prized as one of life's noblest achievements. . . . It is a chief factor to a happy home. There is no loss of prestige in maintaining in a dignified way the standards of the Church. You can be "in" this world and not "of the world." Keep your chastity above everything else! God has commanded that we be chaste.[10]

In The Church of Jesus Christ of Latter-day Saints there is but one standard of morality. No young man has any more right to be unchaste than has a young girl. That young man who asks for a recommend to take a pure girl to the altar is expected to give the same purity that he expects to receive.[11]

Chastity, not indulgence during the pre-marital years, is the source of harmony and happiness in the home, and the chief contributing factor to the health and perpetuity of the race. Loyalty, dependability, confidence, trust, love of God, and fidelity to man are associated with this diadem in the crown of virtuous womanhood and [strong] manhood. The word of the Lord to his Church is: "Keep yourself unspotted from the sin of the world." (See James 1:27; D&C 59:9)[12]

God bless you to keep your lives unpolluted, that you may go in prayer to God and ask him to guide you in choosing your mates, and when chosen, that you will both so live that you can enter the house of God, and if he were present and asked you about your lives, you could answer him honestly, "Yes, we are clean." A marriage begun on that basis, will bring you the happiness, the sweetest joy known in this life, or throughout eternity.[13]

Youth should date appropriately and should carefully evaluate their feelings.

Young people, young girls in high school, [go] daily in courtship with young boys of their age, of the girls' age, in their early 'teens, depriving themselves of becoming better acquainted with other companions; and in that daily courtship in their early age, [become] so intimate as to arouse their passions for an hour's pleasure, bringing misery upon themselves through life. And that is not imagination! You men in the Presidencies of Stakes and Bishoprics of Wards, and you fathers and mothers of some of them, know that that is not imagination.[14]

Young man, always remember when you take [a] girl out to a party that her father and mother trust her to you. She is their most precious possession. If they gave you in trust a thousand dollars, you would not think of misusing it or spending it. They are giving into your keeping something which cannot be priced in money, and you are base indeed if you become disloyal to that trust. . . . I remember my father's admonition when I started in my teens to court a young girl: "David, you treat that young lady as you would have any young boy treat your sister." Young men, follow that advice and you will go through life with your conscience clear, and later in life you can say truthfully that with all your mistakes, you have never wronged a woman.[15]

In choosing a companion, it is necessary to study . . . the one with whom you are contemplating making life's journey. You see how necessary it is to look for the characteristics of honesty, of loyalty, of chastity, and of reverence. But after having found them—"How, then," you ask, "may you tell whether or not there is any consanguinity [or close connection], that something which will make you at least congenial in each other's company?" "Is there," you ask, "some guide?" Though love is not always a true guide, especially if that love be not reciprocated or is bestowed upon a surly creature or a brute, yet certainly there is no happiness without love. "Well," you may ask, "how may I know when I am in love?" That is a very important question. . . .

In the presence of the girl you truly love you do not feel to grovel; in her presence you do not attempt to take advantage of her; in her presence you feel that you would like to be everything that a [great man] should become, for she will inspire you to that ideal. And I ask you young women to cherish that same guide. What does he inspire in you . . . ? When a young man accompanies you after a meeting, or after a dance, and he shows an inclination to use you as a convenience or as a means of gratification, then you may put it down that he is not prompted by love.

Under such circumstances, no matter how fascinated you may be, young women, no matter how confident you may feel that you love him, let your judgment rule and be master of your feelings. It may grieve you not to follow the inclination of your heart, but you had better be pained a little in your youth than to suffer pangs of torture later.[16]

Great blessings await those who properly prepare for an eternal marriage.

Young men and young women who would live the happiest lives would do well to prepare themselves to be worthy of that form of marriage which God has ordained—the union of a man and woman worthy to have their marriage solemnized in the temple of the Most High. There as true lovers kneel . . . , each may cherish the assurance of the following:

First, that their married course begins in purity. The children who come to bless the union are guaranteed a royal birth so far as inheriting a clean body is concerned.

Second, that their religious views are the same. The difficulty of rearing children properly is aggravated when Father and Mother have divergent views regarding doctrine and church affiliation. . . .

Third, that their vows are made with the idea of an eternal union, not to be broken by petty misunderstandings or difficulties.

Fourth, that a covenant made in God's presence and sealed by the Holy Priesthood is more binding than any other bond.

Fifth, that a marriage thus commenced is as eternal as love, the divinest attribute of the human soul.

Sixth, that the family unit will remain unbroken throughout eternity.[17]

Suggestions for Study and Discussion

- How can we help youth understand the sacred responsibilities that come with marriage? (See pages 136–37.) What can we do to help prepare youth for the challenges that inevitably come to a marriage?

- Why is chastity essential in preparing for an eternal marriage and family? (See pages 137–39.) How might being unchaste affect a person's ability to wisely choose an eternal companion? What process must a person go through to completely repent of unchastity? What are some of the blessings of remaining chaste?

- President McKay taught that children are often affected by the actions of the parents before marriage (see pages 137–39). In addition to remaining morally clean, what else can youth and parents do to keep their lives pure and to protect their future children?

- In what ways does the media attempt to influence our views of courtship and marriage? Why do you think President McKay warned against steady dating at an early age? What other safeguards should be observed as people date? (See pages 139–40.)

- What counsel would you give to young people who wonder if they are in love? (See page 140.) What are some qualities that are important in a relationship?

- What is the purpose of marriage? (See pages 136–37.) What are the perils of marrying too soon? What are the perils of delaying marriage too long? How can a couple know when the time to marry is right?

- President McKay taught that those who view marriage as a "divine institution" are strengthened and guided during courtship. Why do you think this is true? How have you seen people blessed as they have lived gospel standards during courtship?

- What similarities do you see in President McKay's teachings for youth and the standards found in *For the Strength of Youth?* How can you help your children understand that the standards you were taught are the same as the standards for them?

Related Scriptures: Jacob 2:28; Alma 37:37; 39:3–5; D&C 132:15–19

Notes

1. In Conference Report, Apr. 1969, 7.
2. Quoted in David Lawrence McKay, *My Father, David O. McKay* (1989), 7–8; paragraphing altered.
3. Quoted in *My Father, David O. McKay,* 8–9; paragraphing altered.
4. In Conference Report, Oct. 1943, 32.
5. In Conference Report, Apr. 1964, 6.
6. *Gospel Ideals* (1953), 466–67.
7. In Conference Report, Apr. 1969, 7.
8. In Conference Report, Apr. 1969, 6.
9. "As Youth Contemplates an Eternal Partnership," *Improvement Era,* Mar. 1938, 139.
10. In Conference Report, Apr. 1969, 6.
11. In Conference Report, Apr. 1969, 9.
12. In Conference Report, Apr. 1964, 6.
13. *Gospel Ideals,* 465–66; paragraphing altered.
14. In Conference Report, Apr. 1958, 90.
15. *Improvement Era,* Mar. 1938, 191.
16. *Gospel Ideals,* 459–60; paragraphing altered.
17. *Gospel Ideals,* 465.

Experiencing Happiness in Marriage

*The exalted view of marriage as held by the Church
is given expressively in five words found in the forty-ninth
section of the Doctrine and Covenants: "marriage
is ordained of God." (D&C 49:15.)[1]*

Introduction

David O. McKay and Emma Ray Riggs were married in the Salt Lake Temple on 2 January 1901, the first couple sealed in that temple that year. Their union of 69 years exemplifies the continuing devotion of a husband and wife to each other. The strength of their marriage was noted by both friends and strangers. Sister McKay once related the following experience:

"I accompanied my husband to a dedication of a meetinghouse in Los Angeles. We stopped on Wilshire Boulevard to get our car washed. I sat on a bench and the President was standing over by the car. Suddenly at my elbow I heard a tiny voice say, 'I guess that man over there loves you.' Surprised, I turned and saw a beautiful boy about seven years of age with dark curly hair and large brown eyes. 'What did you say?'

" 'I said, I guess that man over there loves you.'

" 'Why, yes, he loves me; he is my husband. Why do you ask?'

" 'Oh, 'cuz, the way he smiled at you. Do you know, I'd give anything in the world if my Pop would smile at my Mom that way.' "[2]

Until President McKay was confined to a wheelchair, he always rose when his wife entered the room, held her chair, and opened the car door for her. He also always bade her hello and goodbye with an affectionate kiss. This practice continued when both President and Sister McKay used wheelchairs. Once when

President and Sister McKay enjoyed "that sweet companionship between husband and wife which grows dearer and dearer as the troubles of life come on."

President McKay was being wheeled away for a meeting, he exclaimed: "We have to go back. I didn't kiss Ray goodbye." He was wheeled back for this loving ritual that had become a part of their relationship.[3]

A great tribute to the McKays' marriage was given by a young couple preparing to be married. One of President McKay's sons, David Lawrence McKay, related the experience as follows:

"When Father and Mother were living at 1037 East South Temple [in Salt Lake City], a young couple arrived in a car, got out, and then sat down on the front lawn. There, the young man proposed to the young lady. As he later related the story to a member of the family, it was because 'I want our married life to be as ideal as that of President and Sister McKay.' "[4]

Teachings of David O. McKay

The covenant of eternal marriage brings joy and strengthens love.

In the teachings of the Church of Jesus Christ, the family assumes supreme importance in the development of the individual and of society. "Happy and thrice happy are they who enjoy an uninterrupted union, and whose love, unbroken by any complaints, shall not dissolve until the last day." It will not dissolve when sealed by the authority of the Holy Priesthood throughout all eternity. The marriage ceremony, when thus sealed, produces happiness and joy unsurpassed by any other experience in the world. "What therefore God hath joined together, let not man put asunder." [Mark 10:9.][5]

The eternity of the marriage covenant is a glorious revelation, giving assurance to hearts bound by the golden clasp of love and sealed by authority of the Holy Priesthood that their union is eternal.[6]

A word about the eternity of the marriage covenant. . . . Let's look at the principle of it. Will you name for me in your minds the most divine attribute of the human soul? . . . Love is the most divine attribute of the human soul, and if you accept the immortality of the soul, that is, if you believe that personality persists after death, then, you must believe that love also lives. Isn't that sound? And I ask you this: Whom shall we love when we recognize those personalities in the next world?

True, we are admonished to love everybody. Yes, we should love everybody now; but you and I know that we love those whom we know best. . . . When we meet these personalities in the eternal realm, we shall recognize them, and know them because of these experiences in this life. And that union of loving hearts will be perpetuated after life. That is why we are married—sealed—for time and eternity. It isn't just a mere dogma of the Church—it is a truth fundamental to the life and happiness of all humanity. It is the part of wisdom to choose the House of the Lord in which to [pledge] your love and to consecrate your vows.[7]

With the high ideal of marriage as revealed to the Prophet Joseph Smith, members of the Church should have but one goal, and that is to keep in mind the fact that marriage, the foundation of society, is "ordained of God" [D&C 49:15] for the building of permanent homes in which children may be properly reared and taught the principles of the gospel.[8]

Let us substitute the present tendency toward a low view of marriage with the lofty view which God gives it. Yesterday I stood at the altar of the temple, as I have stood many a time, and saw two hearts—two souls—slipping into one, as two dewdrops on the stem of a rose when the sun comes out in the morning, one slipping into the other, the two becoming one. That high view of marriage in the mind of that young bridegroom, and the appreciation of the sacredness of marriage by the bride, I think is one of the sublimest things in all the world. They had the high view of marriage, not a low view of it as a means of gratifying passion. Let us look upon marriage as a sacred obligation and a covenant as possibly an eternal one.[9]

The marriage bond should be as eternal as love, the most divine attribute of the human soul. Most surely, then, that bond should continue as long as love is an attribute of the spirit.[10]

We must guard against the dangers that threaten marriage.

The signs of the times definitely indicate that the sacredness of the marriage covenant is dangerously threatened. There are places where the marriage ceremony may be performed at any hour of the day or night without any previous arrangement. The license is issued and the ceremony performed while the couple wait. Many couples who have been entrapped by such entice-ments have had their marriages end in disappointment and sor-row. In some instances these places are nothing more than opportunities for legalized immorality. Oh, how far they fall below the true ideal! As far as lies within our power, we must warn young couples against secret and hasty marriages.

It is vital also to counteract the insidious influences of printed literature that speaks of the "bankruptcy of marriage," that advo-cates trial marriages, and that places extramarital relations on a par with extramarital friendships.[11]

Marriage is a sacred relationship entered into for purposes that are well recognized—primarily for the rearing of a family. It is claimed by some careful observers that our present modern life tends to frustrate these purposes.[12]

Sometimes men and women with low ideals and weakened wills permit their passions, like unbridled steeds, to dash aside judgment and self-restraint, and to cause them to commit sin that may sear their conscience and leave in their hearts an ever-lasting regret.

In this day when modesty is thrust into the background, and chastity is considered an outmoded virtue, I appeal to you to keep your souls unmarred and unsullied from this sin, the con-sequence of which will smite and haunt you intimately until your conscience is seared and your character sordid. . . . Remember, too, the significance of the Savior's saying that if any shall com-mit adultery even in his or her heart, he shall not have the Spirit, but shall deny the faith and shall fear [see D&C 63:16].[13]

Twenty-four years ago when the steamship *Marama* dropped anchor outside the coral reef that surrounds the island of Rarotonga, a passenger desiring to go ashore asked the captain why he did not sail nearer to the wharf. In answer, the experienced seaman mentioned treacherous waters and pointed to an engine of one ship, the *Maitai,* and to the bow of another, still protruding out of the water—both carrying mute evidence of the danger of anchoring too close to the shore of this coral-bound island. "We anchor here," said the captain, "because it is safer to avoid being dashed to pieces, as were those two vessels, hulls of which lie on those dangerous reefs."

A flippant attitude toward marriage, the ill-advised suggestion of "companionate marriage," the base, diabolical theory of "free sex experiment," and the ready-made divorce courts are dangerous reefs upon which many a family bark [or ship] is wrecked.[14]

The more you keep in company with your wife, the happier you are. Business takes you away from home. She is there alone. Do not let companionship with other women divide your affection, and that applies to woman as well as to man. At one time I thought that it did not; that man was wholly to blame for the unrest, the disagreements and sorrows that are occurring too frequently, but I have had to modify my opinion. Companionship is the means of perpetuating that love which brought about your union.[15]

Another threat to our society is the increasing number of divorces and the tendency to look upon marriage as a mere contract that may be severed at the first difficulty or misunderstanding that may arise.

One of our most precious possessions is our families. The domestic relations precede, and, in our present existence, are worth more than all other social ties. They give the first throb to the heart and unseal the deep fountains of its love. Home is the chief school of human virtues. Its responsibilities, joys, sorrows, smiles, tears, hopes, and solicitudes form the chief interests of human life. . . .

When one puts business or pleasure above his home, he that moment starts on the downgrade to soul-weakness. When the club becomes more attractive to any man than his home, it is time for him to confess in bitter shame that he has failed to measure up to the supreme opportunity of his life and flunked in the final test of true manhood. . . . The poorest shack in which love prevails over a united family is of greater value to God and future humanity than any other riches. In such a home God can work miracles and will work miracles.[16]

A successful marriage requires continued courtship, effort, and commitment.

I should like to urge *continued courtship,* and apply this to grown people. Too many couples have come to the altar of marriage looking upon the marriage ceremony as the end of courtship instead of the beginning of an eternal courtship. Let us not forget that during the burdens of home life—and they come—that tender words of appreciation, courteous acts are even more appreciated than during those sweet days and months of courtship. It is after the ceremony and during the trials that daily arise in the home that a word of "thank you," or "pardon me," "if you please," on the part of husband or wife contributes to that love which brought you to the altar. It is well to keep in mind that love can be starved to death as literally as the body that receives no sustenance. Love feeds upon kindness and courtesy. It is significant that the first sentence of what is now known throughout the Christian world as the Psalm of Love, is, "Love suffereth long, and is kind." [See 1 Corinthians 13:4.] The wedding ring gives no man the right to be cruel or inconsiderate, and no woman the right to be slovenly, cross, or disagreeable.

The next contributing factor to your happy marriage I would name is *self-control.* Little things happen that annoy you, and you speak quickly, sharply, loudly, and wound the other's heart. I know of no virtue that helps to contribute to the happiness and peace of the home more than that great quality of self-control in speech. Refrain from saying the sharp word that comes to your mind at once if you are wounded or if you see something in the other which offends you. It is said that during courtship we should keep our eyes wide open, but after marriage keep them half-shut. . . .

149

"Marriage is a relationship that cannot survive selfishness, impatience, domineering, inequality, and lack of respect. Marriage is a relationship that thrives on acceptance, equality, sharing, giving, helping, doing one's part, learning together, enjoying humor."[17]

Minimize the faults, commend virtues. After the first thrill of the honeymoon is worn off, couples begin to see frailties, idiosyncrasies which they had not noticed before. Responsibilities of motherhood come to the woman. Difficulties in paying debts come. And so we become prone to find fault. Let us learn to control ourselves in that respect. . . .

I regard it as an incontrovertible fact that in no marriage circle can true peace, love, purity, chastity, and happiness be found, in which is not present the spirit of Christ, and the daily, hourly striving after loving obedience to his divine commands, and especially, the nightly prayer expressing gratitude for blessings received.

God help us to build homes in which the spirit of heaven on earth may be experienced. You and I know that that is possible, it is not a dream, it is not a theory. We may have that sweet companionship between husband and wife which grows dearer and dearer as the troubles of life come on. We can have homes in which children will never hear father and mother wrangle or quarrel. God help us . . . to build such homes, and to teach our young men and young women who are anticipating home life, to cherish such an ideal.[18]

Suggestions for Study and Discussion

- What impresses you about the relationship between President and Sister McKay? How does their relationship enhance his credibility in giving counsel on marriage?

- President McKay taught that love is "the most divine attribute of the human soul" (page 145). Why do you think that is true?

- What do you think it means that "marriage is ordained of God"? (See pages 145–46.) What effect should that knowledge have on our attitude toward marriage? What does "The Family: A Proclamation to the World" teach regarding marriage?

- What are some of the dangers that threaten marriages today? (See pages 147–49.) What is the difference between viewing marriage as a covenant and viewing marriage as a "mere contract"? How can we resolve problems and differences that arise in marriage? (See pages 149–50.)

- Why do some people postpone or avoid marriage? How can we help others regard marriage as the "high ideal" of which President McKay spoke?

- Why is continued courtship essential throughout marriage? (See pages 149–50.) What ways have you found to strengthen your relationship with your spouse? What examples have you seen of other couples who continue to strengthen their marriages?

- Why are harsh words damaging to the marriage relationship? How can we gain greater self-control in this area? (See pages 149–50.)

- President McKay taught that no marriage can thrive without the "spirit of Christ" (page 150). In what ways can we bring the spirit of Christ into marriage?

Related Scriptures: Matthew 19:3–8; Ephesians 5:25; D&C 25:14; 42:22; 49:15–17; 131:1–4

Notes

1. In Conference Report, Apr. 1969, 6–7.
2. Emma Ray Riggs McKay, *The Art of Rearing Children Peacefully* (1952), 10.
3. Quoted in David Lawrence McKay, *My Father, David O. McKay* (1989), 264.
4. *My Father, David O. McKay,* 1.
5. In Conference Report, Apr. 1956, 9; paragraphing altered.
6. *Gospel Ideals* (1953), 463.
7. "As Youth Contemplates an Eternal Partnership," *Improvement Era,* Mar. 1938, 191.
8. In Conference Report, Apr. 1953, 16.
9. *Gospel Ideals,* 478.
10. In Conference Report, Apr. 1947, 119.
11. In Conference Report, Apr. 1969, 7.
12. In Conference Report, Apr. 1945, 141.
13. In Conference Report, Oct. 1951, 8–9; paragraphing altered.
14. *Gospel Ideals,* 508–9.
15. In Conference Report, Apr. 1956, 9.
16. In Conference Report, Apr. 1964, 5.
17. In Conference Report, Apr. 1956, 8–9.
18. In Conference Report, Apr. 1952, 87.

"Let us be more determined to make [righteous] homes, . . . determined that in our homes we are going to have just a little taste of heaven here on this earth."

The Noble Calling
of Parents

*Protect your children. Guide them . . . through the
example of a kind father, a loving mother.*[1]

Introduction

President David O. McKay often expressed appreciation for his
parents and their influence in his life: "From [my father] I
learned the lessons of work and worship which apply to the
moral and spiritual activities as well as the immediate, temporal
things. Whatever duty we assume, whatever task, we must do it
and give our best to it.

"My mother's beautiful example has always remained with me
also—her gentleness and patience and sincerity." [2]

President McKay in turn had a powerful influence as a loving
father. When one of his sons, David Lawrence, was a young boy,
he accompanied his father in a horse-drawn carriage. "We forded
a swollen river in a thunderstorm," David Lawrence later
recalled, "and got caught between that river and a mountain tor-
rent. I thought the end of the world had come, and started to
cry. Father held me on his lap in his arms all night until we were
rescued in the morning. It's hard to disobey a man who loves
you and puts his arms around you." [3]

David Lawrence remembered that David O. and Emma Ray
McKay made their expectations clear to their children and that
they, as parents, "were so self-disciplined that we were never
confused by seeing them behave in a way different from the way
we were supposed to behave. . . . Our parents' expectations provided the path for us to follow, and our love for them provided
an irresistible motivation for us to walk that path. We learned to
love them because they first dearly loved each other and us." [4]

President McKay's example and counsel to Latter-day Saint parents demonstrated his understanding of their important influence and reflected his conviction that "no other success can compensate for failure in the home."[5]

Teachings of David O. McKay

Parents have a divine responsibility to care for and guide their children.

A newborn babe is the most helpless creature in the world. The protecting care of parenthood is essential to its survival, as well as its growth. . . . Our most precious possessions, our treasures of eternity, are our children. These merit and should receive our greatest and our most constant care and guidance. . . .

The bringing of children into the world bears with it great responsibilities and opens to view the noblest purpose of life, namely, a co-partnership with deity "to bring to pass the immortality and eternal life of man." (Moses 1:39.)[6]

The Father of all mankind expects parents, as his representatives, to assist him in shaping and guiding human lives and immortal souls. That is the highest assignment which the Lord can bestow upon man.[7]

Parenthood . . . should be held as a sacred obligation. There is something in the depths of the human soul which revolts against neglectful parenthood. God has implanted deep in the souls of parents the truth that they cannot with impunity shirk the responsibility to protect childhood and youth.

There seems to be a growing tendency to shift this responsibility from the home to outside influences, such as the school and the church. Important as these outward influences are, they never can take the place of the influence of the mother and the father. Constant training, constant vigilance, companionship, being watchmen of our own children are necessary in order to keep our homes intact.[8]

The inspiration of God is seen in requiring the Latter-day Saints to keep their homes intact and to teach their children the principles of the gospel of Jesus Christ. "And they shall also teach their children to pray, and to walk uprightly before the Lord." This command from the Lord, given to us in the Doctrine and Covenants, section 68, verse 28, leaves no question as to the responsibility of parents to teach their children—a responsibility too frequently shifted to the shoulders of the Church, public schools, and officers of the law.[9]

Three groups carry the responsibility of training children: First, the family; second, the Church; third, the state. The most important of these is the family. By divine edict the Lord has placed upon parents the responsibility, first to teach the doctrine of repentance; second, faith in Christ, the Son of the living God; third, baptism and confirmation; fourth, to teach children to pray; fifth, to teach children to walk uprightly before the Lord [see D&C 68:25–28]. Parents who shirk this responsibility will have to answer for the sin of neglect.[10]

The greatest trust that can come to a man and woman is the placing in their keeping the life of a little child. If a man defaults who is entrusted with other people's funds, whether he be a bank, municipal, or state official, he is apprehended and probably sent to prison. If a person entrusted with a government secret discloses that secret, and betrays his country, he is called a traitor. What must the Lord think, then, of parents who, through their own negligence or wilful desire to indulge their selfishness, fail properly to rear their children, and thereby prove untrue to the greatest trust that has been given to human beings? In reply the Lord has said: " . . . the sin be upon the heads of the parents." (D&C 68:25.)[11]

There is nothing temporary in the home of the Latter-day Saints. There is no element of transitoriness in the family relationship. To the Latter-day Saint the home is truly the basic unit of society; and parenthood is next to Godhood. The secret of good citizenship lies in the home. The secret of instilling faith in God, faith in his Son, the Redeemer of the world, faith in the organizations of the Church, lies in the home. There it is centered. God has placed upon parents the responsibility of instilling these principles into the minds of children. Our schools, our Church organizations, and some worthy social institutions are all helps in the upbuilding and guidance of the youth, but none of these—great and important as they are in the lives of our youth—can supplant the permanence and the influence of the parents in the home.[12]

Mothers can have a powerful influence for good on their children.

One of the greatest needs in the world today is intelligent, conscientious motherhood. . . .

Motherhood is the greatest potential influence either for good or ill in human life. The mother's image is the first that stamps itself on the unwritten page of the young child's mind. It is her caress that first awakens a sense of security; her kiss the first realization of affection; her sympathy and tenderness the first assurance that there is love in the world.[13]

The noblest calling in the world is motherhood. True motherhood is the most beautiful of all arts, the greatest of all professions. She who can paint a masterpiece, or who can write a book that will influence millions, deserves the admiration and plaudits of mankind; but she who rears successfully a family of healthy, beautiful sons and daughters, whose immortal souls will exert an influence throughout the ages long after paintings shall have faded, and books and statues shall have decayed or have been destroyed, deserves the highest honor that man can give, and the choicest blessings of God.[14]

Mothers sow the seeds in childhood that determine to a great extent life's harvests in adulthood. A mother who instills into the souls of her children respect for one another and love for motherhood and fatherhood, renders a great service to the Church and to humanity in general. Children from such homes go out into the world as good citizens—citizens who will render the service which their parents have rendered, to fight the battles which their fathers and mothers have fought. . . .

Motherhood is the one thing in all the world which most truly exemplifies the God-given virtues of creating and sacrificing. Though it carries the woman close to the brink of death, motherhood also leads her into the very realm of the fountains of life, and makes her co-partner with the Creator in bestowing upon eternal spirits mortal life.

All through the years of babyhood, childhood, and youth, yes, even after her girls themselves become mothers and her sons become fathers, the mother tenderly, lovingly sacrifices for them her time, her comfort, her pleasures, her needed rest and recreation, and, if necessary, health and life itself. No language can express the power and beauty and heroism of a mother's love. . . .

. . . Among my most precious soul-treasures is the memory of Mother's prayers by the bedside, of her affectionate touch as she tucked the bed clothes around my brother and me and gave each a loving, goodnight kiss. We were too young and roguish then to appreciate fully such devotion, but not too young to know that Mother loved us.

It was this realization of Mother's love, with a loyalty to the precepts of an exemplary father, which more than once during fiery youth turned my steps from the precipice of temptation.[15]

No nobler work in this world can be performed by any mother than to rear and love the children with whom God has blessed her. That is her duty.[16]

Fathers should take an active part in rearing their children.

One evening, about five o'clock, four brethren were riding down Main Street [in Salt Lake City, Utah] in an automobile. Just as they passed First South Street, they heard a little plaintive cry, "Papa! Papa! Papa! wait." The father was the driver, and his ready ear recognized his son's voice. He brought the machine instantly to a standstill. As the men looked out, they saw coming out of that bustling, jostling crowd of humanity, a little nine-year-old boy, out of breath, panting, crying, because of his effort to overtake the machine. . . .

The father said, "Why, where have you been, my son?"

"I have been looking for you."

"Well, did you leave the place where we agreed to meet?"

"Yes, I went up to see where you were."

157

The boy understood that they were to meet in front of the Tabernacle. The father evidently meant to meet the child farther down the street. Through this misunderstanding the son had become separated from his parent, and the little child was thrown into that vast throng, unprotected.

I believe that illustrates the keynote of warning that has been sounded frequently. Fathers, is there a misunderstanding between you and your sons? Is there one wandering amidst the throngs of life, surrounded by all kinds of temptations, and you expecting to meet him at an appointed place which he does not know? He may not come out from that throng and cry, "Father, Father!" and if he should, your ears might be deaf to that call, because of the concentration of your mind upon the affairs of life. So you might speed by him and leave him in the midst of evil, to find his own way home. Take your sons with you along this road of life, that you may have them with you in that eternal home where there is everlasting peace and contentment.[17]

The father who, because of business or political or social responsibilities, fails to share with his wife the responsibilities of rearing his sons and daughters is untrue to his marital obligations, is a negative element in what might and should be a joyous home atmosphere, and is a possible contributor to discord and delinquency.[18]

Parents should lovingly teach obedience and reverence.

Reverence and obedience to law should begin at home. Indeed, too much emphasis cannot be laid upon the responsibility of parents to teach their children reverence for God in all things sacred, and to honor and uphold the law.[19]

Obedience is heaven's first law, and it is the law of the home. There can be no true happiness in the home without obedience—obedience obtained, not through physical force, but through the divine element of love. There is no home without love. You may have a palace and yet not have a home, and you may live in a log house with a dirt roof, and a dirt floor, and have there the most glorious home in all the world, if within those four log walls there permeates the divine principle of love, [which creates] that blessed obedience and compliance that makes life worth while.[20]

There have been rampant some wild theories about the self-determination of children, and the preservation of their individuality. Some of these theorists believe that children should be permitted to solve their own problems without guidance from parents. There is some virtue in this, but there is more error. . . .

. . . The child should learn that there are limits to his actions, that there are certain bounds beyond which he cannot pass with impunity. This conformity to home conditions can be easily obtained with kindness, but with firmness. "Train the child the way he should go: and when he is old, he will not depart from it." [See Proverbs 22:6.][21]

Youth [need] guidance, direction, and proper restraint. "Let thy child's first lesson be obedience, and the second will be what thou wilt," said Benjamin Franklin. . . . The child should learn early that the world is not created for him alone; that he has an obligation to others. . . .

Parents, too, have a responsibility in this training not to provoke children to wrath [see Ephesians 6:4]. They should be considerate not to irritate by vexatious commands or place unreasonable blame. Whenever possible they should give encouragement rather than remonstrance or reproof.[22]

Parental example is a powerful force in the lives of children.

There is a responsibility upon all, and especially upon fathers and mothers, to set examples to children and young people worthy of imitation. Parents must be sincere in upholding law and upholding the priesthood in their homes, that children may see a proper example.[23]

It is the duty of parents and of the Church not only to teach but also to demonstrate to young people that living a life of truth and moral purity brings joy and happiness, while violations of moral and social laws result only in dissatisfaction, sorrow, and, when carried to extreme, in degradation.[24]

It is our duty as adults and [our children's] parents to set them a proper example in the home and in society. It is our responsibility to impress our children with our sincerity in our belief in the gospel of Jesus Christ. Never should parents teach one thing about the gospel and do another. Children are very susceptible to insincerity.[25]

The family gives to the child his name and standing in the community. A child wants his family to be as good as those of his friends. He wants to be able to point with pride to his father, and to feel an inspiration always as he thinks of his mother.[26]

God help us to defend the truth—better than that, to live it, to exemplify it in our homes. . . . God give you power so to have that influence, that your children may be true to the last, to death if necessary, to the truth of the gospel of Jesus Christ.[27]

Let us be more determined to make [righteous] homes, to be kinder husbands, more thoughtful wives, more exemplary to our children, determined that in our homes we are going to have just a little taste of heaven here on this earth.[28]

Suggestions for Study and Discussion

- What are the roles of parents in God's plan "to bring to pass the immortality and eternal life" of His children? (See pages 154–56.) How do fathers and mothers share the responsibility for bringing up children in righteousness? (See pages 156–58.)

- Why should parents make their children and the home their main priority? What kinds of influences or activities compete for family time together? How can parents keep activities outside the home in proper perspective? Why is it important to involve all family members in these decisions?

- What special relationship should exist between a mother and her children? (See pages 156–57.) In what unique ways can mothers influence their children for good?

- What can fathers do to take an active part in rearing their children? (See pages 157–58.) What blessings can come to fathers and children as they spend time together?

- What are some effective ways for parents to teach children obedience and reverence? (See pages 158–59.) Why is love such an important part of this effort? What can parents do when children choose to disobey and become wayward?

- What is the effect on children when parents "teach one thing about the gospel and do another"? How have you seen parental example influence children in positive ways? (See pages 159–60.)

- In what ways can we help single parents who are striving to raise their children in righteousness?

- Why do you think the Lord has placed the responsibilities of parenthood above all other responsibilities? Why is it important to understand that the home is the basic unit of the Church? What similarities do you see between President McKay's teachings on the family and "The Family: A Proclamation to the World"?

Related Scriptures: Colossians 3:20–21; 1 Nephi 1:1; 8:35–38; Enos 1:1–3; Alma 56:41–48

Notes

1. In Conference Report, Oct. 1967, 97.
2. *Secrets of a Happy Life,* comp. Llewelyn R. McKay (1960), xii.
3. Quoted in John J Stewart, *Remembering the McKays* (1970), 30.
4. David Lawrence McKay, *My Father, David O. McKay* (1989), 99; paragraphing altered.
5. Quoted from J. E. McCulloch, *Home: The Savior of Civilization* (1924), 42; in Conference Report, Apr. 1935, 116.
6. In Conference Report, Oct. 1954, 8–9.
7. In Conference Report, Apr. 1955, 27.
8. In Conference Report, Apr. 1969, 7.
9. In Conference Report, Apr. 1966, 107.
10. In Conference Report, Oct. 1954, 8.
11. In Conference Report, Apr. 1955, 25–26.
12. *Stepping Stones to an Abundant Life,* comp. Llewelyn R. McKay (1971), 358.
13. *True to the Faith: From the Sermons and Discourses of David O. McKay,* comp. Llewelyn R. McKay (1966), 167–68.
14. *Pathways to Happiness,* comp. Llewelyn R. McKay (1957), 116.
15. *Man May Know for Himself: Teachings of President David O. McKay,* comp. Clare Middlemiss (1967), 262–65.
16. In Conference Report, Apr. 1951, 81.
17. *Gospel Ideals* (1953), 489–90.
18. In Conference Report, Apr. 1965, 7.
19. In Conference Report, Apr. 1937, 30.
20. In Conference Report, June 1919, 78.
21. In Conference Report, Apr. 1955, 27.
22. In Conference Report, Apr. 1959, 73.
23. In Conference Report, Oct. 1927, 12.
24. In Conference Report, Apr. 1967, 6.
25. In Conference Report, Apr. 1960, 120.
26. In Conference Report, Apr. 1945, 143.
27. In Conference Report, Apr. 1969, 97.
28. In Conference Report, Apr. 1952, 128.

"The most precious thing in the world is a testimony of the truth."

A Testimony of the Truth

*A testimony of the gospel of Jesus Christ is the most
sacred, the most precious gift in our lives, obtained
only by adherence to the principles of the gospel, not
by following the paths of the world.[1]*

Introduction

President David O. McKay often taught about the importance of gaining a personal testimony of the gospel, promising that "the Lord never forsakes those who seek him." While in his youth, David O. McKay desired to obtain his own witness of the truth. Recalling that period of his life, he wrote:

"Somehow in my youth I got the idea that we could not get a testimony unless we had some manifestation. I read of the first vision of the Prophet Joseph Smith, and I knew that he knew what he had received was of God. I heard my father's testimony of a voice that had come to him, and somehow I received the impression that that was the source of all testimony. I realized in my youth that the most precious thing that a man could obtain in this life was a testimony of the divinity of this work. I hungered for it; I felt that if I could gain a testimony, all else would indeed seem insignificant.

"I did not neglect my prayers. I always felt that the secret prayer, whether in the room or out in the grove or on the hills, would be the place where that testimony would come. Accordingly, when I was a boy I knelt in prayer more than once by the serviceberry bush as my saddle-horse stood by the side of the road.

"I remember riding over the hills of Huntsville one afternoon, thinking of these things and concluding that there in the silence of the hills was the best place to get that testimony. I stopped my horse, threw the reins over his head, withdrew just a few steps, and knelt by the side of a tree. The air was clear and pure, the sunshine delightful; the growing verdure and flowers scented the air. . . .

"I knelt down and with all the fervor of my heart poured out my soul to God and asked him for a testimony of this gospel. I had in mind that there would be some manifestation; that I should receive some transformation that would leave me absolutely without doubt.

"I got up, mounted my horse, and as he started over the trail, I remember rather introspectively searching myself and involuntarily shaking my head, saying to myself, 'No, sir, there is no change; I am just the same boy I was before I knelt down.' The anticipated manifestation had not come."[2]

Even though he did not immediately receive the manifestation he expected, President McKay continued to seek a personal witness. He later related that "the spiritual manifestation for which I had prayed as a boy in my teens came as a natural sequence to the performance of duty."[3]

From his own experience President McKay taught that obedience to gospel principles was a key to receiving a testimony. He testified: "If you will undertake to embrace the principles of life everlasting, you will find it instilling upon your soul a benediction of the Holy Ghost which will give you a testimony beyond any possibility of doubt that God lives, that he is indeed our Father, and that this is his work established through the Prophet Joseph Smith. That is my testimony—the most precious thing in life!"[4]

Teachings of David O. McKay

A testimony of the truth is the most precious possession in the world.

There is nothing which a man can possess in this world, which will bring more comfort, more hope and faith than a testimony of the existence of a Heavenly Father who loves us, or of the reality of Jesus Christ, his Only Begotten Son, that those two heavenly personages appeared to the Prophet Joseph and established the Church of Jesus Christ, and that men are officially authorized to represent Deity.[5]

The most precious thing in the world is a testimony of the truth. . . . Truth never grows old, and the truth is that God is the source of [the] Priesthood . . . ; that He lives, that Jesus Christ, the great High Priest, stands at the head of this Church.[6]

We have had testimony of the Spirit that we are children of our Father in heaven. We have had testimony that God is a living being. We have had testimony that Christ, who was crucified and who rose the third day a resurrected being, is the head of his Church. We have had testimony of the Spirit that he has revealed in this dispensation the gospel of Jesus Christ, which is again established on earth in all its fullness. The gospel of Jesus Christ, as revealed to the Prophet Joseph Smith, is in very deed in every way the power of God unto salvation [see Romans 1:16]. It gives to every man the perfect life here, and through obedience to gospel principles it gives us eternal life.[7]

Cherish in your hearts the testimony of truth; make it as solid and as firm and unwavering as the fixed stars in the heavens. May there come into everyone's heart and into all our homes the true Spirit of Christ, our Redeemer, whose reality, whose inspiring guidance I know to be real.[8]

As we are obedient, we receive a testimony through the Spirit.

Purity of thought, and a *sincere heart seeking* the Savior's *guidance daily* will lead to a testimony of the truth of Christ's Gospel as sure and permanent as that which Peter possessed . . . after seeing the transfiguration of Christ, and hearing the voice of God testify to His divinity [see Matthew 17:1–5].[9]

I have wondered how many of us are showing . . . [the youth] *how* they may [receive a testimony]. Are we sufficiently emphasizing the fact that they will never know it if they indulge in sin; they will never find it out if they live to gratify their passions and appetites. "My spirit shall not always strive with man." (Gen. 6:3; D&C 1:33; Moses 8:17.) His spirit will not dwell in unclean tabernacles. ("The Spirit of the Lord doth not dwell in unholy temples." Helaman 4:24.) And you cannot have a testimony without the Spirit of God. . . .

165

. . . The question arises—How may I know? Jesus has answered it, as he has shown the way in every aspect of life. One day, when he bore testimony to his divinity, that his teachings were of God, the Pharisees and others around him said, "How knoweth this man letters, having never learned?" How do we know (that was their question), that you are divine? And he gave a simple answer: "If any man will do his will, he shall know of the doctrine, whether it be of God, or whether I speak of myself." (John 7:15, 17.) There is a definite answer—a clear-cut statement. . . . "If ye will do the will, ye shall know." And, "to know God, and Jesus Christ, whom he has sent, is eternal life." [See John 17:3.][10]

It is given unto some, says the Lord in the Doctrine and Covenants, to know by the Holy Ghost that Jesus is the Son of God and that He was crucified for the sins of the world [see D&C 46:13]. It is to these I refer who stand firm upon the rock of revelation in the testimony that they bear to the world. But the Lord says further there are others to whom it is given to believe upon the testimony of others' words, that they may also receive salvation if they continue faithful [see D&C 46:14]. To all these, however, there comes the testimony also of daily experience.

The Latter-day Saints throughout the world find confirmation of their testimony in every performance of duty. They know that the gospel teaches them to be better individuals; that obedience to the principles of the gospel makes them stronger men, and truer women. Every day such knowledge comes to them, and they cannot gainsay it; they know that obedience to the gospel of Jesus Christ makes them better and truer husbands, true and honored wives, obedient children. They know that obedience to the principles of the gospel makes them in every respect ideal home-builders; the ideal is there, they sense it in their minds, they cannot gainsay it, they know it, and they know that transgression of these principles will have the opposite effect upon their individual lives and upon their home lives. They know that obedience to the gospel fosters true brotherhood and fellowship among mankind; they know that they are better citizens by virtue of obedience unto the laws and ordinances. So, as they go through their daily acts, and apply religion in their vocation, the truth of the Gospel becomes exemplified in their lives.[11]

You, no doubt, have met people who . . . wonder how it is that this Church manifests such vitality and growth. The secret is this, that every true Latter-day Saint possesses individually the assurance that this is the work of God, the same power that gave Peter and John strength to stand before their accusers and declare openly and boldly in the Sanhedrin that "Jesus whom ye crucified is the power by which this man was made whole," that His name is the only name given among men by which they can be saved [see Acts 4:10, 12].

The secret lies in the testimony possessed by each individual who is faithful in the membership of the Church of Christ, that the gospel consists of correct principles. . . . This testimony has been revealed to every sincere man and woman who has conformed to the principles of the gospel of Jesus Christ, obeyed the ordinances and become entitled to and have received the Spirit of God, the Holy Ghost, to guide them. Every individual stands independent in his sphere in that testimony, just as [the] thousands of incandescent lamps which [make] Salt Lake City . . . so brilliant at night, each one of which stands and shines in its own sphere, yet the light in it is produced by the same power, the same energy, from which all the other lights receive their energy. [12]

If we receive the witness of man, the witness of God is greater, for this is the witness of God which he has testified of his Son: "He that believeth on the Son of God hath witness in himself." [1 John 5:10.] There is a witness of the Spirit. God does reveal today to the human soul the reality of the resurrection of the Lord, the divinity of this great work, the truth, the divine and eternal truth, that God lives, not as a power, an essence, a force, as electricity, but as our Father in heaven. . . . God reveals to the soul his existence. He reveals the deity of the Lord Jesus Christ, who came to earth to give to men the great reality of the existence of God and his Son. [13]

With truth as our guide, our companion, our ally, our inspiration, we may tingle with the consciousness of our kinship with the Infinite, and all the petty trials, sorrows, and sufferings of this life will fade away as the temporary, harmless visions seen in a dream. That is our privilege through God's blessing and guidance if we apply in daily activity the spiritual blessings and privileges of the gospel of Jesus Christ.[14]

A testimony of the gospel is an anchor to the soul.

The testimony of the gospel is an anchor to the soul in the midst of confusion and strife. . . . Knowledge of God and His laws, means stability, means contentment, means peace, and with that a heart full of love reaching out to our fellow man offering the same blessings, the same privileges.[15]

We cannot truly believe that we are the children of God, and that God exists, without believing in the final inevitable triumph of the truth of the gospel of Jesus Christ. If we believe that, we shall have less worry about the destruction of the world and the present civilization, because God has established his Church never to be thrown down nor given to another people. And as God lives, and his people are true to him and to one another, we need not worry about the ultimate triumph of truth.

. . . If you have that testimony [of truth] on your side, you can pass through the dark valley of slander, misrepresentation, and abuse, undaunted as though you wore a magic suit of armor that no bullet could enter, no arrow could pierce. You can hold your head high, toss it fearlessly and defiantly, look every man calmly and unflinchingly in the eye. . . . You will know that all will come out right in the end; that it must come; that all must flee before the great white light of truth, as the darkness slinks away into nothingness in the presence of the sunburst.[16]

Suggestions for Study and Discussion

- What does it mean to have a testimony of Jesus Christ and His gospel? Why is a testimony the most precious possession we can obtain? (See pages 164–65.) Why is it essential that we each have an individual testimony?

- What must we do to receive a witness of the truth? (See pages 165–68.) Why is obedience an integral part of a strong testimony? What part does the Holy Ghost have in our obtaining a testimony?

- Why is it important to continue to strengthen our testimonies throughout our lives? What ways have you found to nourish your testimony?

- What can we do to help our children receive a testimony of Jesus Christ and His gospel?

- President McKay taught that a "testimony of the gospel is an anchor to the soul" (page 168). Why do we need a testimony to anchor our souls? (See page 168.) How has your testimony protected and strengthened you through the trials of life?

- Why is it important that we share our testimonies with others? What blessings have you experienced as a result of bearing testimony?

Related Scriptures: Matthew 16:13–17; Luke 22:32; John 7:17; 14:26; Ether 12:4; Moroni 10:3–5; D&C 1:39; 93:24–28

Notes

1. *Treasures of Life,* comp. Clare Middlemiss (1962), 228.
2. *Treasures of Life,* 228–30.
3. *Cherished Experiences from the Writings of President David O. McKay,* comp. Clare Middlemiss, rev. ed. (1976), 7.
4. *Treasures of Life,* 232.
5. In Conference Report, Oct. 1953, 88.
6. In Conference Report, Apr. 1948, 172.
7. In Conference Report, Oct. 1966, 136.
8. In Conference Report, Oct. 1965, 145–46.
9. *Ancient Apostles* (1918), 49.
10. In Conference Report, Oct. 1953, 88–89.
11. In Conference Report, Oct. 1912, 121; paragraphing altered.
12. In Conference Report, Oct. 1912, 120–21.
13. In Conference Report, Oct. 1925, 111.
14. In Conference Report, Apr. 1958, 130.
15. In Conference Report, Oct. 1912, 122.
16. In Conference Report, Apr. 1969, 152.

"Through the mist of his bitter tears, [Peter] saw all the true attributes of manhood as they were personified in Jesus—Reverence, Brotherliness, Patience, Sincerity, Courage."

Courage to Live Righteously

*The greatest need in the world today is faith
in God and courage to do his will.[1]*

Introduction

In a general conference address, President David O. McKay related a story told by a man named James L. Gordon:

"A young boy . . . decided to be an apprentice in one of the carpenters' societies. He was a bright young boy in his teens, and the men were very glad to admit him. They said, 'Come on, let's drink to the entrance of this young man to our group!' They poured out the beer [and] handed him the glass.

"He said, 'No, thank you, I do not drink.'

" 'Well,' said a gruff old member, 'we're not going to have any teetotalers [or nondrinkers] in our group.'

" 'Well,' said the young boy, 'you'll have one if you have me.'

"Another seized him by the collar and said, 'Young man, you'll have this beer either inside or outside!'

" 'Very well, I came here with a clean jacket and a clear conscience. You may soil my jacket if you wish, but you shall not soil my character.'

Referring to the young man in the story, President McKay observed:

"He had been trained—I use that word properly—not only taught, but trained to avoid the use of tobacco and strong drink, intoxicating liquor. That is what I mean by moral courage. The greatest need in the world today is faith in God and courage to do his will."[2]

Teachings of David O. McKay

The Savior is the supreme example of courage.

He who is or should be the guide of our lives was the most courageous of all men. "In Jesus we find bravery at the best; courage at its loftiest; heroism at its climax." True heroism defends the right and faces disaster without cringing. In this regard the Savior was the personification of true courage and heroism. Illustrative of this I need only mention the cleansing of the temple [see Matthew 21:12–13]; or his fearlessly speaking the truth when his home folk turned him from Nazareth [see Luke 4:16–32, 43–44]; or when the five thousand in Capernaum . . . [were reduced in number and] he turned [to the Twelve] and said, "Will ye also go away?" [See John 6:66–67.] Never once, however, did the Master despair or turn from his destined course. This is the kind of courage we need in the world today.[3]

As soldiers went to lay hands upon Jesus, Peter . . . jumped to the rescue of his Master, "drew his sword, and smote a servant of the high priest and cut off his ear." [See John 18:10.]. . . "Put up thy sword into the sheath," commanded the Savior, "the cup which my Father hath given me, shall I not drink it?" [John 18:11.] What a lesson to Peter! Even though duty led to suffering and death, yet would the Lord not waver in His strength. . . .

Peter's strength and loyalty were wavering; but he could not bring himself to flee with the others. Neither could he conclude that it was best to go with Jesus; so he did neither, but "followed Him afar off, even unto the palace of the high priest." [Mark 14:54.] At first, he remained on the outside, but later ventured in where the servants were sitting. . . .

[After Peter had denied knowing the Lord three times], the Savior . . . "turned and looked upon Peter." Then recalling the words of his Lord, "Before the cock crow twice, thou shalt deny me thrice," Peter went out and wept bitterly. [See Luke 22:54–62.]

It is said when Peter "went out speechless from the face of all . . . and filled the silence, weeping bitterly," that his grief was so heavy that he remained alone all day during Friday and Saturday following the Savior's crucifixion. If so, his sorrow for what he had done was made all the more acute as he recalled the many kind words the Savior had spoken to him, and the many, many happy moments he had spent in the Lord's company. Every word and act and look associated with his Master would flash upon his mind with a new meaning. . . . Through the mist of his bitter tears, he saw all the true attributes of manhood as they were personified in Jesus—Reverence, Brotherliness, Patience, Sincerity, Courage.[4]

The world's hope and destiny are centered in the Man of Galilee, our Lord and Savior, Jesus Christ. In your moment when you are fighting out the battle of the day, will you look introspectively and see whether you really believe that? [A writer] once asked this question: "Is Jesus only a legendary figure in history, a Saint to be painted in the stained glass of church windows, . . . not to be approached and hardly to be mentioned by name, or is he still what he was when he was in the flesh, a reality, a man of like passions with ourselves, an elder brother, a guide, a counselor, a comforter, a great voice calling to us out of the past to live nobly, to guide bravely, and keep up our courage to the last." What is he to you, my fellow laborer?[5]

Courage springs from faith and hope.

We have greater responsibility than ever to learn and to live the Gospel of Jesus Christ. We have greater tasks before us. The final work is not all done yet. . . . We need courage to enter into those new realms; we need courage to meet our present situations and conditions, and that is why I have chosen the text, "Be of good courage, and he shall strengthen your heart, all ye that hope in the Lord." [Psalm 31:24.]

In this promise are two principles that should be cherished by every truly religious man—faith and courage. What is implied in this text? We know with assurance that the Lord is keeping faith with his people; therefore, let none despair, but take courage and their hope shall not be in vain. Faith in God, trust, confidence in our fellowmen, the courage of our convictions, will enable us eventually to achieve any righteous cause.[6]

With faith in an over-ruling power, in the personal, intimate protection of our Father—and we like to consider him such, a loving Father—let us face our difficulties with courage.[7]

Young people must develop courage
to maintain spiritual values.

[Maintaining] our ideals is another field in which we can manifest courage, and merit the approval of God in whom we trust. These are times when men should keep their heads, and not be swept from their moorings by every will-o'-the-wisp theory that is offered as a panacea [or cure-all] of our present ills. The times call for courageous youth to hold aloft the moral standard. In that field we can find the truest moral courage. It is said that heroism is concentrated courage. Well our greatest heroes are not always found on the battle field. I think we find them also among our youth. Young men and young women who, when put in social groups, will stand up fearlessly and denounce those things which we know sap the character, the very life energy of youth.

"Never was there a time in the history of the world," says [one writer], "when moral heroes were more needed. The world waits for such. The providence of God has commanded science to labor and prepare the way for such. For them she is laying her iron tracks, and stretching her wires, and bridging the oceans. But where are they? Who shall breathe into our civil and political relations the breath of a higher life?" "The most important thing in the world," says a great scientist, "is not the discovery of Galileo, Faraday, and others, but a belief in the reality of moral and spiritual values." I appeal to youth to be courageous in maintaining the moral and spiritual values of the Gospel of Jesus Christ. After all, "What is a man profited, if he shall gain the whole world, and lose his own soul? or what shall a man give in exchange for his soul?" [Matthew 16:26.] [8]

The aim of education is to develop resources in the child that will contribute to his well-being as long as life endures; to develop power of self-mastery that he may never be a slave to indulgence or other weaknesses, to develop [strong] manhood, beautiful womanhood that in every child and every youth may be found at least the promise of a friend, a companion, one who later may be fit for husband or wife, an exemplary father or a loving intelligent mother, one who can face life with courage, meet disaster with fortitude, and face death without fear. [9]

Like Helaman's young warriors, we should be "exceedingly valiant for courage, and also for strength and activity" and "true at all times" (Alma 53:20).

I have read from the fifty-third chapter of Alma, which gives an account of young men who were exceedingly valiant for courage, for strength, and activity—men who were true at all times in whatsoever thing they were entrusted. Who were these young men? They were sons of parents who were equally true to every trust. Their parents were converted Lamanites who, when the Spirit of God came upon them, devoted their lives to the service of their fellow men, and in their ministry in the Church covenanted that they would never more take up arms against their brethren, never more go to war. Such was their oath; such was their covenant; and they were true to it even unto death.[10]

I appeal to the youth to be courageous in maintaining the moral and spiritual values of the gospel of Jesus Christ. The world needs moral heroes![11]

In the words of [one writer]: . . . "Two ways lie open for you—one leading to an ever lower and lower plane, where are heard the cries of despair . . . ; and the other leading to the highlands of the morning where are heard the glad shouts of humanity and where honest effort is rewarded with immortality." . . .

In making the choice, . . . God give you clear vision, clear seeing, strong wills, courageous hearts. Having chosen wisely, may you walk with heads erect, with countenance open indicating that you have wronged no one. Even though the tasks of life become heavy and sorrow weighs upon you, may the light of the Christ life beckon you on still undismayed.[12]

With moral courage, we can overcome life's adversities.

Courage is that quality of the mind which meets danger or opposition with calmness and firmness, which enables a man to face difficulties that lie in his pathway to righteous achievement. . . . Courage implies facing difficulties and overcoming them.[13]

It is easy enough to do right when in good company, but it is not easy to defend the right when the majority of the crowd are opposing it; and yet, that is the time to show true courage. The Prophet Joseph, for example, was reviled and persecuted for saying that he had received a vision, but he always remained true to his testimony. Though he "was hated and persecuted yet he said it was true that God had spoken to him," and *"All the world could not make him think or believe otherwise."* [See Joseph Smith—History 1:24–25; italics added.]

Such is the courage and firmness everyone should have. When one knows what is right one should always have the courage to defend it even in the face of ridicule or punishment.[14]

Let us be courageous in defense of the right. Be not afraid to speak out for the right. Let us be true.[15]

May God give us courage to choose the right, ability to appreciate the good things of life, and power faithfully to serve Him and our fellow men.[16]

Truth is loyalty to the right as we see it; it is courageous living of our lives in harmony with our ideals; it is always power.[17]

Suggestions for Study and Discussion

- What is courage? (See page 176.) Why is moral courage more important than physical courage? How can we increase or strengthen our moral courage? How might we live the gospel with quiet, daily courage?

- What are some examples from the scriptures of the Savior and others showing perfect moral courage? (See pages 172–73.) How has their example strengthened you?

- What is the relationship between faith and courage? (See page 173.) How does the Lord help us to face seemingly over-whelming opposition? What must we do to receive His help?

- Discouragement is to lose one's courage. Why is discourage-ment such a dangerous tool of the adversary? How can we guard against and overcome discouragement?

- What kinds of social or other situations require extraordinary courage? How can Latter-day Saints show courage in these sit-uations? How can we help and encourage the children and youth of the Church to be courageous in maintaining gospel standards? (See pages 174–76.) How can the publication *For the Strength of Youth* help in this effort?

Related Scriptures: Deuteronomy 31:6; 2 Kings 6:16; Romans 15:13; 1 Nephi 3:7; D&C 121:7–9

Notes

1. In Conference Report, Apr. 1963, 95.
2. In Conference Report, Apr. 1963, 95; story taken from James L. Gordon, *The Young Man and His Problems.*
3. In Conference Report, Apr. 1936, 58.
4. *Ancient Apostles* (1918), 63–66; para-graphing altered.
5. In Conference Report, Oct. 1954, 84; paragraphing altered.
6. In Conference Report, Apr. 1936, 57–58; paragraphing altered.
7. In Conference Report, Apr. 1936, 61.
8. In Conference Report, Apr. 1936, 60–61; paragraphing altered.
9. *Gospel Ideals* (1953), 436.
10. In Conference Report, Oct. 1927, 11–12.
11. In Conference Report, Apr. 1969, 152.
12. *Whither Shall We Go?* Brigham Young University Speeches of the Year, 10 May 1961, 7.
13. In Conference Report, Apr. 1936, 58.
14. *Ancient Apostles,* 185; paragraphing altered.
15. In Conference Report, Oct. 1968, 145.
16. In Conference Report, Apr. 1940, 118.
17. In Conference Report, Apr. 1959, 73.

*"True Christianity is love in action. . . . With faith, with kindness,
let your heart be filled with the desire to serve all mankind. The spirit of
the gospel comes from service in the good of others."*

The Divine Nature of Service

The noblest aim in life is to strive to live to make other lives better and happier.[1]

Introduction

President David O. McKay frequently taught that service to others brings true happiness and that the Lord guides and blesses those who serve. In 1921, one such instance of the Lord guiding His servants occurred while Elder David O. McKay and Brother Hugh J. Cannon were fulfilling an assignment from the First Presidency to visit Church members throughout the world. One part of their assignment was to visit the members of the Church in Armenia. Because of the effects of World War I and difficult conditions in the region, little was known about the state of Church members there. Elder McKay recorded:

"In March 1921, we learned that on a special fast day, contributions in the amount of several thousand dollars had been made for relief of the destitute in Europe and the suffering Armenians in Asia. We learned, too, that the First Presidency contemplated sending a special messenger to Syria to render personal aid to our Armenian Saints."

Because Elder McKay and Brother Cannon were not scheduled to visit the Church members in Armenia until much later in their trip, they continued their travels, visiting such areas as Australia, New Zealand, and many islands. For several months, they heard nothing about conditions in Armenia or whether anyone had been sent with the relief funds. Finally, on 2 November 1921, while in Jerusalem, they received word that a man named J. Wilford Booth had been sent by Church headquarters to meet them. However, no one knew his schedule or whereabouts. That day, Elder McKay recorded in his diary, "We have no idea where he is, but shall leave Jerusalem for Haifa, en route to Aleppo [Syria], tomorrow morning. Have concluded to go by auto through Samaria, visiting Bible scenes." Before leaving, Elder McKay and Brother Cannon ascended the Mount of Olives, chose a secluded spot, and prayed that the Lord would guide them on their trip.

After the prayer, Elder McKay recalled, "Upon returning to the hotel, I felt strongly impressed that we should go by train and not auto to Haifa." Brother Cannon agreed, and they continued their trip to Haifa, hoping to find Elder Booth there. Elder McKay recorded: "Our greatest desire as we neared this mission was to meet Elder Booth. Indeed, it seemed that our trip to Syria would be useless unless we should meet him. We were strangers. We knew no one. . . . We had some names and addresses; but we could not read them, since they were written in the Turkish language."

When Elder McKay and Brother Cannon arrived at the train station, they were delayed in leaving the station as they tried to find information on a suitable hotel. After the delay, Elder McKay approached the station door just as another traveler did. The man touched him on the shoulder and said, "Isn't this Brother McKay?"

Elder McKay recorded the results of the encounter as follows: "Astonished beyond expression to be thus addressed in so strange a town, I turned, and recognized Elder Wilford Booth, the one man above all others whom we were most desirous of meeting. We had met, too, at the most opportune time and place. . . . It could not have been better had we been planning it for weeks! As we recounted to each other our experiences, we had no doubt that our coming together was the result of divine interposition. . . . Indeed, had it not been for our having met at Haifa, our trip to the Armenian Mission would have been, so far as human wisdom can tell, a total failure. As it was, among many duties and experiences, we organized the Armenian Mission."[2]

Teachings of David O. McKay

It is the Lord's will that we serve one another.

The will of God is [that you] serve your fellowmen, benefiting them, making this world better for your having lived in it. Christ

180

gave his all to teach us that principle. And he made the statement: "Inasmuch as ye have done it unto one of the least of these my brethren, ye have done it unto me." (Matt. 25:40.) This is the message God has given to us. This Church is God's Church, which is so perfectly organized that every man and every woman, every child, may have an opportunity to do something good for somebody else. It is the obligation of our priesthood members, it is the responsibility of the auxiliary organizations and of every member to serve and do God's will. If we do, and the more we do it, the more we shall become convinced that it is the work of God, because we are testing it. Then, *by doing the will of God, we get to know God and get close to him and to feel that life eternal is ours.* We shall feel to love humanity everywhere, and we can cry out with the apostles of old, "We know that we have passed from death unto life, because we love the brethren." (1 John 3:14.)[3]

It has been said that "the race of mankind would perish if they ceased to aid one another." One man, from whom I quote, says that "from the time that the mother binds the child's head until the moment that some kind assistant wipes the death-damp from the brow of the dying, we cannot exist without mutual help." . . . The Church, with all its quorums and organizations, is God's plan for rendering mutual aid.[4]

There come to mind some . . . to whom I wish to express gratitude. . . . They are the men and women throughout the entire Church who are contributing of their time and means to the advancement of the truth—not just in teaching, but in genuine service in many ways. Some of these are struggling to make their own living. Some of them are wealthy men and women who have retired and who count their wealth in millions. . . . God bless those who are rendering such service, and bless you all, for I think we can say for the Church, "We are striving to be one, Father, as thou and thy Son are one."[5]

Are you willing to serve? Do you have the vision King Benjamin had when he said, ". . . when ye are in the service of your fellow beings, ye are only in the service of your God"? (Mosiah 2:17.) True Christianity is love in action. There is no better way to manifest love for God than to show an unselfish love for one's fellowmen. . . .

181

. . . With faith, with kindness, let your heart be filled with the desire to serve all mankind. The spirit of the gospel comes from service in the good of others.[6]

Service brings happiness to the giver and the receiver.

Happiness is the end, really, of our existence. That happiness comes most effectively through service to our fellow men.[7]

All mankind desire happiness. Many also strive sincerely to make the most and best of themselves. Surprisingly few, however, realize that a sure guide to such achievement may be found in the following declaration by Jesus of Nazareth: "Whosoever will save his life shall lose it: And whosoever will lose his life for my sake shall find it." [Matthew 16:25.] This significant passage contains a secret more worthy of possession than fame or dominion, something more valuable than all the wealth of the world.

It is a *principle* the application of which promises to supplant *discouragement* and *gloom* with *hope* and *gladness;* to fill life with *contentment* and *peace* everlasting. This being true its acceptance would indeed be a boon today to this distracted, depression-ridden world. Why, then, do men and nations ignore a thing so precious?

Is the truth in the paradoxical statement, losing one's life to find it, so elusive that mankind cannot grasp it? Or is it so in conflict with the struggle for existence that men consider it impractical?

Even so, the fact remains that He who is "The Way, the Truth and the Life" [see John 14:6] has herein set forth an immutable law. . . .

Specifically stated, this law is, *"We live our lives most completely when we strive to make the world better and happier."* The law of pure nature, survival of the fittest, is *self-preservation at the sacrifice of all else;* but in contrast to this the law of true spiritual life is, *deny self for the good of others.* . . .

With this end in view, [thousands of] men and women, serving willingly without salary, offer every week to [tens of thousands of] children and youth instruction and guidance in character building and spiritual growth. In addition to this army of officers and teachers, . . . men ordained to the priesthood have accepted the obligation to devote their time and talents as far as possible to the scattering of sunshine, joy, and peace among their fellowmen.[8]

There is more spirituality expressed in giving than in receiving. The greatest spiritual blessing comes from helping another. If you want to be miserable, just harbor hate for a brother, and if you want to hate, just do your brother some injury. But if you would be happy, render a kind service, make somebody else happy.[9]

Let sincere men and women the world over unite in earnest effort to supplant feelings of selfishness, hatred, animosity, greed, by the law of service to others, and thereby promote the peace and happiness of mankind.[10]

We need to follow the example of the Savior in rendering service.

When the Savior was about to leave his Apostles, he gave them a great example of service. You remember he girded himself with a towel and washed his disciples' feet. Peter, feeling it was a menial work for a servant, said, ". . . dost thou wash my feet? . . . Thou shalt never wash my feet."

The Savior answered "If I wash thee not, thou hast no part with me."

"Nay then," said the chief Apostle, "Not my feet only, but also my hands and my head."

"He that is washed needeth not save to wash his feet, but is clean every whit.

"What I do thou knowest not now; but thou shalt know hereafter." [See John 13:6–10.]

And then he washed his feet, and those of the others also. Returning the basin to the side of the door, ungirding himself, and putting on his robe, he returned to his position with the Twelve, and said:

"Ye call me Master and Lord: and ye say well; for so I am.

"If I then, your Lord and Master, have washed your feet; ye also ought to wash one another's feet." [John 13:13–14.]

What an example of service to those great servants, followers of the Christ! He that is greatest among you, let him be least. So we sense the obligation to be of greater service to the membership of the Church, to devote our lives to the advancement of the kingdom of God on earth.[11]

Just think! The only reason the world knows anything about them [Jesus' Apostles] is because having met the Savior, they made Him their guide in life. If they hadn't, nobody now would know that such men had ever lived. They would have lived and died and been forgotten just as thousands of other men in their day lived and died and nobody knows or cares anything about them; just as thousands and thousands are living today, wasting their time and energy in useless living, choosing the wrong kind of men for their ideals, turning their footsteps into the road of Pleasure and Indulgence instead of the road of Service. Soon they will reach the end of their journey in life, and nobody can say that the world is any better for their having lived in it. At the close of each day such men leave their pathway as barren as they found it—they plant no trees to give shade to others, nor rosebushes to make the world sweeter and brighter to those who follow—no kind deeds, no noble service—just a barren, unfruitful, desert-like pathway, strewn, perhaps, with thorns and thistles.

Not so with the disciples who chose Jesus for their Guide. Their lives are like gardens of roses from which the world may pluck beautiful flowers forever.[12]

The most worthy calling in life . . . is that in which man can serve best his fellow man. . . . The noblest aim in life is to strive to live to make other lives better and happier.[13]

Suggestions for Study and Discussion

- Why does the Lord command us to serve one another? (See pages 180–82.) What are some opportunities we have for service within the Church? What kinds of service can we render outside of formal Church callings?

- The Lord taught that "whosoever will save his life shall lose it: and whosoever will lose his life for my sake shall find it" (Matthew 16:25). What does this scripture have to do with service? What eternal blessings come from selflessly serving others? What is the difference between serving because we are commanded to and serving because we want to? (See also D&C 58:26.)

- What have you experienced as you have given of yourself in service to others? How are happiness and service connected? How does service help us overcome feelings of selfishness, unhappiness, or depression? (See pages 182–83.) How can service to others help us overcome unkind feelings toward them?

- What impresses you about Jesus' many examples of service? (See pages 183–84.) What can we learn from Him as we strive to serve others? Why is it important to seek divine guidance as we serve?

- Why is it sometimes difficult to allow others to serve us? Why is it important to graciously accept service? How have you or your family been blessed by the service of others?

Related Scriptures: Matthew 25:40; Mark 8:35; Galatians 5:13; Mosiah 4:15; D&C 18:10, 15–16

Notes

1. *Two Contending Forces,* Brigham Young University Speeches of the Year (18 May 1960), 7.

2. See *Cherished Experiences from the Writings of President David O. McKay,* comp. Clare Middlemiss, rev. ed. (1976), 101–4; paragraphing altered.

3. In Conference Report, Oct. 1966, 137.

4. In Conference Report, Oct. 1962, 119.

5. In Conference Report, Oct. 1968, 143.

6. In Conference Report, Oct. 1969, 88–89.

7. In Conference Report, Oct. 1953, 132.

8. In Conference Report, Apr. 1936, 45–46; paragraphing altered.

9. In Conference Report, Oct. 1936, 104–5.

10. In Conference Report, Apr. 1936, 46.

11. In Conference Report, Apr. 1951, 158–59.

12. *Ancient Apostles* (1918), 5–6.

13. *Two Contending Forces,* 7.

President McKay loved to teach the gospel. To his fellow teachers, he said:
"On with your noble work! There is none greater; none more righteous!
Yours is the joy promised by the Savior."

Teaching, a Noble Work

*God help our teachers to feel the
responsibility that comes to them, and to remember
that responsibility is not measured alone by
what they say, but by what they do. . . . Oh, how
mighty is the responsibility of a teacher![1]*

Introduction

President David O. McKay was a teacher most of his life. He fulfilled this role in such capacities as missionary, schoolteacher, administrator, Apostle, Church President, and father.

In a message directed primarily to priesthood holders, he shared an experience that relates to all who have the opportunity to teach:

"The other day it was my privilege to drive through the fields in my old home town. I passed through two farms up near the mountain canal. I saw one that had yielded an exceptionally good crop of oats. Notwithstanding the drought, the cold in the spring, and other disadvantages, the farmer had [produced] an excellent yield. Just over the fence was another oat field, but a failure, comparatively speaking. I said to the man: 'Why, what is the matter? You must have planted poor seed.'

" 'No, it is the same seed that my neighbor has.'

" 'Well, then it was planted too late, and you did not have enough moisture in the ground to bring it up.'

" 'It was sown the same afternoon that he sowed his.'

"Upon further inquiry, I learned that the first man had plowed his in the fall; then he had disked it carefully in the spring, making a mulch on the surface, and by such tilling had conserved the moisture of the winter. His neighbor, on the other hand, had plowed his late in the spring, had left the furrows unharrowed;

187

the moisture had evaporated. Following the sowing of the seed came four weeks or six weeks of [drought], and there was not sufficient moisture to germinate the seed. The first man had made preparation, the proper kind of preparation, and nature yielded the increase. The second man labored hard, but his preparation was poor; indeed, he had made inadequate preparation."

President McKay used this story to illustrate the influence of teachers. He said: "In God's great garden have been placed overseers called teachers, and they are asked to nourish and to inspire God's children. I venture the thought that the Great Gardener in looking over his fields can see some that are thriving in righteous activity and others are starving because of the drought of neglected duty, of the chilling atmosphere of vanity, or the blight of intemperance. Why? Perhaps because the gardeners, the overseers, had not made necessary preparations, or performed their duty well." [2]

Whether referring to parents, classroom instructors, or home teachers and visiting teachers, President McKay devoted much of his ministry to helping Church members understand the great importance and influence of effective teaching.

Teachings of David O. McKay

In the Church we have many opportunities to teach others and develop personal strength.

We are a Church of teachers. In the Latter-day Saint home the father and mother are required to be teachers of the word—expressly required so by the revelation of the Lord. Every auxiliary organization, every quorum, is made up of a body of men and women . . . who are in the ultimate sense of the word, teachers. [3]

I am grateful for membership in a Church whose religion fits men for the struggle with the forces of the world and, which enables them to survive in this struggle. One of these acting forces is the responsibility of teaching, and the opportunity afforded in this Church for so many to share this responsibility. . . .

Now in furnishing opportunity for so many to get the development that comes to the true teacher, think what the Church is doing to help this army of teachers as individuals to become strong in the battle against the forces of the world!

First, it places upon them the obligation of teaching their fellow men by example; and there is no better safeguard placed upon an honest man or a sincere woman.

Second, it develops the divine attribute of love for others. Jesus said to one of his Apostles, "Simon, son of Jonas, lovest thou me more than these? . . . Yea, Lord, thou knowest that I love thee. . . . Feed my lambs." (John 21:15.) Love should precede the responsibility of feeding those lambs. And these tens of thousands of teachers must have in their hearts the love of teaching, the love of fellow men, and a willingness to accept this responsibility with the divine attribute of love.

Then there is a third requirement, namely: purity of life. I cannot imagine one who has soiled himself, teaching successfully purity to boys. I cannot imagine one who has doubt in his mind about the existence of God, teaching impressively the existence of a Deity to young boys and girls. He cannot do it. If he act the hypocrite and attempt so to teach, what he is will speak louder than what he says—and that is the danger of having doubting men as teachers of your children. The poison sinks in, and unconsciously they become sick in spirit, because of the poison which the person in whom they have confidence has insidiously instilled into their souls. The thought of teachers attempting to teach youth faith in God, when they haven't it, is irreconcilable with consistency, if not indeed unthinkable. So the third qualification is purity of life and faith in the gospel of Jesus Christ.

Finally, it gives them an opportunity to serve their fellow men, and therein magnify the calling which has come to them, and indeed prove that they are real disciples of Christ.[4]

In the formation of character and guidance of childhood, parental influence is greatest; next comes the teacher's. . . . "There is true nobility in the soul of that man or woman who sincerely desires and strives to lead children out of contaminating influences into an environment of high ideals and lofty endeavor."[5]

Effective teachers prepare through
study, faith, and prayer.

The great obligation upon a teacher is to be prepared to teach. A teacher cannot teach others that which he himself does not know. He cannot make his students feel what he does not feel himself. He cannot attempt to lead a young man or young woman to obtain a testimony of the gospel of God if the teacher does not have that testimony himself or herself.

There are three things which must guide all teachers: first, get into the subject; second, get that subject into you; third, try to lead your pupils to get the subject into them—not pouring it into them, but leading them to see what you see, to know what you know, to feel what you feel.

Every teacher must be prepared on his or her lesson when he or she meets those boys and girls of the class; for, mind you, your presentation of that lesson, your attitude toward the truth in that lesson will largely determine the boys' and girls' attitude toward it and their attitude toward Church activity in general. If you turn them away after class with the feeling in their youthful hearts that they have received nothing by coming, you will find difficulty in getting them to come back the following week. But on the other hand, if you have thrilled them, or if unable to do that, if you have given them one thought which has appealed to them, you will find that their intention and desire to return will be manifest by their presence one week later. . . .

Simply reading the lesson manual before time is not enough. In so doing I have not yet made that lesson mine, and until it is mine, until I feel that I have a message to give to my class members, I am not prepared as the Lord has asked me to prepare when he calls upon me to give his word. It must be mine; what I want to give to the boys and girls is what will count when I meet them. I can make that lesson in a manual mine by study, faith, and prayer.[6]

To give a lesson well prepared is like mercy—it blesses him that gives and him that receives. It is true in teaching as in life—"Give to the world the best you have, and the best will come back to you.". . .

. . . Teachers, begin the preparation of your lessons in prayer. Teach your lessons with a prayerful heart. Then pray that God will enrich your message in the souls of your children through the influence of his holy Spirit.[7]

Order and reverence in Church classrooms help young people learn respect and self-control.

I believe that discipline in the classroom, which implies *self-control,* and which connotes *consideration for others,* is the most important part of teaching. . . .

The best lesson a child can learn is self-control, and to feel his relationship to others to the extent that he must have respect for their feelings. . . .

A disorderly environment, one in which disrespect is shown to the teacher and to fellow pupils, is one that will stifle the most important qualities in character.[8]

Our classrooms are sometimes places of boisterousness. Here is where we need good teachers. A teacher who can present a lesson interestingly will have good order, and when he or she finds students who are rebellious, flipping papers, paying no attention, stumbling, kicking one another, he or she may know that the lesson is not being properly presented. Perhaps it was not even properly prepared. . . .

In the classrooms children should be taught, should be free to discuss, free to speak, free to participate in classwork, but no member of the class has the right to distract another student by jostling or making light and frivolous remarks. And I think in this Church, in the priesthood quorums and classes and in auxiliaries, teachers and [leaders] ought not to permit it. Disorder injures the child who makes it. He should learn that when he is in society there are certain things which he cannot do with impunity. He cannot trespass upon the rights of his associates.

Let children learn this lesson in youth because when they get out in society and try to trespass against the law, they will feel the restraining hand and probably suffer punishment.

Good order in the classroom is essential to instill into the hearts and lives of young men and young women the principle of self-control. They want to talk and they want to whisper, but they cannot do it because it will disturb somebody else. Learn the power and lesson of self-mastery.[9]

The Sunday School looks forward to the time when in every class in the Sunday School the principles of punctuality, courtesy, self-control, respect for authority, studiousness, responsiveness, and, particularly, reverence and worship, will . . . [fill] the atmosphere.[10]

In our efforts to teach truth, Jesus Christ is our great Exemplar.

In the realm of personality, in the kingdom of character, Christ was supreme. By personality, I mean all that may be included in individuality. Personality is a gift from God. It is indeed a pearl of great price, an eternal blessing.

Fellow teachers, you and I cannot hope to exert, even to a small degree, the personality of our great Teacher, Jesus Christ. Each one's personality may be to the Savior's only as one little sunbeam to the mighty sun itself; and yet, though infinitely less in degree, each teacher's personality should be the same in kind. In the realm of character, each teacher may be superior and be such a magnet as will draw around him in an indescribable way those whom he would teach.

But no matter how attractive his personality may be to the members of the class, that teacher fails in his work who directs the love of the child only to the teacher's personality. It is the teacher's duty to teach the child to love—not the teacher only, but the truth also. Always, everywhere, we find Christ losing himself for his Father's will; and so the teacher, so far as his personality is concerned, should lose himself for the truth he desires to teach.[11]

The teacher must know whom she teaches, to be able to discern, to a degree at least, the mentality and capability of the members of her class. She should be able to read the facial expressions and be responsive to the mental and spiritual attitude of those whom she is teaching. The Great Teacher had this power of discernment in perfection. He could read the hidden thoughts and interpret the very feelings of the persons whom He taught. In the acquisition of this power the sincere teacher may approach Him only partially. Too few teachers develop this gift, even to a necessary degree; notwithstanding every teacher has the responsibility of determining how best to approach the members of the class in order to make appeals that will be lasting.[12]

Use the things around you. Show the example of the Great Teacher who sat with his disciples and looked down on the farmers putting in their spring grain. He said, "Some seed fell on good ground, some on stony ground." [See Mark 4:3–8.] There was a lesson of life. The woman of Samaria who came to quench her thirst at the well is another example. Jesus told her that the water he would give her would be a well of water springing up into everlasting life [see John 4:14]. Gather in experiences, and then illustrate each point. I think that is a lesson to every teacher—you who have a lesson to prepare—not a speech, but a message.[13]

Worthy servants of Christ, you are! Teachers! Followers of the true Teacher, the great Exemplar of all! On with your noble work! There is none greater; none more righteous! Yours is the joy promised by the Savior.[14]

Suggestions for Study and Discussion

- What are a teacher's responsibilities? (See pages 188–91.) Why is it important that gospel teachers have personal testimonies?

- What blessings have you received as you have taught the gospel? How has your life been blessed or changed by faithful, effective teachers?

- In what ways does a well-prepared lesson influence both teacher and student? (See pages 190–91.) What are some of the ways that teachers can prepare? (See pages 190–91.) What resources are available in the Church for the improvement of teaching?

- What can we do to promote order and respect in Church classrooms? (See pages 191–92.) How do young people benefit when there is order in the classroom? What can parents do to support teachers in their efforts to maintain orderly classrooms?

- What is the difference between "teaching a lesson" and teaching people? How did the Savior exemplify this skill? What else can we learn from Jesus Christ's example as the Master Teacher? (See pages 192–93.)

- What can a teacher do to ensure that class members love "not the teacher only, but the truth also"?

- How can we use President McKay's counsel to improve the teaching in our homes? What ways have you found to effectively teach your children?

Related Scriptures: John 21:15–17; 3 Nephi 27:21; D&C 11:21; 42:14; 88:77–80, 118; 132:8

Notes

1. "The Teacher," *Improvement Era*, Sept. 1951, 622.
2. In Conference Report, Oct. 1916, 58–59; paragraphing altered.
3. " 'That You May Instruct More Perfectly,' " *Improvement Era*, Aug. 1956, 557.
4. "The Teacher," 621–22.
5. *Gospel Ideals* (1953), 214.
6. " 'That You May Instruct More Perfectly,' " 557.
7. *Gospel Ideals*, 222–23.
8. *Man May Know for Himself: Teachings of President David O. McKay,* comp. Clare Middlemiss (1967), 337–38.
9. In Conference Report, Oct. 1950, 164–66.
10. *Gospel Ideals*, 221.
11. "To the Teacher," *Improvement Era*, Aug. 1955, 557.
12. *True to the Faith: From the Sermons and Discourses of David O. McKay,* comp. Llewelyn R. McKay (1966), 251.
13. "We Believe in Being True . . . ," *Improvement Era*, Sept. 1959, 647.
14. *Gospel Ideals*, 135.

The First Principles and Ordinances of the Gospel

I know the gospel is divine, and the world needs it.[1]

Introduction

President David O. McKay was always kind and respectful to people of other faiths, and he praised the good work of all churches. However, he was firm in his testimony that the fulness of the gospel is found only in The Church of Jesus Christ of Latter-day Saints. To teach the importance of obeying the principles and ordinances of the restored gospel, he spoke of membership in the Church as citizenship in a great kingdom:

"All churches and all creeds contain some good which lead toward the kingdom of our Father; but to become a citizen of that kingdom everyone must conform to the requirements made by the King. Indeed, there is only *one way* in which entrance into the Church of Jesus Christ may be obtained, and that is the way marked out by Jesus Christ, the Lord. 'I am the way, the truth, and the life: no man cometh unto the Father, but by me.' (John 14:6.)

"The means of obtaining citizenship in the Church of Jesus Christ are very explicit; so clear, indeed, that it is surprising that so many seemingly intelligent and well-read people . . . [assume] that they can gain entrance by other and various means.

"There is only one who has the right to prescribe the means of human salvation. Surely he spoke not meaninglessly when he said what is necessary to citizenship in his kingdom.

"Note how explicit are his words: 'Except a man be born again, he cannot *see* the kingdom of *God.*' [John 3:3; italics added.] In explanation of this seemingly enigmatical saying to Nicodemus, the Master continued:

195

" 'Except a man be born of water and of the Spirit, he *cannot* enter into the kingdom of God.' [John 3:5; italics added.]

"Evidently Peter, the chief Apostle, attached significance to this requirement as an essential means of gaining not only citizenship in the Church, but also salvation in the kingdom of God, for, when the multitude pricked in their hearts cried out, 'Men and brethren, what shall we do?' [Acts 2:37] he answered and said:

" 'Repent, and be baptized every one of you in the name of Jesus Christ for the remission of sins, and ye shall receive the gift of the Holy Ghost.' (Acts 2:38.) Thus are given the four requirements, the four essential principles and ordinances, obedience to which are essential to membership in Christ's Church: [namely,] faith, repentance, baptism, and the reception of the Holy Ghost. . . .

"There are many roads being pointed out as leading to the kingdom of God, but there is only one gate through which entrance and citizenship therein may be obtained. Christ plainly pointed this out when he was among men; and he has again revealed it through the Prophet Joseph Smith. The way is simple and easy to find, and as infinitely sublime as it is eternal.

"There are many roads . . . leading sincere people *toward* the church and kingdom of God, but those who would participate in the privileges and blessings of citizenship therein must obey the principles and ordinances of the gospel of Jesus Christ."[2]

Teachings of David O. McKay

Faith in Jesus Christ is the most fundamental principle of the Church.

An unwavering faith in Christ is the most important need of the world today.[3]

What does it mean to keep the faith? It means first, that we accept Jesus Christ, not merely as a great teacher, a powerful leader, but as the Savior, the Redeemer of the world. . . . He who keeps the faith will accept Jesus Christ as the Son of God, the Redeemer of the world. I would have all men keep that faith. I think it is fundamental to man's happiness, fundamental to his peace of mind. I think it is the cardinal principle of the Church of Jesus Christ.[4]

It is such faith as must have sustained the eleven Apostles and at least seventy disciples who met Christ after the resurrection. In their minds there was absolutely no doubt of his personality. They were witnesses of the fact. They knew because their eyes beheld, their ears heard, their hands felt the corporeal [bodily] presence of the risen Redeemer.

It is that unwavering faith which brought forth this glorious vision given to the Prophet Joseph Smith:

"And now, after the many testimonies which have been given of him, this is the testimony, last of all, which we give of him: That he lives!

"For we saw him, even on the right hand of God; and we heard the voice bearing record that he is the Only Begotten of the Father—

"That by him, and through him, and of him, the worlds are and were created, and the inhabitants thereof are begotten sons and daughters unto God." (D&C 76:22–24.)

Those who have such assurance in their hearts accept him as "The Way, the Truth, and the Life," as the one safe guide in this perplexing universe.[5]

Faith in the Gospel is the first step toward true knowledge, and leads thru sacrifice, to wisdom and happiness.[6]

Faith in God cannot of course be other than personal. It must be yours; it must be mine; and, to be effective, must spring from the mind and heart.[7]

What we need today is faith in the living Christ, which is more than a mere feeling, but a power that moves us to action—a faith that will put purpose into life and courage into the heart. We need the gospel of application.[8]

The Church does not accept the doctrine that a mere murmured belief in Jesus Christ is all that is essential to salvation. A man may say he believes but if he does nothing to make that belief or faith a moving power to do, to accomplish, to produce soul growth, his protestation will avail him nothing. "Work out your own salvation" is an exhortation to demonstrate by activity, by thoughtful obedient effort the reality of faith.[9]

Repentance involves a change of life, thought, and action.

It is inconceivable to think that anyone can even question the essentiality of repentance. Every principle of the gospel when studied carefully reveals a harmony with truth that is simply sublime. Each seems to be all comprehensive, either leading into or embracing other principles. Thus, faith in a perfect being, inspiring one to live righteously, seems to include repentance.[10]

The message of [the Church] is to help men recognize their weaknesses and to help man overcome those sins and weaknesses. Here we have not time to discuss what sin is, but John Wesley's mother [John Wesley was a noted theologian] reputedly has given us this:

"Would you judge of the lawfulness or unlawfulness of pleasure? Take this rule: Now note—whatever weakens your reason, impairs the tenderness of your conscience, obscures your sense of God, takes off your relish for spiritual things, whatever increases the authority of the body over the mind, that thing is sin to you, however innocent it may seem in itself."

The message of [missionaries] who are going in all parts of the world, the message of the Church to all the world is: Repent of those things which contribute to the superiority of the physical senses over our love for spirituality. That is why they cry repentance! What does repentance mean? A *change* of life, a *change* of thought, a *change* of action. If you have been angry and hateful, change that hatred and enmity to love and consideration. If you have cheated a brother, let your conscience smite you and change that, and ask his forgiveness, and never do it again. In thus changing your life from those things which are on the animal plane, you repent of your sins. If you profane Deity, never do it again! Instead of profaning his name, worship him! And once that feeling of change comes to the soul, you desire to be born again, to have a new life. . . .

"Repentance is the turning away from that which is low and the striving for that which is higher."

This changing of life, this repenting is what the world needs. It is a change of heart. Men must change their way of thinking! Change their way of feeling! Instead of hating and fighting and crushing one another, they should learn to love![11]

Repentance is the turning away from that which is low and the striving for that which is higher. As a principle of salvation, it involves not only a desire for that which is better, but also a sorrow—not merely remorse—but true sorrow for having become contaminated in any degree with things sinful, vile, or contemptible.

It is not uncommon for people to have remorse for mistakes made, for follies and sins committed, but to have no turning

199

away from such frailties and evils. They may even feel penitent; but "penitence," we are told, "is transient, and may involve no change of character or conduct." Repentance, on the other hand, "is sorrow for sin with *self-condemnation,* and complete turning away from the sin." It is, therefore, more than mere remorse; "it comprehends a change of nature befitting heaven."[12]

True faith and repentance lead to baptism.

When an applicant for baptism stood at the water's edge, before being buried with Christ in baptism, he possessed an implicit faith that the Church of Jesus Christ is established upon the earth, and that this organization is the best in the world today for the fostering of spiritual life, for the attaining of true religious development, for the salvation of the soul.

I repeat that this implicit faith was within him; and with that, there was a true repentance, and that repentance carried with it a desire to leave off everything in the past life that was contrary to the teachings of the gospel or the Church. His old life, and the sins, if there were any connected with it, he truly repented of. He looked forward to the time when he would be born anew in the kingdom of God. He was about to go through the ordinance of baptism, typical of the burial of his old life, and with it all the imperfections, the frailties, the evils, the sins that accompanied that old living. He was to be buried by baptism, that as Christ was raised from the dead by the power and the glory of the Father, so he might come forth in newness of life, a member of the Church of God, a child of the Father, a citizen in the kingdom of Christ. By baptism he was born again, and became a fit recipient of the Holy Spirit. His body came forth anew, and the Holy Ghost was bestowed upon him; he was confirmed a member of the Church of Jesus Christ. That is where we all stood at one time. Those were our feelings, our faith, our hope.[13]

To Nicodemus Jesus said, "Except a man be born of water and of the Spirit, he cannot enter into the kingdom of God." (John 3:5.)

To the members of the Church, Paul and Peter wrote, "For ye are all the children of God by faith in Christ Jesus. For as many of you as have been baptized into Christ have put on Christ." (Gal.

3:26–27.) "The like figure whereunto even baptism doth also now save us . . . by the resurrection of Jesus Christ." (1 Peter 3:21.)

In these three instances we have set forth clearly the threefold purpose of the ordinance of baptism, [namely]:

(1) A rite established by God himself and associated with the eternal principle of righteousness, compliance with the law, therefore, being established to man's salvation.

(2) An initiatory ordinance—the gateway leading to membership in the fold of Christ.

(3) A beautiful and sublime symbol typifying the burial of the "former" man with all his weaknesses and impurities, and the coming forth into a newness of life.

The ordinance of baptism is a law of God, obedience to which, in sincerity, in purity, in simplicity, brings inevitably the promised blessing of the Comforter, a divine Guide. . . . Though men may scoff at it, ridicule it, and doubt its efficacy, baptism remains ever, even in its simplicity, not only one of the most beautiful symbols known, but also one of the most effective laws operating for the salvation of man.[14]

God help us all to proclaim to the world the necessity of repentance, the importance of baptism, first to fulfil all righteousness, second as the entrance into the kingdom of God, the doorway into his Church, and third to bury our old life and be guided by his holy spirit.[15]

After we sincerely exercise faith, repent, and are baptized, we receive the gift of the Holy Ghost.

Only those who sincerely believe in Jesus Christ as the Redeemer of the World and who repent of their sins receive the Holy Ghost. Those who are baptized without faith and repentance are mere pretenders.[16]

The channel of communication is open, and the Lord is ready to guide, and does guide, his people. . . . The testimony of the Holy Ghost is a special privilege. It is like tuning in the radio and hearing a voice on the other side of the world. Men who are not within that radiation cannot hear it, but we hear it, and we are entitled to that voice and the guidance of it. It will come to us if we do our part.[17]

God help us all to keep our consciences clear, our characters sound, responsive to the whisperings of the Holy Spirit, which is real, if we shall but put our ears and listen to it.[18]

I testify to you that divine inspiration is a reality. Men and women who obey the principles of life and salvation, sincerely repent of their sins, and as sincerely strive to live in accordance with the principles of the gospel, are guided and inspired by the Holy Ghost, and are shown things to come. I testify that that guidance is with this Church and has been since the Prophet Joseph Smith established it.[19]

The Latter-day Saints have learned the truth that the everlasting Gospel has been restored. And what does this knowledge bring to them? It brings to all, who have honestly and sincerely obeyed the principles of repentance and baptism, the gift of the Holy Ghost, which enlightens their minds, quickens their understandings, and imparts unto them a knowledge of Christ.

The Latter-day Saints have a guide, a help, a means to assist in their acquisition of truth, in their desire to know what their duty is, that the world does not possess. And this guide is necessary; man cannot find out truth; he cannot find out God by intellect alone. It has been said that no man can find out God by a microscope. Reason alone is not a sufficient guide in searching for truth. There is another, higher, more sure guide than reason. . . .

[Faith is] that principle which draws our spirit into communion with the Higher Spirit which will bring all things to our remembrance, show us things to come, and teach us all things. To acquire that Spirit is the responsibility of the Latter-day Saint who would know truth.[20]

Suggestions for Study and Discussion

- What is faith in Jesus Christ? (See pages 196–98.) Why is faith in Jesus Christ the fundamental principle of the gospel? (See pages 196–98.) What must we do to develop and strengthen our faith in Him?

- In what ways can we put our faith in Jesus Christ into action? How have you been blessed as you have exercised such faith in Jesus Christ?

- Why does true faith in Jesus Christ lead to repentance? How is repentance more than simply stopping a certain behavior? (See pages 198–200.) What must we do to completely repent of our sins? What are the risks of failing to repent?

- What is the symbolism of the ordinance of baptism? (See pages 200–201.) What covenant or promise do we make at baptism? What does the Lord promise in return? How can we remember our baptismal covenant and continue to enjoy the blessings associated with it?

- What is the mission of the Holy Ghost? (See pages 201–2.) What is required of us to be in tune with the promptings of the Holy Ghost? (See pages 201–2.) Why is receiving the gift of the Holy Ghost necessary to return to our Father in Heaven?

- How can we recognize when we are being guided by the Holy Ghost? What experiences have you had in which you were guided by inspiration from the Holy Ghost?

Related Scriptures: John 14:26; James 2:14–20; 2 Nephi 2:21; 32:5; Mosiah 18:8–10; Alma 32:21; Moroni 10:5; D&C 11:13–14; 58:43; 121:26

Notes

1. *Gospel Ideals* (1953), 329.
2. *Gospel Ideals,* 117–18.
3. In Conference Report, Apr. 1966, 58.
4. In Conference Report, Oct. 1928, 36–37.
5. *Gospel Ideals,* 42.
6. *Ancient Apostles* (1918), 258.
7. *Gospel Ideals,* 11.
8. In Conference Report, Apr. 1968, 144–45.
9. In Conference Report, Apr. 1938, 17.
10. *Gospel Ideals,* 12.
11. *Gospel Ideals,* 327–28.
12. *Gospel Ideals,* 13.
13. In Conference Report, Apr. 1960, 26–27; paragraphing altered.
14. *Gospel Ideals,* 16–17.
15. *Gospel Ideals,* 329.
16. *Ancient Apostles,* 92.
17. *Cherished Experiences from the Writings of President David O. McKay,* comp. Clare Middlemiss, rev. ed. (1976), 128; paragraphing altered.
18. In Conference Report, Apr. 1963, 95.
19. In Conference Report, Oct. 1929, 15.
20. In Conference Report, Oct. 1906, 112–13; paragraphing altered.

*Because Heavenly Father has given us the gift of agency,
we can choose to follow Jesus Christ.*

Agency and Responsibility

*What you make of yourself depends upon
you as an individual. You are in this world to
choose the right or the wrong, to accept
the right or yield to temptation. Upon that choice
will depend the development of the spiritual
part of you. That is fundamental in the
gospel of Jesus Christ.[1]*

Introduction

President David O. McKay served for more than six decades as a General Authority, and during this time he witnessed many notable events in the world's history. He saw global upheaval, including two world wars, widespread regional conflicts, and the rise of superpower nations on the brink of nuclear war. He also lived through significant economic and social changes, such as the Great Depression and the world's growing acceptance of instant gratification through promiscuity and illicit drugs. As an inspired witness of history, he spoke to Church members many times about agency and individual responsibility. In a conference address given after the United States had entered World War I, Elder McKay (then a member of the Quorum of the Twelve Apostles) spoke of the tragic events that encompassed the world:

"I do not believe that God has caused the misery, the famine, the pestilence, and the death that are now sweeping the war-torn countries of Europe. I do believe that the conditions of the world today are a direct result—an inevitable result, of disobedience to God's laws. . . . Men may choose the right or they may choose the wrong; they may walk in darkness or they may walk in the light; and, mind you, God has not left his children without the light. He has given them in the various dispensations of the world the light of the gospel wherein they could walk and not stumble, wherein they could find that peace and happiness which he desires, as a loving Father, his children should enjoy, but the Lord does not take from them their free agency."[2]

Although President McKay recognized the tragedies that can occur when people choose evil, he remained ever grateful for the gift of agency. He understood the blessings that come from righteous choices, and he reminded those he taught that the freedom to choose is an essential part of the plan of salvation. In his discourses on the subject of agency, he often referred to it as "God's greatest gift to man."

Teachings of David O. McKay

The eternal gift of agency allows us to progress and gain exaltation.

Free agency is the impelling source of the soul's progress. It is the purpose of the Lord that man become like him. In order for man to achieve this it was necessary for the Creator first to make him free.[3]

There is a significant reference in the [book of Revelation] to "a war in heaven." (Rev. 12:7.) It is not only significant, but seemingly contradictory, for we think of heaven as a celestial abode of bliss, an impossible condition [for] war and contention [to] exist. The passage is significant because it implies a freedom of choice and of action in the spirit world. In the Pearl of Great Price we are given this account: "Wherefore, because that Satan rebelled against me, and *sought to destroy the agency of man,* which I the Lord God, had given him, and also, *that I should give unto him mine own power;* by the power of mine Only Begotten, I caused that he should be cast down;

"And he became Satan, yea, even the devil, the father of all lies, to deceive and to blind men, and to lead them captive at his will, even as many as would not hearken unto my voice." (Moses 4:3–4; italics added.)

Two things you will note in that passage: one, that Satan was determined to destroy the free agency of man. Free

206

agency is a gift of God. It is part of his divinity. The second point is that he desired to supplant God. I quote, "Give me thy glory." [See Moses 4:1.]

The world does not comprehend the significance of that divine gift to the individual. It is as inherent as intelligence which, we are told, has never been nor can be created [see D&C 93:29].[4]

Freedom of the will and the responsibility associated with it are fundamental aspects of Jesus' teachings. Throughout his ministry he emphasized the worth of the individual, and exemplified what is now expressed in modern revelation as the work and glory of God—"To bring to pass the immortality and eternal life of man." [Moses 1:39.] Only through the divine gift of soul freedom is such progress possible.

Force, on the other hand, emanates from Lucifer himself. Even in man's [premortal] state, Satan sought power to compel the human family to do his will by suggesting that the free agency of man be inoperative. If his plan had been accepted, human beings would have become mere puppets in the hands of a dictator, and the purpose of man's coming to earth would have been frustrated. Satan's proposed system of government, therefore, was rejected, and the principle of free agency established.[5]

Although God has created the universe and all therein, "man is the jewel of God." This is just another way of saying that the earth was created for man and not man for the earth. God gave to man part of his divinity. He gave man the power of choice, and no other creature in the world has it. So he placed upon the individual the obligation of conducting himself as an eternal being. You cannot think of any greater gift that could come to a man or woman than the freedom of choice. You alone are responsible, and by wielding and exercising that freedom of choice, you grow in character, you grow in intelligence, you approach divinity, and eventually you may achieve that high exaltation. That is a great obligation. Very few people appreciate it. The roads are clearly marked—one offering animal existence, the other life abundant. Yet, God's greatest creation—*man*— often is content to grovel on the animal plane.[6]

Next to the bestowal of life itself, the right to direct that life is God's greatest gift to man. . . . Freedom of choice is more to be treasured than any possession earth can give. It is inherent in the spirit of man. It is a divine gift. . . . Whether born in abject poverty or shackled at birth by inherited riches, everyone has this most precious of all life's endowments—the gift of free agency; man's inherited and inalienable right.[7]

References in the Scriptures show that [agency] is (1) essential to man's salvation; and, (2) may become a measuring rod by which the actions of men, of organizations, of nations may be judged.

"Therefore, cheer up your hearts, and remember that ye are free to act for yourselves—to choose the way of everlasting death or the way of eternal life." (2 Nephi 10:23.)[8]

With agency comes personal responsibility to fulfill the "true purpose of life."

The responsibility is upon each individual to choose the path of righteousness, of faithfulness and duty to fellowmen. If he [chooses] otherwise, and as a result [meets] failure, misery and death, he alone is to blame. As President [Brigham] Young said on one occasion:

"If Brother Brigham should take a wrong track and be shut out of the kingdom of heaven, no person will be to blame but Brother Brigham. I am the only being in heaven, earth, or hell, that can be blamed.

"This will equally apply to every Latter-day Saint. Salvation is an individual operation. . . . When salvation is sent to me, I can reject or receive it. In receiving it, I yield implicit obedience and submission to its great Author throughout my life, and to those whom he shall appoint to instruct me; in rejecting it, I follow the dictates of my own will in preference to the will of my Creator." [See *Discourses of Brigham Young,* sel. John A. Widtsoe (1954), 390.][9]

With free agency there comes responsibility. If a man is to be rewarded for righteousness and punished for evil, then common justice demands that he be given the power of independent action. A knowledge of good and evil is essential to man's progress on earth. If he were coerced to do right at all times, or

"Actions in harmony with divine law and the laws of nature will bring happiness, and those in opposition to divine truth, misery."

were helplessly enticed to commit sin, he would merit neither a blessing for the first nor punishment for the second. . . .

. . . Man's responsibility is correspondingly operative with his free agency. Actions in harmony with divine law and the laws of nature will bring happiness, and those in opposition to divine truth, misery. Man is responsible not only for every deed, but also for every idle word and thought. Said the Savior:

". . . every idle word that men shall speak they shall give account thereof in the day of judgment." (Matthew 12:36.) [10]

Earth in all its majesty and wonder is not the end and purpose of creation. ". . . *my glory,*" says the Lord himself, *"(is) to bring to pass the immortality and eternal life of man."* (Moses 1:39.) And man in exercising the divine gift of free agency should feel in duty bound, should sense the *obligation* to assist the Creator in the accomplishment of this divine purpose.

The true end of life is not mere existence, not pleasure, not fame, not wealth. The true purpose of life is the perfection of humanity through individual effort, under the guidance of God's inspiration. [11]

There are a few simple but fundamental things which everyone can do. One of these is for each individual to work out his own salvation. An outstanding doctrine of the Church is that each individual carries this responsibility, and that the salvation of man is a process of gradual development. . . . We should seek the strength and grace of God for inspiration to obtain the final victory.

However, to work out one's salvation is not to sit idly by, dreaming and yearning for God miraculously to thrust bounteous blessings into our laps. It is to perform daily, hourly, momentarily, if necessary, the immediate task or duty at hand, and to continue happily in such performance as the years come and go, leaving the fruits of such labors either to self or to others to be bestowed as a just and beneficent Father may determine.

I am not unmindful of the scripture that declares, "By grace are ye saved through faith, and that not of yourselves; it is a gift of God." [See Ephesians 2:8.] That is absolutely true, for man in his taking upon himself mortality was [powerless] to save himself. When left to grope in a natural state, he would have become, and did become "carnal, sensual and devilish by nature." [Alma 42:10.] But the Lord through His grace appeared to man, gave him the Gospel or eternal plan whereby he might rise above the carnal and selfish things of life and obtain spiritual perfection.

But he must rise by his own efforts and he must walk by faith.[12]

Choosing to obey gospel principles brings happiness, peace, and salvation.

Conformity to the Lord's word or law will invariably contribute to man's happiness and salvation. Those who do not what the Lord commands, we are told, will be subjected to justice and judgment. In other words, there is eternally operative in the moral world a law of compensation and retribution—compensation commensurate with conformity to law; retribution in actual degree to the extent of disobedience.[13]

The peace of Christ does not come by seeking the superficial things of life, neither does it come except as it springs from the individual's heart. Jesus said to His disciples: "Peace I leave with you. My peace I give unto you; not as the world giveth, give I unto you." [John 14:27.] Thus the Son of Man as the executor of his own will and testament gave to his disciples and to mankind the "first of all human blessings." It was a bequest conditioned upon obedience to the principles of the Gospel of Jesus Christ. It is thus bequeathed to each individual. No man is at peace with himself or his God who is untrue to his better self, who transgresses the law of right either in dealing with himself by indulging in passion, in appetite, yielding to temptations against his accusing conscience, or in dealing with his fellowmen, being untrue to their trust. Peace does not come to the transgressor of law; peace comes by obedience to law, and it is that message which Jesus would have us proclaim among men.[14]

Jesus Christ, the Savior of the world, has given us the means whereby man may obtain eternal happiness and peace in the kingdom of our Father, but man must work out his own salvation through obedience to the eternal principles and ordinances of the gospel.[15]

As members of society, we should appreciate freedom and promote the responsible use of it.

Freedom of speech, freedom of action within boundaries that do not infringe upon the liberty of others are . . . divine gifts "essential to human dignity and human happiness."[16]

Liberty may be either helpful or fatal according to the use made of it. . . . "Liberty is an atmosphere of the higher life. . . . Liberty?—it is respect. . . . Men must be made capable and worthy of [liberty], otherwise public life becomes impossible."[17]

True liberty in individuals consists in the enjoying of every right that will contribute to one's peace and happiness, so long as the exercise of such a privilege does not interfere with the same privilege in others. It consists not in doing what one likes to do, but in doing what one ought to do. It is the right of each individual to be master of his own time and actions consistent with fairness and justice to his fellow men and with harmony with the laws of God. . . . It is freedom of choice, a divine gift, an essential virtue in a peaceful society.[18]

In these days of uncertainty and unrest, liberty-loving people's greatest responsibility and paramount duty is to preserve and proclaim the freedom of the individual, his relationship to Deity, and . . . the necessity of obedience to the principles of the gospel of Jesus Christ—only thus will mankind find peace and happiness.[19]

If we would make the world better, let us foster a keener appreciation of . . . freedom and liberty.[20]

Suggestions for Study and Discussion

- Why did God give us agency? (See pages 206–8.) Why did Satan want to deprive us of our agency? (See pages 206–7.)

- In what ways does Satan continue to try to influence our agency? How can we resist those attempts?

- What guidance has the Lord provided to help us use our agency righteously? What counsel could you give someone who is struggling to discern between right and wrong?

- In what ways can parents teach and train their children until they are mature enough to decide for themselves? How can we honor the agency of family members and at the same time help them make correct decisions? How can we help family members understand the consequences of their decisions?

- President McKay taught that life's purpose is "the perfection of humanity through individual effort, under the guidance of God's inspiration" (page 209). How can agency help us fulfill this divine purpose? (See pages 208–10.) What are our individual responsibilities in exercising our agency? (See pages 208–10.)

- How are personal agency and the Atonement of Jesus Christ related?

- How does our righteous use of agency make us free?

- How can we help preserve liberty and promote the responsible use of individual freedoms? (See pages 211–12.)

Related Scriptures: Joshua 24:15; 2 Nephi 2:14–16, 26–28; Alma 5:40–42; Helaman 14:30–31; D&C 58:26–28; 130:20–21; Abraham 3:24–28

Notes

1. In Conference Report, Apr. 1967, 134–35.
2. In Conference Report, Apr. 1917, 46–47; paragraphing altered.
3. In Conference Report, Apr. 1950, 32.
4. In Conference Report, Oct. 1965, 7.
5. In Conference Report, Apr. 1950, 34–35.
6. In Conference Report, Oct. 1969, 6–7.
7. In Conference Report, Apr. 1950, 32.
8. In Conference Report, Apr. 1940, 116.
9. In Conference Report, Apr. 1938, 18.
10. In Conference Report, Apr. 1950, 33.
11. In Conference Report, Oct. 1963, 7.
12. In Conference Report, Apr. 1938, 17–18; paragraphing altered.
13. In Conference Report, Oct. 1951, 6.
14. In Conference Report, Oct. 1938, 133.
15. *Gospel Ideals* (1953), 8.
16. *Pathways to Happiness,* comp. Llewelyn R. McKay (1957), 166.
17. In Conference Report, Apr. 1937, 29; paragraphing altered.
18. *True to the Faith: From the Sermons and Writings of David O. McKay,* comp. Llewelyn R. McKay (1966), 139.
19. In Conference Report, Apr. 1950, 37.
20. In Conference Report, Oct. 1940, 104.

"*There has been but one perfect character in this world—the peerless personality of Jesus of Nazareth, the Son of God, the Redeemer of the world. No man can do better than to accept Christ as the great Exemplar and the safest Guide.*"

Developing a
Christlike Character

*Man's chief concern in life should not be
the acquiring of gold, or of fame, or of material
possessions. It should not be the development
of physical prowess, nor of intellectual strength,
but his aim, the highest in life, should be
the development of a Christ-like character.[1]*

Introduction

President David O. McKay understood the importance of developing a righteous character patterned after that of the Savior. This was evident in both his public and his private life. His son Robert once said of him, "In all of my years of close association in the home, on the farm, in business, in the Church, there has never been shown to me one action nor one word, even while training a self-willed horse, which would throw any doubt in my mind that he should be and finally did become the representative and prophet of our Heavenly Father."[2]

President McKay taught that the building of a Christlike character is an ongoing, daily process for which each of us must take responsibility. To illustrate this principle for the youth, he described an occasion when he visited a sculptor's yard in Florence, Italy: "Scattered about were unbroken, irregular pieces of granite from which a sculptor was preparing to cut out a vision which he saw in his mind. . . .

"If you had stood in that yard, and a man had placed in your hands a chisel and a hammer, would you have dared to take one of the shapeless blocks of stone and carve a human image out of it? You could not do it. Or if someone had placed before you a canvas and given you paints and put in your hands a brush, would you have undertaken to paint on that canvas the picture of an ideal soul? You probably would have said to the first, 'I am not a sculptor,' and to the second, 'I am not a painter. I cannot do it.'

"Nevertheless, each of us is carving a soul this very minute— our own. Is it going to be a deformed one, or is it going to be something admirable and beautiful?

"Yours is the responsibility. Nobody else can carve it for you. Parents may guide, and teachers may help with suggestions, but each young man and young woman has the responsibility to carve his own character."

President McKay went on to describe the results of carving an upright character: "If you keep your character above reproach, no matter what others may think or what charges they make, you can hold your head erect, keep your heart light, and face the world undauntedly because you, yourself, know that you have kept your soul untarnished."[3]

Teachings of David O. McKay

We should strive to follow the Savior's supreme example.

There has been but one perfect character in this world—the peerless personality of Jesus of Nazareth, the Son of God, the Redeemer of the world. No man can do better than to accept Christ as the great Exemplar and the safest Guide.[4]

If we desire to learn the ideal life to lead among our fellow-men, we can find a perfect example in the life of Jesus. Whatsoever our noble desires, our lofty aspirations, our ideals in any phase of life, we can look to Christ and find perfection. . . .

The virtues that combined to make this perfect character are truth, justice, wisdom, benevolence, and self-control. His every thought, word, and deed were in harmony with divine law and, therefore, true. The channel of communication between him and the Father was constantly open, so that truth, which rests upon revelation, was always known to him.

His ideal of justice is summed up in the admonition: "Do unto others as you would have others do unto you." (See Matt. 7:12.)

His wisdom was so broad and deep that it comprehended the ways of men and the purposes of God. . . . Every act that is recorded of his short, though eventful, life was one of benevolence that comprehends charity and love. His self-control, whether exemplified in his power over his appetites and passions or his dignity and poise when before his persecutors, was perfect—it was divine.[5]

There are [certain] pictures upon which I always love to look. The first of these is the picture of Christ before Pilate when that Roman official said to the angry mob, "Behold the man!" (John 19:5.) As he said it, he pointed to Jesus, crowned with thorns, bearing upon his shoulders the purple robe. He pointed to one at whom the angry mob sneered, condemned as a felon and blasphemer, and yet when he said, "Behold the man!" he described one who was perfect in character, who was conqueror over weaknesses and temptations, and who could say, as he did to his fellow workers, "These things I have spoken unto you, that in me ye might have peace . . . be of good cheer; I have overcome the world." (John 16:33.) He is our pattern.[6]

As individuals we should emulate Jesus Christ because of His divine character. . . . Christians do not honor Him, even with the honor they give Him, because He was a great poet, because He was a great scientist, because He was a great discoverer, a great inventor or great statesman or a great general. They honor Him because He was a great man. In the realm of character He was supreme.[7]

Maintaining righteous thoughts is critical to the development of a righteous character.

The kind of life you live, your disposition, your very nature, will be determined by your thoughts, of which your acts are but the outward expression. Thought is the seed of action.[8]

Character springs from the depths of the soul. You tell me what you think about when you do not have to think, and I'll tell you what you are.[9]

Thoughts make us what we are. As definitely and surely as the weaver shapes his flowers and figures out of the warp and woof of his loom so every moment the shuttle of thought moves back and forth forming character and even shaping the lineaments of our features. Thoughts lift your soul heavenward, or drag you toward hell.[10]

No principle of life was more constantly emphasized by the Great Teacher than the necessity of right thinking. To Him, the man was not what he appeared to be outwardly, nor what he professed to be by his words: what the man *thought* determined in all cases what the man *was*. No teacher emphasized more strongly than He the truth that "as a man thinketh in his heart, so is he" [see Prov. 23:7]. . . .

His teachings regarding man's duty to himself, as well as man's duty to his neighbor, are pervaded with the truth that thought in all cases determines the man's right to happiness or his condemnation for sin. . . .

Whether found out or not, all who commit sin pay the penalty of sin and of indiscretion. The intent that precedes the act leaves its indelible impression upon the character. And though the culprit might offer a balm to his conscience by saying . . . that he will not count "this one," yet, deep down in the nerve tissue, it is counted just the same, and the marks in his character will stand against him in the day of judgment. No one can hide from his thoughts, nor escape from their inevitable consequences.[11]

The Savior knew that if the mind could be directed rightly; if the evil thought and tendency could be resisted, the evil act would be minimized. Jesus does not lessen the seriousness of these acts, nor say that we should not punish them; but he emphasizes the greater need of keeping the thought clean, the mind pure. An evil tree will bring forth evil fruit; a good tree will bring forth good fruit. Keep the tree pure, the thoughts pure, and the fruit will be pure and the life pure.[12]

An upright character is the result only of continued effort and right thinking, the effect of long-cherished associations with Godlike thoughts. He approaches nearest the Christ spirit who makes God the center of his thoughts; and he who can say in his heart, "Not my will, but thine be done" [see Luke 22:42], approaches most nearly the Christ ideal.[13]

Over time, the "little things" in our lives shape our character.

As straws tell which way the wind blows, so little things indicate the direction of a person's feelings and thoughts.[14]

Little things are but parts of the great. The grass does not spring up full grown by eruption. It rises up and increases as noiselessly and gently as not to disturb an angel's ear, perhaps is invisible to an angel's eye. The rain does not fall in masses but in drops; the planets do not leap in their orbits, but inch by inch and line by line they circle the orbits. Intellect, feeling, habit, character, all become what they are through the influence of little things, and in morals and religion, it is by little things, by little actions, that every one of us is going—not by leaps, yet surely by inches—either to life or death eternal.

The great lesson to be learned in the world today is to apply in the little acts and duties of life the glorious principles of the Gospel. Let us not think that, because some of the things may seem small and trivial, they are unimportant. Life, after all, is made up of little things. Our life, our being, physically, is made up of little heart beats. Let that little heart stop beating, and life in this world ceases. The great sun is a mighty force in the universe, but we receive the blessings of his rays because they come to us as little beams, which, taken in the aggregate, fill the whole world with sunlight. The dark night is made pleasant by the glimmer of what seem to be little stars; and so the true Christian life is made up of little Christ-like acts performed this hour, this minute—in the home, in the quorum, in the organization, in the town, wherever our life and acts may be cast.[15]

What a man is today will largely determine what he will be tomorrow. What he has been during the past year to a great extent marks his course throughout the year before him. Day by day, hour by hour, man builds the character that will determine his place and standing among his associates throughout the ages.[16]

We develop a Christlike character through obedience and self-control.

Character is built by adherence to principles. Character grows from within just as a tree grows, just as every living thing grows. There is no outward thing to be put on to make yourself beautiful; [products from] the drug store [help], it is true, but it is only superficial and temporary. Real beauty, as character, comes from within, and that which contributes to strength of character is in compliance with those principles enunciated by the Prophet Joseph, and by the Savior Himself: virtue, uprightness, holiness—keeping the commandments of God [see *History of the Church*, 5:134–35].[17]

In the building of character as in the transforming of a landscape, the laws of peace and of happiness are ever operative. Effort, self-denial, and purposeful action are the stepping-stones of progress. Indulgence and sin are vandals and destroyers of character. Only regret and remorse follow in their wake.[18]

Self-control means the government and regulation of all our natural appetites, desires, passions, and affections; and there is nothing that gives a man such strength of character as the sense of self-conquest, the realization that he can make his appetites and passions serve him and that he is not a servant to them. This virtue includes temperance, abstinence, bravery, fortitude, hopefulness, sobriety, chastity, independence, tolerance, patience, submission, continence, purity.[19]

What is the crowning glory of man in this earth so far as his individual achievement is concerned? It is character—character developed through obedience to the laws of life as revealed through the gospel of Jesus Christ, who came that we might have life and have it more abundantly [see John 10:10]. Man's chief concern in life should not be the acquiring of gold, or of fame, or of material possessions. It should not be the development of physical prowess, nor of intellectual strength, but his aim, the highest in life, should be the development of a Christ-like character.[20]

Through our influence and teaching, we can help children and youth build a Christlike character.

Children at birth are the most dependent and helpless of all creatures, yet they are the sweetest and greatest of all things in the world. . . . Their souls are as stainless white paper on which are to be written the aspirations or achievements of a lifetime.[21]

As a child grows physically by eating regularly at intervals, by breathing fresh air constantly, by resting at stated intervals, so character is built by little things, by daily contacts, by an influence here, a fact or truth there.[22]

"Man's greatest duty in [the] family is to rear boys and girls possessing health of body, vigor of mind, and higher even than these, a Christ-like character."

Fundamentally, our characters are formed in the home. The family is a divine organization. Man's greatest duty in that family is to rear boys and girls possessing health of body, vigor of mind, and higher even than these, a Christ-like character. Home is the factory where these products are made.[23]

Of what infinite value to the community are teachers and trainers of youth who carve and shape the moral atmosphere in which the people live. Flowers shed beauty and fragrance for a brief time, then fade and die and are gone forever; but children who, through instruction from noble teachers, become imbued with eternal principles of truth, radiate an influence for good which, like their own souls, will live forever.[24]

Suggestions for Study and Discussion

- What are the hallmarks of the Savior's character? (See pages 216–17.) How can we incorporate these traits into our own lives?

- Why are noble thoughts the foundation for building a Christlike character? (See pages 217–18.) How would you explain President McKay's statement, "You tell me what you think about when you do not have to think, and I'll tell you what you are"? What can we do to develop pure thoughts?

- What are some of the "little things" in your life that have helped shape your character? What can you do every day to become more Christlike? (See also D&C 64:33.)

- In what ways is obedience to the gospel of Jesus Christ a critical factor in developing strength of character? (See page 220.) How do self-control and service contribute to this development? (See page 220.)

- What can we as parents and teachers do to help young people build a Christlike character? (See pages 221–22.)

Related Scriptures: Philippians 4:8; Mosiah 4:30; 3 Nephi 27:27; D&C 64:33; 93:11–14

Notes

1. In Conference Report, Oct. 1926, 111.
2. In Conference Report, Apr. 1967, 84.
3. *Secrets of a Happy Life,* comp. Llewelyn R. McKay (1960), 145–46, 147.
4. In Conference Report, Oct. 1945, 132.
5. In Conference Report, Apr. 1968, 7.
6. *Gospel Ideals* (1953), 355.
7. *True to the Faith: From the Sermons and Discourses of David O. McKay,* comp. Llewelyn R. McKay (1966), 133.
8. *Treasures of Life,* comp. Clare Middlemiss (1962), 200.
9. *Pathways to Happiness,* comp. Llewelyn R. McKay (1957), 257.
10. *Secrets of a Happy Life,* 160.
11. " 'As a Man Thinketh . . . ,' " *Instructor,* Sept. 1958, 257–58.
12. *Man May Know for Himself: Teachings of President David O. McKay,* comp. Clare Middlemiss (1967), 8–9.
13. In Conference Report, Oct. 1953, 10.
14. *True to the Faith,* 270.
15. *True to the Faith,* 153.
16. "Man's Soul Is as Endless as Time," *Instructor,* Jan. 1960, 1.
17. *True to the Faith,* 95–96.
18. *True to the Faith,* 29.
19. In Conference Report, Apr. 1968, 8.
20. In Conference Report, Oct. 1926, 111.
21. "The Sunday School Looks Forward," *Improvement Era,* Dec. 1949, 804.
22. "The Home and the Church as Factors in Character Building," *Instructor,* Apr. 1946, 161.
23. *True to the Faith,* 107.
24. *True to the Faith,* 248.

President McKay followed the Savior's admonition:
"Let your light so shine before men, that they may see your good works,
and glorify your Father which is in heaven" (Matthew 5:16).

"Let Your Light So Shine"

*May the Spirit of the Lord abide in your hearts,
and in your homes, that people partaking of
your radiation of honesty, integrity, uprightness,
and faith in our Lord Jesus Christ will be led
to glorify our Father in heaven.[1]*

Introduction

President David O. McKay received the following letter from
Harold L. Gregory, who served as president of the East German
Mission in the early 1950s:

"Dear President McKay:

"You will be interested to hear of an experience I had this week.
Two men about forty years of age, poorly dressed, came to see me
during the week. They told me they had lost their faith, and yet
they could not turn to any of the other sects or religious organizations they knew. Mr. Braun (as one was called) had prevailed
upon his friend, Mr. Fascher, to come and see me. He told Mr.
Fascher that he knew of our church and that we would help them.
Fascher objected strenuously for two days, but finally came along.

"Mr. Braun began by saying that he was standing on a street
corner one day when he noticed hundreds of people going by. He
asked one where he was going, and he said, 'To see the Prophet.'
Mr. Braun went along. It was the dedication of the meetinghouse
in Berlin-Charlottenburg, and the Prophet was Brother McKay.

"He said (and I will quote him roughly): 'I had never sensed
such a spirit of love and good will as I did among those people
that day. And then the Prophet, a tall man in his eighties, with a
full head of hair—all white—stood up and addressed the body. I
have never seen such a young face on a man that age. When he
spoke, something went through me. Afterwards as he was getting

into his car, I noticed he was shaking hands with the members, and even though I was not one of them I pressed forward and shook his hand too. Something warm and lovely went clear through my body, and I marveled again at his young, clear features. Through worldly cares and extreme economic difficulties the memory was somewhat beclouded, but I knew that I had to come back to find out more.'

"Mr. Fascher told me that Braun could say nothing but words of amazement and wonderment at the man he had seen. The two sat in my office and listened intently to the message of the restoration which I gave them, as if hanging on every word. They were penniless and miserable, but they were humble and dissatisfied with the churches of men. I lent them a Book of Mormon, and they promised to be to church Sunday. I believe these two men (both Russian war prisoners) are ready for the gospel.

"May the Lord bless you, Brother McKay. You and all our brethren at the head of our church are shining examples of all that is righteous and good." [2]

Many people saw in David O. McKay what these two men saw—an example of a true disciple of Christ. The story is told of a newspaper photographer who saw President McKay for the first time:

"Arrangements had been made for pictures to be taken, but the regular photographer was unable to go, so in desperation the United Press picked their crime photographer—a man accustomed to the toughest type of work in New York. He went to the airport, stayed there two hours, and returned later from [the] dark room with a tremendous sheaf of pictures. He was supposed to take only two. His boss immediately chided him, 'What in the world are you wasting time and all those photographic supplies for?'

"The photographer replied very curtly, saying he would gladly pay for the extra materials, and they could even dock him for the extra time he took. . . . Several hours later the vice-president called him to his office, wanting to learn what happened. The crime photographer said, 'When I was a little boy, my mother used to read to me out of the Old Testament, and all my life I have wondered what a prophet of God must really look like. Well, today I found one.' "[3]

Teachings of David O. McKay

We influence others by what we say, what we do, and who we are.

Every person who lives in this world wields an influence, whether for good or for evil. It is not what he says alone, it is not alone what he does. It is what he is. Every man, every person radiates what he or she is. Every person is a recipient of radiation. The Savior was conscious of that. Whenever he came into the presence of an individual, he sensed that radiation—whether it was the woman of Samaria with her past life; whether it was the woman who was to be stoned or the men who were to stone her; whether it was the statesman, Nicodemus, or one of the lepers. He was conscious of the radiation from the individual. And to a degree so are you, and so am I. It is what we are and what we radiate that affects the people around us.

. . . As individuals, we must think nobler thoughts. We must not encourage vile thoughts or low aspirations. We shall radiate them if we do. If we think noble thoughts, if we encourage and cherish noble aspirations, there will be that radiation when we meet people, especially when we associate with them.[4]

The effect of our words and acts is tremendous in this world. Every moment of life you are changing to a degree the lives of the whole world. . . . So, it's not the surroundings, it isn't the positions; the thing that will influence [others] in this world, are personalities. No matter what you are people will feel and recognize this. You radiate, you can't hide it. You may pretend something else, but that will not affect people.[5]

It is important . . . that we seek, both in life and in books, the companionship of the best and noblest men and women. [Thomas] Carlyle, a great English writer, says that "Great men taken up in any way are profitable company. We cannot look, however imperfectly, upon a great man, without gaining something by him. He is the living 'light-fountain,' which it is good and pleasant to be near."

If you will study the lives of these great "light-fountains" of the world, you will learn of at least one thing that has made their

227

names endure. It is this: Each one has given something of his life to make the world better. They did not spend all their time seeking only pleasure and ease, and a "good time" for themselves alone, but found their greatest joy in making others happy and more comfortable. All such good deeds live forever, even though the world may never hear of them.[6]

No good deed, no kind word can be spoken without its effect being felt for good upon all. Sometimes the good may be infinitesimal, but as a rock that is thrown in a pool starts a wave from the center which continues to enlarge until every part of the shore is touched, so your deeds, silent, many of them, unknown, unspoken, unheralded, continue to radiate and touch many hearts.[7]

God bless you, my dear fellow workers, you General Authorities, stake presidencies, bishoprics, every officer and teacher throughout the land, every member. May the Spirit of the Lord abide in your hearts, and in your homes, that people partaking of your radiation of honesty, integrity, uprightness, and faith in our Lord Jesus Christ will be led to glorify our Father in heaven.[8]

Latter-day Saint homes can be examples of harmony and love.

Our homes radiate what we are, and that radiation comes from what we say and how we act in the home. . . . You have to contribute to an ideal home by your character, controlling your passion, your temper, guarding your speech, because those things will make your home what it is and what it will radiate to the neighborhood. . . .

A father visited his son's new home. The son was proud to show him the new bedroom, the new installations in the kitchen. After they were through with their visit, the father said, "Yes, it is beautiful, but I see no signs of God in your home." And the son said, "I went back, and as I looked through the rooms, I noticed I had nothing suggestive of the presence of the Redeemer or the Savior."

What I am saying is, we [have a] greater responsibility than ever before, as men of the priesthood, as women of the Church, to make our homes such as will radiate to our neighbors harmony, love, community duties, loyalty. Let our neighbors see it and hear

As we follow the Savior's example, we will "radiate strength, control, love, charity, . . . consideration, best wishes for all human beings."

it. Never must there be expressed in a Latter-day Saint home an oath, a condemnatory term, an expression of anger or jealousy or hatred. Control it! Do not express it! . . .

The Savior set us the example, always calm, always controlled, radiating something which people could feel as they passed. . . . God help us to radiate strength, control, love, charity, which is another name for love, consideration, best wishes for all human beings.[9]

God bless you, my dear fellow workers. Bless you in your homes. Make your faith shown by your works in your home.

Husbands, be true to your wives, not only in act, but in thought; wives, be true to your husbands. Children, be true to your parents; do not [assume] that they are old-fashioned in their beliefs and that you know more than they do. Girls, follow that sweet mother and her teachings. Boys, be true to your fathers, who want happiness and success for you, which come only through living the principles of the gospel. Strangers, seeing such homes, will say, "Well, if that is the result of Mormonism, I think it is good." You will show by your faith and acts in everyday life what you really are.[10]

Let the sincere investigators who believe more from what they see than from what they hear, find, upon investigation, that "Mormons" prove by example in the home, by devotion, and in their service to God, that they believe and know that God is their Father.[11]

If we live according to our beliefs, our good example will anchor the Church and be a light to the world.

God help us to go forth . . . imbued with the Spirit of the Lord, that every man and woman who has an opportunity to work in the Church—and that means all—may be determined to live a life of virtue and purity that will command the strength of the world, and the admiration of it. In short, let us provide things honest in the sight of all men. If it be possible, so far as in us lies, let us live peaceably with all men—not overcoming evil by evil, or being overcome by evil, but overcoming evil with good. Then will the Church stand as a light to the world. That is her destiny.[12]

Let your light so shine among men that they seeing your good works may be led to glorify our Father which is in heaven [see Matthew 5:16; 3 Nephi 12:16]. In probably no more effective way can the truth be witnessed before men than for every Latter-day Saint to maintain and foster the confidence of our outside friends in a faithful member of the Church of Christ.

Now, in order to do that we must be honest in all things. If we are contractors, and agree to put in such and such material in a building, let us put that material in. If we agree to the stipulations of a contract, to put in one hundred and fifty feet of [heating materials] in the building, let us put in one hundred and fifty feet. Those are details, aren't they, but those are the details by which the men whom you deal with will judge your actions. If we are taking to market potatoes of a particular grade, and we so describe that grade, let us know that an investigation will prove our statements true. I was grieved when I heard a wholesale dealer say that he has opened sacks of produce, brought in from the farm, and found foreign material, such as rocks and dirt, placed in to make up weight. I did not ask him for the religion of those men; I asked for no name; but such things are dishonorable, no true member of the Church of Christ can stoop to such trickery. Let your light shine before men. In this world today there needs to be an ensign, a people standing out in bold relief as an example to the world in honesty and fair-dealing. [13]

If we can only maintain the standards of the gospel of Jesus Christ, the future of the Church is secure. Truly, men and women will see a light that is not hidden under a bushel, but one that is set upon a hill, and they will be attracted by it, and will be led to seek the truth more by our acts and deeds and by what we radiate in virtue and integrity, rather than by what we say. [14]

Let us set an example of harmony and peace to the world. Let us prove that whether we're in Africa, South America, New Zealand, or Australia, we're all one in Christ. We have only one object in view: to declare to the world that the gospel of Jesus Christ is restored in its fulness, and that the gospel of Jesus Christ is the only plan given to man by which the peace of towns, the peace of nations may eventually come. [15]

May there come into everyone's heart, and into all our homes, the true spirit of Christ, our Redeemer, whose reality, whose inspiring guidance I know to be real.

The gospel is our anchor. We know what it stands for. If we live it, feel it, and bear record to the world by the way we live, we will contribute to its growth and upbuilding. Speak well of it, of the priesthood, of the Authorities; let the standards of the gospel radiate in our lives. [16]

Suggestions for Study and Discussion

- Why is it important to remember that "the effect of our words and acts is tremendous in this world"? (See pages 227–28.) How have you seen that small acts of righteousness can have a far-reaching influence?

- In what ways do our thoughts and actions influence what we radiate to others?

- What can we do in our marriages and with our families to show that we are disciples of Christ? (See pages 228–30.)

- Who are some people whose examples have influenced you? Why have these people been so influential in your life?

- In what ways can our example make a difference in our homes, workplaces, and communities? (See pages 230–31.) What can you do today to radiate the light of Christ in your life?

- Why is example an important part of missionary work? What experiences have you had in which Latter-day Saints' good examples have inspired others to investigate the Church?

Related Scriptures: Matthew 5:14–16; Alma 5:14; 17:11; 3 Nephi 12:14–16; 18:16, 24

Notes

1. In Conference Report, Apr. 1953, 138.
2. Quoted in *Cherished Experiences from the Writings of President David O. McKay,* comp. Clare Middlemiss, rev. ed. (1976), 109–10.
3. Arch L. Madsen, quoted in "Memories of a Prophet," *Improvement Era,* Feb. 1970, 72.
4. In Conference Report, Apr. 1963, 129.
5. "Talk by President David O. McKay Given to the North British Mission 1 March 1961," Family and Church History Department Archives, The Church of Jesus Christ of Latter-day Saints, 3.
6. *Ancient Apostles* (1918), 2–3.
7. In Conference Report, Apr. 1953, 137.
8. In Conference Report, Apr. 1953, 138.
9. In Conference Report, Apr. 1963, 129–30; paragraphing altered.
10. In Conference Report, Oct. 1967, 152.
11. In Conference Report, Oct. 1922, 78.
12. In Conference Report, Apr. 1912, 57.
13. In Conference Report, Oct. 1910, 48–49; paragraphing altered.
14. In Conference Report, Apr. 1968, 94.
15. *Cherished Experiences,* 189.
16. In Conference Report, Oct. 1967, 149.

List of Paintings

Index